AF564622

ROBERT CLIVE TO JAWAHARLAL NEHRU

India: New Historical Interpretations

ROBERT CLIVE
TO
JAWAHARLAL NEHRU

India: New Historical Interpretations

DR. B.M. SANKHDHER
C.P. MATHUR
KALPANA SANKHDHER
DR. K.B. SRIVASTAVA

DEEP & DEEP PUBLICATIONS PVT. LTD.
F-159, Rajouri Garden, New Delhi - 110027

ROBERT CLIVE TO JAWAHARLAL NEHRU
India: New Historical Interpretations

ISBN 978-81-8450-424-8

Typeset by THE LASER PRINTERS, 8/15, 3rd Floor, Subhash Nagar, New Delhi-110027.

Printed in India at MAYUR ENTERPRISES, WZ Plot No. 3, Gujjar Market, Tihar Village, New Delhi - 110 018

Published by DEEP & DEEP PUBLICATIONS PVT. LTD.,
F-159, Rajouri Garden, New Delhi-110027. Phones: 25435369, 25440916.
E-mail: ddpubs@yahoo.com • ddpubs@gmail.com
Sales Showroom: 2/13, Ansari Road, Daryaganj, New Delhi-110002
Phone/Fax: 23245122

Contents

Acknowledgements

The authors are indebted to the following institutions for providing invaluable source materials:

India Office Library and Records, London.
National Archives of India, New Delhi.
British Museum, London.
Royal Commission on Historical Manuscripts, London.
Central Secretariat Library, New Delhi.
University of Delhi, Delhi.
University of Allahabad, Allahabad.
University of London, London
Jawarharlal Nehru University, New Delhi.
Maharashtra State Archives, Bombay.
National Library, Calcutta.
Asiatic Society of Bombay, Bombay.
Indian Institute of Mass Communication, New Delhi.
Indian International Centre, New Delhi.
British Council, New Delhi.
Lala Hardayal Public Library, Delhi.
Gandhi Smarak Samiti, New Delhi.
University of Bombay, Bombay.
Gandhi Peace Foundation, New Delhi.
Theosophical Society of India, Adyar.
Raman Kendra, New Delhi.
Press Institute of India, New Delhi.

INS, New Delhi.
Bristol Museum, Bristol.

The authors express their gratitude to the following eminent scholars and friends, who provided them invaluable help, guidance and cooperation in the preparation of this work:

Dr. S.N. Prasad
Dr. O.P. Kejnwal
Dr. S Bhattacharya
Dr. R.K. Perti
Miss E. David
Dr. K.C. Yadav
Professor Emeritus S.R. Mehrotra
Dr. Sudhir Chandra
Dr. V. C. Bhutani
B.N. Rao
Dr. Kireet Joshi
Professor C.B. Tripathi
Mrs. Kamal Pachori
Dr. Dayal Dass
Dr. T.R. Sareen
Dr. Kalpana Dasgupta
Professor H.P. Kaushik
K.S. Talwar
Dr. Mallar Ghosh
Kartar Singh
Mrs. Kusum Sharma
Dr. Chhaya Sharma
Navin Mahajan
Dr. Usha Mathur
Sneh Saxena
L.S. Ramaiah
Devendra Swarup
Urmilla Bhargava
Subhash Vyas

Dr. Ishwari Prasad
Padmashri Dr. Shyam Singh Shashi
Dr. Ram Prakash 'Saras'
Dr. S.P. Sudhesh
Prof. G.K. Chaddha
Sudha Rani Sarma
Gayatri Vashishtha
Dr. Shitla Prasad
Dr. Mushiral Hasan
Dr. S.R. Kidwai
Archana Sharma
Dr. Rajendra Singh Vats
Dr. Rekha Joshi
Padmashri Santosh Yadav
Dr. Radhakant Bharati
Dr. Shardendu Sharma
B.M. Lall
Jayanti Das
Mandhur Bundopuanyaye
Arnold Harrison
Professor Nirmal Singh
Professor B.K. Shrivastava
Dr. Suresh Chand Mishra
Professor M.M. Sankhdher
Mandakani Sankhdher
Shri R.M. Sankhdher
Smt. Shivani Sankhdher

Their thanks are also due to Shri Shyam Sunder Sankhdher, (December 30, 1903–September 17, 1994) an eminent educationist and a constant source of inspiration.

Introduction

'Robert Clive to Jawaharlal Nehru—India: New Historical Interpretations' is an extremely interesting and absorbing work covering the whole of Modern India from the mid-eighteenth century to India's Independence on August 15, 1947 and even later.

It throws excellent light on many episodes, individuals, institutions and ideas, which collectively form a solid foundation on which Modern India has been erected.

This is a new interpretation.

Countless original sources and recent researches have been thoroughly examined and utilized to make this study absolutely authentic and dependable.

The incidents covered in this work are full of extremely interesting details and insights.

The purpose of this study is to examine and analyse certain extremely interesting and absorbing developments in the annals of Modern India. It is unfortunate that countless scholars have not scrutinized many historical events, individuals and institutions from a close angle with the help of countless new historical sources. Historical facts, therefore, require a proper understanding and interpretation.

Why the great founder of the British Empire in India, Robert Clive had to commit horrible suicide by slashing his own throat with a sharp knife on November 22, 1774, when he was alone in his house and his entire family had gone out. Why the British Parliament found it impossible to pardon Robert Clive for his maladministration, bribery, corruption, intrigues and other such misdeeds?

Was he desperate or disappointed?

Why a great writer from Denmark, Captain M. Niebour, who had lived in India for some time, described India as the most civilized country of the world in 1764?

The most interesting themes covered in this study are as follows:

How Nawab Hyder Ali's Government enchained or handcuffed the British Military officer Captain Donald Campbell, without a deadline with a British Soldier, even when the soldier had died?

Why an outstanding world orientalist, a linguist and the founder of the Asiatic Society, Calcutta, could not write Shakuntala, Saraswati, Gautam, Kapil, Manu, Ahilaya, Upanishad, Charak, Valmiki, Dharma, etc. correctly in his literary works? Was it a product of his total ignorance?

How Abhigyan Shakuntalam, first translated into English by Sir William Jones in Calcutta in 1789 created a stir in the west and was translated in quick succession in various western languages?

How an eminent scholar from Kashmir, Goverdhan Kaul, who was overwhelmed by the study of Indian literature wrote in 1788 about the Infinity of Indian Literature. He remarked that one lifetime was not sufficient for the study of Indian Literature.

How a member of the British Supreme Council in India, Sir Philip Francis lost all balance of mind on December 8, 1778 night and in total darkness entered secretly like a robber a lonely Danish Beauty Catherine Grand's house in Calcutta! He was caught while running away and charged with Criminal Conspiracy and fined an extremely heavy amount by his own Government. Humiliated and wounded, he had to return to England after a Savage, Uncivilized bloody Duel with the British Governor General Lord Warren Hastings. The duel took place in Calcutta on August 17, 1780.

How the Mughal Emperor Shah Alam wept and cried, when he had to undergo unlimited, unendurable tortures and humiliations in the Delhi Red Fort in 1788? And why it became unavoidable to turn him blind?

What happened when the Tiger of Mysore Tipu Sultan lost the Battle of Serringapatam and who cut to pieces? How the invaluable gems and gold jewelery, etc. which he was wearing disappeared within no time. Why the searches proved completely futile and why the culprits could not be traced by the British Government?

How the powerful British forces under Lord Lake, despite countless efforts failed disastrously to register a single complete victory against Maharaja Ranjit Singh at Bharatpur? Why the British forces met their Waterloo in Bharatpur? How the British forces were massacred and humiliated in Bharatpur and the British humiliation was so frustrating that the British Governor General Lord Wellesley was immediately recalled to England in 1805. The British forces were no match to the Bharatpur forces either in valour or heroism or the war strategy.

Why Lord Lake shamelessly misbehaved with the bewitching Kashmir Beauty Begum Zebunnussa Samru and committed an unpardonable crime on February 20, 1805, when she arrived with her bodyguards at Lord Lake's British military camp?

How an extraordinary and excellent and most powerful song in Brajbhasha, against the British rule in India, produced 58 years before Bankim Chandra Chatterjee's immortal 'Vandematram', was traced and published in England in 1824?

What efforts did the British Governor General Lord William Bentinck make so that Jaipur could be annexed and how all his plans could not be materialized when William Blake was cut to pieces in Jaipur on June 4, 1835? What was the nature of the Jaipur Revolt of 1835?

How the great British scholar Thomas Macaulay's achievements were evaluated after his return from India to England? Why the Prime Minister of England Lord Melbourne displayed his extreme dislike for Thomas Macaulay? Why some British newspapers of London described Thomas Macaulay as a swindler?

Why an extremely enlightened Indian leader and social reformer Rammohan Roy did not consider it imperative to write or raise his powerful voice against many blatant autocratic British policies and blunders in India? Why his newspapers did not condemn British tyranny and injustice?

Why countless people in England while greeting Rammohan Roy, who moved magnificently on the streets in England in 1831 and later shouted time and again Hail Tippoo Saheb, King of Ingee? Was it an abysmal ignorance about India? Rammohan Roy was not an Indian sovereign and Tipu Sultan of Mysore had died in the Battle of Serringapatam, more than three decades back on May 4, 1799.

How the powerful Sikh sovereign of Panjab Maharaja Ranjit Singh played Holi with the British Governor General Lord William Bentinck and Lady William Bentick in Panjab on October 31, 1831?

This work also comprises excellent account of some individuals, institutions and ideas pertaining to mid-nineteenth century particularly on themes connected with the Great Indian Revolt of 1857.

An eminent Indian scholar of Kashipur, Lokratna Pant, produced excellent poems in Hindi condemning the British maladministration in India and on national unity and India's Independence many years before the Great Indian Revolt of 1857. He should be described as an inspirer of the great Indian revolt of 1857.

In 1857, the great Indian scholar and a social reformer Radhakent Dev demonstrated a rare sense of philanthropy by saving an eminent scholar of Sanskrit from Germany Dr. L. Schntz from total ruin and bankruptcy through a rare monetary gesture. The German scholar wanted to sell all his Sanskrit works to save himself from financial disaster.

How the British Governor General Lord Dalhousie, offended the people of India by handing over most precious royal jewels of the Maharanis of Nagpur to a private British firm for open public auction around 1857?

Why did an outstanding journalist James Buckingham, who was humiliated, punished and thrown out of India for his bold criticism of the East India Co's maladministration in India, on reaching England made it impossible for the British Government in India to breathe and how did he prepare a 'Plan for the Future Government of India' and pleaded for India's representation in the British Parliament prior to the Great Indian Revolt of 1857? Was he an inspirer of the Revolt of 1857?

How Delhi achieved its Independence in 1857, when the Indian revolutionaries, through their heroic efforts, achieved the downfall of the British Tyranny and Injustice, how countless British soldiers and civilians were cut to pieces and how Bahadurshah Zafar, the Mughal Emperor organized a Victory Procession in Delhi, marked by the 'blooming' of countless guns at Red Fort?

The bravery and heroism of Maharaja Bhaskarrao Nargundkar who during the Great Indian Revolt of 1857, defeated the powerful British forces under Charles Maclean, massacred the British forces in total darkness at the dead of night on May 26, 1858, and rejected point blank all British proposals for the annexation of Nargund.

How the greatest urdu Poet of the nineteenth century India, Mirza Ghalib, who was extremely sad due to British tyranny and tortures during the Great Indian Revolt of 1857, escaped himself, after arrest, from execution in Delhi, during the Revolt of 1857 through his humour and the ODE to Queen Victoria, which he had sent to England before 1857?

The open British treachery when William Hodson shot dead the Mughal Princes Mirza Mughal, Mirza Sultan and Abu Bakr, while they were returning from Humayun's Tomb to Red Fort in Delhi on September 22, 1857 under British protection. They were mercilessly shot dead by William Hodson, without any reason or provocation.

A great leader of the great Indian revolt of 1857, Begum Hazrat Mahal, who did not understand the autocratic and tyrannical British policy and the annexation of Oudh before the Great Indian Revolt of 1857, condemned the Queen of England for her unethical, autocratic policies. She wondered why she was not permitted to rule Oudh after the Revolt of 1857. She always felt that the British promises and assurances had absolutely no foundation. Those were a way to deceive the people of India.

How the great Indian Rajput revolutionary leader Amar Singh was captured and tortured to death in prison in Gorakhpur? He was young, bold and courageous; the British Government wrote that he had died due to illness, on February 5, 1860.

How one of the greatest British scholars in India Sir Charles Trevelyan was kicked out of the British Government by the Governor

General and Viceroy Lord Canning for his condemnation of British policies in India in 1860?

How Maharani Jind Kaur, of Punjab, who served as a flame, during the Great Indian Revolt of 1857 was tortured and thrown out of India and who died in total disappointment and isolation in England on August 1, 1863?

Ruthless suppression of the Revolt of 1857 and the mysterious death of Viceroy Lord Elgin on November 26, 1863 in ice-cold weather in Dharamshala. Was he afraid to remain in Calcutta after the Revolt? What was he doing on a hill station during the extreme cold weather?

Eminent Indian Scholar Michael Madhusudan Dutt had tremendous love for the French beauty Emilla Sophia, his wife, whom he considered as inseparable and when she died on June 26, 1873, the shock of this tragedy proved fatal. On receiving the news of her death, Michael Madhusudan Dutt recited 'Tomorrow and Tomorrow' from William Shakespeare's Mecbeth and within no time, breathed his last.

The great Indian barefoot Mahatama Booth Tucker, a British Civil servant, completely transformed himself and behaved exactly like an Indian 'sannyasi' or Yogi, even begged in the Indian streets to impress the Indians and to propagate Christianity in India. He was also a Christian missionary.

Why was it so unavoidable that the British Government in India demonstrated its total inhumanity, racism, pride and arrogance and could not consider the claims of an outstanding Indian educationist and scholar Pandit Ishwarchandra Vidyasagar for highest appointments in India? Why a policy of blatant discrimination was adopted by the administration in dealing with this great Sanskrit genius?

Based on countless archival and non-archival historical sources, this work, also highlights the following individuals, ideas and institutions: how a poor village young man from Tirutani, becomes a celebrity overnight, when as a Scholar, studying in the University of Madras, he produced as a part of his MA Paper a dissertation 'the Ethics of the Vedanta', which was extremely scholarly and deep and which became a talk of the intellectual circles immediately after its publication, even before, he was awarded his Master's degree.

Total fearlessness of Shaheed Madanlal Dhingra, who had shot dead Curzon Wyllie in London and who rejected every offer of legal assistance in fighting his case after arrest by the British police and said that he wanted to die or get hanged, he did not want any mercy by the British Government and got executed in England on August 17, 1909?

Aurobindo Ghosh's unique metamorphosis, after escape from Calcutta to Pondicheery, where this diehard Indian revolutionary, instead of actively participating in revolutionary terrorism for the overthrow of British Colonialism, decided to concentrate on Yoga and write literary, philosophical works such as 'Savitri and Life Divine', after 1910.

How Indian revolutionaries or freedom fighters brilliantly interpreted Viceroy Lord Hardinge's University of Calcutta Convocation Address of March 16, 1912, "be true to your country" and soon threw bombs on Lord Hardinge so that they could perform their duties towards the Motherland, by achieving the Downfall of the British Government and attainment of Swarajya in 1913. How an outstanding Indian scholar and revolutionary, who had founded the Yugantar Ashram in Stockton, USA, for the achievement of Independence for India created a miracle and countless Indians left foreign countries and reached India in order to sacrifice themselves for the achievement of Swarajya. This great revolutionary Dr. Har Dayal had written in 1912: "draw your swords, it is time to fight. sweep all the Bristish from India."

How the great political leader and poetess Sarojini Naidu, could not tolerate British inhumanity, pride and torture in Amritsar, during the Jallianwallahbagh Massacre on April 13, 1919 and reached England and condemned fearlessly the British tyranny and cruelty in India.

The British Government had imposed all kinds of restrictions on Indian educationists and scholars to prevents their participation in any form in India's Struggle for Independence, but the Indian patriots continued to play their own role in the Freedom Movement,

Sir Asutosh Mukherjee, who was serving as the Vice-Chancellor of the University of Calcutta, was not prepared to lower his voice he wanted to provide his own inspiration to the fighters for freedom. In a convocation address at the University of Calcutta, he created his own effect and instead of reciting the Vandematram, which he knew was intolerable to the British Government, he concluded his Convocation Address by reciting a patriotic song by a British war poet and said: 'I vow to thee my country...'

An attempt has been made to understand how Pandit Motilal Nehru created a Thunder in Indian Politics on March 9, 1926, when he warned the British Empire that in case it did not adopt a sympathetic attitude towards the aspirations of the Indian people 'anarchical societies' would raise their heads in different parts of the country, how Winston Churchill out of total disappointment and panic after the commencement of Mahatma Gandhi's historic Dandi March on March 12, 1930 condemned the British Government and wondered why the Indian National Congress was not 'broken up', when the British Union Jack was burnt to ashes in Lahore, how Pandit Motilal Nehru emerged as the Uncrowned Sovereign of Allahabad and was not prepared to walk in the shadow of others, how Ganesh Shankar Vidyarathi, a great patriot, decided to sacrifice himself for peace, national unity and harmony in Kanpur and died on March 25, 1931, while trying to restore love and mutual understanding, how Indian political leadership was hypnotized and how the British diplomacy succeeded during the World War in obtaining the resignation of all the Indian Ministers by the end of 1939 and making them completely ineffective. How Gurudev Rabindranath Tagore surprised everyone, when he attended a special convocation at Shantiniketan, in which he was honored by the University of Oxford, England with a Doctorate and how when the university representative read out the Bendecation in unintelligible Latin, Rabindranath Tagore decided to accept the honor not in English, or Latin but in Sanskrit.

The British Government demonstrated its injustice and blatant racism and discrimination, when because of his boldness, courage and patriotism it refused to grant extension as Vice-Chancellor to Sir Asutosh Mukherjee around 1923.

This study also concentrates on some of the most notable themes such as when before the Quit India Movement, countless Indians looked helpless and disappointed a brilliant political leader Chakravarty Rajagopalachari, in a powerful and inspiring address on December 13, 1941, said: "The greatness of India is not dead, build, build daily."

How Mahatma Gandhi treated the uncontrollable Indian revoltionaries, who believed in the doctrine of Dagger and Bomb for the achievement of Swarajya when they came to seek an interview with him, in total darkness, at the dead of night, and how Mahatma Gandhi had developed a unique philosophy of Total Involvement for nation-building, which was also the greatest secret of his tremendous success in almost every field of endeavour; how Netaji Subhash Chandra Bose's air crash death report was also publicized during his lifetime, Rajarshi Purushottamdas Tandon's extraordinary sense of sacrifice and commitment and the Ramlila in Allahabad, and the extraordinary Univeristy of Allahabad Convocation in which Jawaharlal Nehru was awarded a Doctorate on December 13, 1947.

These interpretations are totally independent.These are not directly connected with each other.

1

When Lord Clive Cut his own Throat with a Sharp Knife. The Mystery of the Founder of the British Empire's Suicide

Lord Clive is considered as the founder of British Empire in India. He defeated Nawab Sirajuddaullah in the battle of Plassey, with the help of Mir Jaffar and a follower of Guru Nanak Seth Amichand. He amassed a lot of wealth through all kind of ways; fair or foul. Through conspiracies and intrigues, he got rid of Nawab Sirajuddaullah and collected a huge amount from Mir Jafar.

Lord Clive had to pay more than Rs. 30,000,00 to Seth Amichand for help in the overthrow of the Nawab of Bengal but Lord Clive had no intension of paying that amount. He had shown some fictitious documents, treaty or agreement to one of the richest businessman of Bengal: Amichand.

In mysterious circumstances Seth Amichand died immediately after the Battle of Plassey.

Lord Clive had also succeeded in obtaining Mughal Emperor Shah Alam's permission for collecting land revenue from Bengal, Bihar and Orissa. Lord Clive agreed to pay Rs. 30,000,00 to Shah Alam every year for the permission.

When Lord Clive retired and returned to England in 1767, he

was surprised that the press, the parliament and the people all were hostile. They considered him as an unprincipled individual who had no sense of morality and truthfulness. A man who could go to any extent to amass wealth and power. The people did not like the way he intrigued to dethrone Nawab Sirajuddaullah.

Lord Clive was made 'baron Clive of Plassey' in England in 1762. He became KCB in 1764. He also became a member of British Parliament.

He was also described as the "Heaven Born General".

But his life was completely devoid of any peace or pleasure. He was all the time in panic. He had lost his courage, his confidence and his nerves. He was an epitome of self-distrust. After his return from India, there was not even a single moment in his life when he did not undergo severe, unbearable physical pain and nervousness.

His health had deteriorated and despite medical treatment, increasing use of heavy drugs and opium, there was hardly any relief.

His loving wife and four children Edward, Rebecca Charloote, Magaret and Robert no one provided him relief from insufferable, unendurable pain and anxiety.

Lord Clive was a portrait of disappointment, disenchantment and disillusionment after his return from India.

He live luxuriously in his newly purchased comfortable houses. He had all the amenities of life, including domestic aids, and countless millions of rupees, plundered from India, through bribes and frauds, but nothing could provide him much pleasure.

His ordeal became all the more distressing, when the British Parliament decided to debate his misdeeds and he was questioned about his fictitious treaty with Mir Jaffar. The Black Hole of Calcutta, in which more than 145 British had to die due to suffocation, was considered by the people of England as a consequence of his unpardonable policies adopted by the servants of the East India Company in India. Lord Clive also almost wept in the Parliament and said:

"Taken my fortune but save my honour".

Lord Clive was made the governor of Bengal by the East India

Company for about 2 years. He was also made the Commander-in-Chief for some time but in the parliament he was treated as a 'criminal' who had set a wrong example in India.

Countless British Members who remained furious up to the last days of Lord Clive's life were H. Johnstone, Burgoyne and the chairman of the East India Company Sullivan. Another Member of Parliament, who had made it impossible for Robert Clive to breath was Stanley, who wanted an answer for every crime committed by Lord Clive in India.

Attacks on Lord Clive continued both in the Press and the Parliament. Lord Clive had no peace of mind and he was suffering from maddening physical pain.

On November 22, 1774, something extraordinary, unbelievable happened. When Lord Clive's wife and his children and other relations had gone out, he took up a sharp knife and brutally cut his throat. He fell down on the ground and died.

When his wife returned home, she found Lord Clive lying in a pool of blood.

Some newspapers, however, wrote that Lord Clive had killed himself with a revolver under a tree.

Even today some people are not prepared to accept that Lord Clive committed suicide. They for their own reasons believe that the founder of the British Empire in India died a . . . natural deaths.

2

Captain M. Niebuhr of Denmark and a Rare Pen-Portrait of Eighteenth Century Indian Society, Politics and Culture

India is singularly fortunate that countless outstanding scholars from all over the world came here since times immemorial and drew their brilliant pen portraits of Indian society, politics and culture. Their rare accounts are an immortal source of information for research and other historical investigations.

One such eminent scholar—a man of highest integrity and objectivity-was Captain M. Niebuhr from Denmark, who visited India more than 240 years ago, after the fall of the Mughal Empire and when England, Holland, France and other western powers were trying to establish their hold in India. It was much before the American War of Independence and the Great French Revolution of 1789.

India provided M. Niebuhr, author of 'Travels Through Arabia' a great inspiration and he found India 'the earliest civilized nation in the world'. He was full of admiration for the people of India, whom he described as 'magnificent and enlightened' and also "mild, laborious and naturally virtuous in their disposition."

In 1764, this great writer from Denmark, paid a marvellous tribute to India, when he remarked: 'The inhabitant of other countries of the East, the Greeks, and perhaps the Egyptians drew the first elements of their knowledge from India'.

India was not merely the 'most civilized' but also the most 'ancient of nations and Indians, according to the Denmark intellectual genius had 'retained their ancient usages and opinions in an admirable manner', even in the eighteenth century.

M. Niebuhr was full of admiration for the women of India, who appeared to him extremely industrious and active. He also praided the 'benevolence', probity and 'patience' of the Indian people.

Surprisingly, unlike some Christian missionaries and British administrators, who condemned the 'infant marriages' in India, during the eighteenth and nineteenth centuries. Niebuhr demonstrated a remarkable restraint, when he did not find anything alarming or intolerable about 'marriages at the age of 6, a pratice quite popular among some people in some parts of India. The reason was quite simple'. The boys and girls had to remain totally separate till their maturity.

Niebuhr wrote:

> 'They give their children in marriage at six years of age but the young couple continue to be separate in the house of their patents, till they attain puberty.'

M. Niebuhr was great defender of India's 'varna-vyavastha' or caste system. The reason was that he did not observe any rigidities or exploitation in the system.

He was extremely happy when he found prohibition on Widow-burning or sati in Poona, M. Niebuhr wrote:

> 'The Marathas seldom allow the living wife to burn herself on the funeral pile of the deceased husband.'

Niebuhr must have laughed wildly when he noticed 'Yogis' or 'fakirs' in India fully 'armed' and who moved with powerful troops in thousands, ready for terrible, bloody combats and as a contrast, he also discovered a 'fakir' at Surat, who had lived, shut up in a cage, for 20 years and who kept both his arms 'constantly raised'.

The Denmark scholar had great admiration for the Government of Poona. He wrote: 'Justice is impartially administered, Agriculture and manufactures flourish and the country is very populous.'

What impressed Niebuhr the most in economic matters was the astonishing affluence and a remarkably successful and flourishing international trade at Surat, in which countless countries: Portugal, China, Arabia, Denmark, Persia, France, England, etc. were deeply involved. It was supported by an excellent, most modern and flourishing ship-building complex. Made of teak wood and fully protected against all odds, the Indian ships strong and sturdy, were perhaps 'the best in the world'. The ships were quite economical. Niebuhr perhaps could not believe his eyes when he saw a 'ninety year old' Indian ship ready for sea-voyage.

Niebuhr could not ignore certain horrible, ghastly and savage customs and practices. He was perhaps stunned or shocked when he saw a 'Tower of Death' in Bombay.

Some Parsis brought their dead to the Tower of Death to be devoured by birds of prey. Niebuhr wrote:

> 'They still retain the singular control of exposing their dead to be eaten by birds of prey, instead of interring or burning them. When the flesh is devoured they remove the bones into two chambers at the bottom of the Tower.'

Niebuhr was rather hypercritical or unduly pessimistic about the Muslims. He wrote: 'It is folly to suppose that any literary art can make progress among the 'mahometans', while despotism, indolence, and superstition—the great enemies of literary improvement continue to retain their ground among them'.

M. Niebuhr was critical of British policies in India. He was writing after the Battle of Plassey, the murder of Sirajuddaullah and Lord Clive's maladminstration, plunders and other intrigues. Niebuhr was convinced that India would emerge as a great flourishing country, immediately after the decline or downfall of the British power. He wrote:

> 'It is the exorbitant power of the English that at present retards

the progressive improvement, but when this colossal statue, whose feet are of clay, and which has been raised by conquering merchants, shall be broken in pieces—an event which may fall out sooner than is supposed, then shall 'Indostan' become again a flourishing country.'

He returned to Denmark from Bombay on March 24, 1864 and joined the service of the King of Denmark as a 'Captain of Engineers'.

3

Hyder Ali and the Horrible Handcuff of Captain Donald Campbell with a Dead Soldier without a Deadline

The East India Company's Government in India was a horrible blend of thoroughly unprincipled and corrupt traders, totally unqualified and ignorant clerks, stupid, untrained soldiers and narrow-minded, almost blind, missionaries, whose paramount concern was conversion of 'heathens' and spread of Christianity from one part of India to the other, through every possible trick or trap, including temptations, force, inducements and monetary incentives.

The result was ruin and disaster.

Countless innocent Britons, men, women and children, had to part with their lives due to unimaginative, aggressive and inhuman policies of British colonialism.

Many British thinkers or intellectuals condemned the East India Company's injustice and corruption and warned the Company from time to time.

Mad with power and racial arrogance, many officials of the Company humiliated all the people and the sovereign in India.

They indulged in tyranny, torment and torture. The Company adopted all kinds of ways to achieve its ambitious objects, such as acquisition of more and more territory, power and wealth.

Before commanding suicide, Lord Clive, had indulged in India, in endless conspiracies, intrigues, murder, blackmail, exploitation, briberies and violence.

He, like many other employees of the East India Company, wanted to return to England, as a 'nabob', loaded with Indian wealth.

The Company's employees indulged in worst kind of corruptions and spying. They had no shame in torturing even the men of respectability and power, including the rulers of the Indian states. It was impossible to put a check on the ambitions of the British mercantile firm or to check its horrible activities.

Out of disgust and disappointment, the Indian elite described the Britons as 'malechehs'. They were openly indulging in drinking, smoking, eating of pork and beef and dancing with other men's wives, which was intolerable to the Indian people.

The Company's had no chance of success in Indian politics or society, trade or commerce without the active cooperation of regular informers, spies or intelligence network. A disorganized powerful spy-ring, therefore, came into operation. Countless employees of the Co's and outsiders, therefore, worked as detectives, espionage-agents, detectors, dowsers, political surveyors, political-excavators, under-cover fact-finders and even criminologists.

They kept the Company's fully informed about the activities of different political powers in this country, through all kinds of probes, hunts and explorations.

Hyder Ali, 1722-82, the ruler of Mysore was one of the greatest threats and dangers to the East India Company. He was an extraordinary General, who was far-sighted, brave, courageous and extremely well informed. He knew the British designs thoroughly, and he knew how to out—Herod. He had captured Bednore, Malabar, and invaded Carnatic. He had defeated the powerful British forces and captured Arcot in 1780.

Hyder Ali was the deadliest enemy of the British and wanted to throw them out of India with the help of France. He was critical of the British policies and attitudes in India.

He was always in search of an opportunity to their teach the British a lesson for their tortures and inhumanity in India.

An opportunity presented itself when Hyder Ali's forces captured, with tremendous difficulty, an English captain Donald Campbell and his associates, including Hall. They were suspected by the Mysore Government of spying or espionage.

The Government of Mysore tried to extract all possible information from these militarymen. They were tortured and thrown into a dungeon.

The Mysore officials wanted to torture them. Unable to endure the pain and punishment, Hall breathed his last, in captivity. He had been thrown into the torture cell along with Captain Donald Campbell. Both these suspected blood-hounds or gum-shoes had been handcuffed or enchained together.

When Hall died, deadbeat and fatigued, he should have been separated from Captain Donald Campbell and buried with military honour, but the Government of Mysore did not separate the dead-body from the Captain. For several long days and nights, without a deadline, Donald Campbell remained constantly, inseperably enchained with the dead-body of Hall.

It was a most horrible sight. It was totally unbearable. It was inhumane and uncivilized.

Ultimately, when Hall was reduced to a deadwood, the dead-body was separated for final burial.

Such a doom, death and decay was never witnessed in the history of Mysore. Such a ghastly incident never happened under Emperor Ashok or Chandragupt Maurya. Such inhumanity was never demonstrated under the Great Mughals. Even in the history of the British Empire and perhaps the world such death in shackles, chains or irons and torture has, perhaps, no parallel. This was unprecedented and shocking in the extreme.

Captain Donald Campbell returned to England, after this horrible experience, and died there on June 5, 1804.

4

Sir William Jones, an Outstanding World-Orientalist and the Founder of the Asiatic Society

Sir William Jones was an eminent world orientalist and the founder of the Asiatic Society of Bengal. He was deeply influenced by India and its immortal Sanskrit Literature. He had read Bhagvad Gita, Manu-Smriti, Meghadoot, Abhijan Shakuntalam, Ramayan and the Vedas. He was so much influenced by the profundity and richness of Indian Philosophy, Science and Literature, that he devoted a major part of his life in India in their understanding and appreciation. He knew more than two dozen languages of the world and his comments on Indian Literature created almost a commotion in the realm of ideas. He translated Kalidas's immortal Sanskrit classic; Abhijan Shakuntalam into English and the result was that the work was not merely reprinted a number of times in Calcutta, London, Boston, etc., but Russia, Germany, France, Italy, etc. also got it translated into their own languages.

Sir William Jones was also a brilliant poet. He founded the '*Asiatic Miscellany*' and the '*Asiatic Researches*'.

In this poem, Lord Teignmouth or better known Sir John Shore tries to provide an estimate of the character and achievement of his distinguished scholar-friend, Sir Willaim Jones. He portrays him as a man of unbounded learning—upright, pure, gentle, faithful and friendly to the whole mankind. He borrows Dr. Samuel Joanson's expression, when he describes Sir William Jones as The Most Enlightened to sons of men.

Unbounded learning, thoughts by genius framed
To guide the bounteous labours of his pen,
Distinguished him, whom kindred sages named,
'The most enlighten'd of the sons of men.'

Upright through life, as in his death resign'd.
His actions spoke a pure and ardent breast:
Faithful to God, and friendly to mankind,
His friends rever'd him, and his country bless'd.

Admir'd and valued in a distant land,
His gentle manners all affection won
The prostrate Hindu own'd his fostering hand
And Science mark'd him for her favourite son.

Regret and praise the general voice bestows,
And public sorrows with domestic blend;
But deeper yet must be the grief of those,
Who, while the sage they honour'd, love'd the friend.

Sir William Jones found India a lovely country. He wrote:

"To the east a lovely country wide extends,
India, whose borders the wide ocean bounds,
On this the sun, new rising from the main,
Smiles pleased, and sheds his early orient beam.

The rich soil,
Washed by a thousand rivers, from all sides,
Pours on the natives wealth without control."

Sir William Jones, however, created the greatest mystry of all times. Till today the mystry remains unresolved. Sir William Jones used wild spellings of Indian names etc. in his brilliant writings. Why was he not careful or meticulous or absolutely accurate is beyond understanding.

His spellings do not reflect his genius, his calibre and competence, his intellect or his supreme brilliant scholarship or wisdom.

It seems, he used the most absured, inappropriate, and ludicurous spellings both in his original writings and translations.

His absentmindedness or lack of total concentration seems to be inexcusable. For Shakuntala, he wrote Sacontla, for Saraswati he wrote Seraswaty and for Shankar he used Sancarea.

Such spellings were simply preposterous and disgusting.

In place of Gautam, he wrote Gotama, and for Kapil, he wrote Capila. He did not write the correct names of even Kalidas, Manu, Ahilaya, Goverdhan, Valmiki, and Charak.

He wrote Calidas, Menu, Ahalya, Goverdhena, Valmici and Chereca.

Sir William Jones demonstrated his total unfamiliarity with spellings when he wrote Upanisat instead of Unpanishad.

It is astonishing that a linguist of the stature of Sir William Jones could not write 'dharma' and 'Dara Shukoh' correctly.

The result was diasterous. Hundreds of British officials in India, including Governors-General and Viceroys continued to use the most absured spellings of Indian names etc.

Sir Monier Williams, who translated 'Abhigyan Shakuntalam' in 1857 however used much better spellings.

5

When Sir William Jones Published Excellent Translations of Oriental Poetry Produced by Jayadev, Hafiz, Meer Durd, Sadiq, etc. along with the Originals, In 'the Asiatic Miscellany', Calcutta, Founded in 1785

THE ASIATIC MISCELLANY
THE FIRST JOURNAL OF THE ASIATIC SOCIETY OF BENGAL

Sir William Jones was not merely a linguist and a scholar of Indian or oriental literatures, but was also a great journalist of his age. The *Asiatic Miscellany*, and the *Asiatic Researches*, the two journals which he established in India immediately after the foundation of the Asiatic Society of Bengal, demonstrate his great capacity as a journalist. In later years, the *Gleanings in Science* (1829) and the *Journal of the Asiatic Society of Bengal* (1830), were established as the mouthpiece of the Society. These also unmistakably bore the impress of his personality though he was no more in this world to conduct them. He did on April 27, 1794.

The *Asiatic Miscellany* was founded in 1785. Its main objective was to introduce oriental literature to those who had no idea about its profundity and richness. It was a quarterly publication. Its first two numbers were published in the quarto size, which was reduced to octovo size in 1787 as it was found unwieldy by the management. Its price was also reduced in accordance with the size of the periodical. In 1787, its name was slightly altered and it became *The Asiatic Miscellany and Bengal Register.* It was a significant change as it also included now a Register of Occurrences, and a brief commentary on Indian politics. In the Preface to the Third Number of the *Asiatic Miscellany* the editor remarked, 'The original design of the *Miscellany* was to collect instructive and amusive essays relative to Asia, to find an easy means of circulating occasional productions too short for distinct publication, to rescue from oblivion the most interesting local descriptions of former travelers and to disseminate the Oriental languages; to review new books published in India; and by a variety of its materials to be at once entertaining, curious, and instructive. These objects will, all of them, be still kept in view; but more especially the diffusion of many of the Eastern dialects; the study of which is now become so essentially useful, that the attainment of them cannot be too much recommended and assisted; and in addition, A Register of Occurrences will be inserted for the sake of convenient reference. The publication will hereafter be termed the *Asiatic Miscellany* and *Bengal Register* ?

The following was its plan for the future:

> 'The work to consist, as at present, of original productions, Translations, Historical, Moral, and Poetical, with the originals on the opposite page of all except the first; the style of which being in general dry and unengaging, the English version to be given alone, authenticated by the name of Translator. Also of a Review and Chronicle at the end of each number, the former containing a brief account of all new publications in Bengal, during the preceding quarter; the latter, a compendious Register of all Oriental Occurrences of Worthy notice; of Births, Marriages, Deaths, Arrivals and Departures of all Ships, at and from Calcutta; and Promotions of the Hon. Company's Civil and Military Servants in Bengal. II. The number of pages to be as hitherto 128 but of octovo size, containing about two-thirds of the present quarto page besides the Review and Chronicle, more or less, as may be occasionally required. III. The price of

each number to be eight sicca Rupees to Subscribers. To non-Subscribers Twelve.'

The Third Number of the *Asiatic Miscellany* contained translations of certain extracts from Firishtah by I.H. Harington and *Seyrul Mutakhereen* by J. Anderson. These related to the conquest of Bengal by the Muslims and the rise of Marathas respectively. Under the title Love and Beauty it published poetry of Neemut Khan in Persian with its English translation.

'The tale of Love adorns my teeming prose,
With flame like ardour on my tongue it glows.
Free shall my pen intoxicated rove;
Let every Lover list the lore of Love.'

Moola Togra's Persian eulogy on Kashmir was translated by some one under the pen 'H.H.' The Eulogy runs as follows:

'...where captive birds for ever join their strains,
Where herbs and flowers for ever grace the plains,
And gild the hills—whose beauteous summits rise
Decked with their garlands, to the starry skies,
Flowers fill the scented air—
and flowers the ground:
Overland and water blooming flowers abound:
Nature with all her gifts Kushmeer has crown'd.'

Similarly a translation of Elagiac Verses of Moola Wehshee addressed to his mistress was published in the *Asiatic Miscellany* in 1787. It shows how much effort was made by the journal to translate oriental poetry into English.

How long the rose-like, wilt thou smile on all?
How long with others recreation take?

Ah! think if thy embrace these oft receive,
Hereafter wilt thou feel repentant shame.

The crowd shall fly, and leave thee in despair,
Lost in confusion then, as I am now.
When I depart, they wayward cruelties
Who will endure? who suffer for thy sake?

Thou must not seek my rival's house by night;
Nor with light another's gloom dispel.
Nor everywhere, to all, affection show;
Nor foster him will afflict thy heart.

Translations of certain works of Jayadev, Abu Nasirudding, Meer Durd, Hafiz, Hamasah, Sadiq with their originals, and hymns to Durga, Bhawani, Prakriti in English were published in the Third Nukber of the *Asiatic Miscellany*. This was about the Miscellany. The Bengal Register contained review of new Publications; Miscellaneous Occurrences; Indian Politics; Proceedings of the Supreme Court; Theatrical Intelligence; Sporting Intelligence, an account of births, deaths, and marriages, Arrivals and Departures of Ships; Civil and Military Promotions. All these items covered the period of three months from October to December 1787.

Review of New Publications contained a brief editorial note which is remarkable for its reflection on the editorial policy. It said, 'The confined society of Europeans in this country will not admit of free criticism; to censure where every author is so well known to every reader, would be invidious, and painful, independent of which, we are conscious of our weak pretensions to preside in the tribunal of literature. We shall, therefore, as proposed, merely describe such books as have been published within the last quarter, in a brief analysis of their subjects and designs; leaving it to every reader to pass his own decision on their merits and demerits. The books which were reviewed in the *Asiatic Miscallany* during the year 1787 included *Original Persian Letters* translated into English by John Mulcock, *The*

Volunteers, or a Trip to Bengal, in the year 1783 by a Gentleman at Calcutta; the *Oriental Asylum* by J.O. Reilly: *a Treatise of Horses* translated by Joseph Earles, *a Narrative of Transactions in Bengal* translated by F. Gladwin, *Letters of the Emperor Aurangzeb to his sons,* translated by Joseph Earles and the *Memoirs of Khojeh Abdul Kureeem* by F. Gladwin.

The *Asiatic Miscellany* ceased publication in 1788 when its place was taken by the *Asiatic Researches,* the well known Journal of the Asiatic Society of Bengal.

6

'Abhigyan Shakuntalam' and the Intellectual Stir in the West

Sir William Jones (1786-94), one of the greatest world-orientalists of all times and the founder of the Asiatic Society, Calcutta (1784), created an unparalleled stir in the world of Literature, when he translated into English, in 1789, Mahakavi Kalidas's immortal Sanskrit classic Abhigyan Shakuntalam. This translation created a commotion in the western world. The scholars felt deeply impressed and they raised Abhigyan Shakuntalam to the highest pedestral.

Immediately after its publication from Calcutta in the year of the French Revolution, the Abhigyan Shakuntalam was published from London in 1790. Seen in 1792, another edition had to be produced there. Sir William Jones died in Calcutta on April 27, 1794 but the demand for Abhigyan Shakuntalam continued to increase and in 1796, it was republished from Edinburgh. Scholars in England found it extremely interesting and extraordinary. They praised not only the translator, but also Mahakavi Kalidas for his excellent literary accomplishment.

The Analytical Review, London, Published its appreciation of Sir William Jones's translation in thirteen long pages in August 1790. *The Gentlemen's Magzine*, London, compared Kalidas in November 1790, with William Shakespeare. The *Oriental Review*, London, the

Annual Register, London, etc. congratulated Sir William Jones on his great discovery.

The eighteenth century could not come to its close without the publication of yet one more edition of Abhigyan Shakuntalam in London in 1799.

The beginning of the nineteenth century witnessed the publication of Abhigyan Shakuntalam from Boston in 1805. London was not lagging far behind and in 1806, another edition of Abhigyan Shakuntalam came out from that metropolis. The interest did not end there. On the contrary it continued to increase further and many more editions came out in quick succession from different parts of the world.

Abhigyan Shakuntalam thus succeeded in introducing Indian Literature to England and in bringing India, subsequently, into closer cultural contact with the west. In decades to come, it generated a lot of goodwill, understanding and appreciation for India abroad.

Sir William Jones was not the sole translator of Kalidas's Abhigyan Shakuntalam, though he was the pioneer in English. The German orientalist Professor George Forster translated it into German in 1791. In 1790, he had brought a copy of Sir William Jones' translation from England. To him it was 'Worthy of close attention' and 'embodied subtelity, sentiment, poetic fervour and tenderest emotions.'

In 1792, a great Russian Scholar and an outstanding literary genius of his age, Nikulai Mihallovich Karamzin (December 12, 1766 to June 3, 1826) translated it into Russian. Nikolai Mihallovich Karamzin was also a poet, linguist and a historian. He was a friend of the Russian Emperor Tsar Alexander and he produced a 12 volume History of the Russian State, which became a landmark in the History and Literature of that country. He also edited the Moscow Journal and the Bulletin of Europe. The Abhigyan Shakuntalam was not merely serialized in the Moscow Journal by Nikulai Karamzin, but it was also staged in Russia due to the efforts of that great Russian man of letters.

In the Foreword to his translation of Abhigyan Shakuntalam Nikolai Karamzin made it clear that the creative spirit of man did not reside in Europe alone, but its character is universal and that the man with his sensitive heart and deep imagination, is everywhere the same. In the mirror of his imagination, the man, according to Nikolai Karamzin, 'holds both Heaven and Earth'. Nikolai Karamzin's translation of Abhigyan Shkuntalam was based on the translations of Sir William Jones and professor George Forster.

E.M. Post translated this classic into Dutch in 1792 and in 1793 it was translated into Danish by Hans West.

The classic continued to inspire countless scholars and A. Bruguiere translated it into French in 1803 and Professor Luicidoria translated it into Italian in 1815.

Abhigyan Shakuntalam was thus becoming a sensation.

August W. Schlegel, Johann Herder and J.W. Goethe—all were full of praise. John Herder was of the firm opinion that Abhigyan Shakuntalam was more invaluable than the Vedas. He remarked that such masterpieces appeared only in two thousand years. To Goethe Kalidas's Abhigyan Shakuntalam was 'a strand that braides earth and heaven into one.'

In France, perhaps, the greatest admirers of Abhigyan Shakuntalam were Professor A.L. Chezy, who translated this 'work of unfathomable depth', into French in 1830, and Fauche, who found it worthy of deep appreciation in 1854. Some critics felt that in the whole Greek antique, there were 'no poetic portrayal of beautiful womanhood' 'that came anywhere near' Abhigyan Shakuntalam.

An excellent English translation of Abhigyan Shakuntalam came out in 1853. It was produced by an eminent English scholar Sir Monder Williams.

These translations inspired a host of other translations of the Indian classics, such as the Meghadut, the Geet Govind, the Hitopdesh, the Maltlmadhav, the Manu Smriti, the Mahabharat, the Ramayan and the Vedas in different parts of the world, Shrimad Bhagvad Gita had already been translated into English in 1785, by Charles Wilking.

These literary endeavours not merely led to a better understanding between India and the rest of the world, but they also shattered the powerful British colonial or Christian missionary myth against India, in the eighteenth and early nineteenth centuries that India was a land of darkness and its people were uncivilized, and uncultured. These translations served as a floodgate which connected the powerful stream of Indian thought with the ocean of world literature.

The most concrete accomplishment of these oriental studies was the establishment of a large number of permanent literary and cultural institutions, all over the world, devoted exclusively to oriental investigations and research, such as the Asiatic Society of St. Petersburge, 1810, The Societe Asiat IQUE, Paris, 1822, the Royal Asiatic Society of Great Britain and Ireland, London, 1823, Detsche Morgenland Ische Gesellschaft and Sir Monier Williams'. The Indian Institute Oxford, 1883.

Not only this, the Court of Directors of the East India Company, was so much impressed by Sanskrit Literature that it commissioned from Germany, one of the greatest orientalists known to human history, Dr. Friederich Maxmuller, (1823-1900), to edit in 1846, the world- famous Sanskrit treasure the Rigveda. This great German translator of Hitopadesh (1843), performed a miracle. He dedicated his entire life to the study and translation of Sanskrit classics. He spent about 25 years to provide a glimpse of oriental literature to the entire mankind, before his death in 1900, and produced the 51 volume world-famous English literary series: The Sacred Books of the East.

These translations led to a fresh appraisal of Indian classical literature in India too. One of the greatest national leaders and an eminent English poet, Sri Aurobindo's writing about the literary contribution of Kalidas described him as 'a consumate artist, profound in conception and suave in execution.'

7

Goverdhan Kaul and Infinity of Indian Literature

Sir William Jones, H.H. Wilson, John Gilchrist, H.T. Colebrooke and many other orientalists had a deep understanding of Indian works of Literature. They were greatly impressed by the Vedic wisdom and other Indian works of literature, philosophy and science. They were appreciative of the originality, dept and extraordinary vastness of Indian scholarship, including Srimad Bhagvad Gita, Ramayan, Geet-Govind, Mahabharat, Upanishads and the Vedas. Even in the western world, there were some scholars in the closing decades of the eighteenth century, who were well acquainted with Indian's great, glorious culture inheritance. They admired the philosophical ideas of Italy, German, Greece, France, England and thousands of years old Indian Literature. However, many ignorant, blindfolded, unenlightened civil and military employees of the East India Company demonstrated their total lack of understanding and comprehension about India and its encyclopaedic Literature. Out of sheer ignorance, unwittingly some British soldiers, traders and missionaries remained completely in the dark and in the most stupid and naïve manner condemned some of the most profound and inspiring works of Sanskrit Literature.

Many Indian outstanding intellectuals did not like the criticism and condemnation of Indian physiology, science and literature by unqualified, uninitiated, uninstructed backward obscurantists. Even some of the highest officials and policy-makers of the Company, betrayed a complete lack of understanding about the most outstanding and enlightening works of great glorious Vedic Literature.

It seems, Goverdhan Kaul, an extraordinary Sanskrit genius from Kashmir, felt greatly disappointed by the ignorance of the western world about India. It seems, he was determined to destroy or demolish the prevailing myths and misunderstandings about India. He wanted to enlighten the entire intellectual world about the vastness and profundity of India's scholarship right from the earliest times. Sir William Jones, founder of the Asiatic Society, provided him the most appropriate opportunity by establishing an annual in Calcutta, the *Asiatic Researches* in 1788.

This was much before the apostle of Indian awakening Rammohan Roy has emerged on the national horizon or Justice Radhakant Dev, Bal-Shastri Jambhekar, Jaggannath Shankar seth, Jamshedji Jijabhsi, Lokratna Pant, Dwarkanath Tagore, Henry Derozio, Ishwarchandra Gupta, Rassikkrisna Mallick, Prassannakumar Tagore and Kasiprasad Ghosh had started making their presence felt in Indian politics, society or culture.

This was indeed pioneering, unprecedented and unparalleled.

In his brilliant contribution to *the Asiatic Researches*, Calcutta, Goverdhan Kaul tried to provide an excellent assessment of the entire Sanskrit literature in a most objective and scholarly manner.

He enlightened the western world and conclude his article with the following remarks:

> 'Whenever we direct our attention to Hindu Literature, the notion of infinity presents itself and the longest life would not be sufficient for the perusal of near 500000 stanzas in the Purans with a million more perhaps in the other works'.

This was followed by scholarly contributions of other Indian scholars such as Radhakant Sarman, Ramlochan Pandit, and Akhtar Ali Khan.

Because of these contributions there was a tremendous demand for the Asiatic Researches in England, and a pirated edition of the journal was published in 1798 in London. The demand spread like a wild fire and M.A. Labaume published a French translation of the annual, with scholarly comments from M. Langles and M.M. Cavier, under the title 'Resarches Asiaticque'.

Countless scholars and members of the Asiatic Society were appreciative of Goverdhan Kaul's ideas and estimates. The article had a great impact on the western thinkers. However, the officials of the East India Company who wanted to grope in the dark throughout their lives, such as Thomas Macaulay, Sir Charles Trevelyan, John Wilson, Alexander Duff and Sir Charles Wood and who wanted to play politics, continued to underestimate the Indian languages and Indian Literatures and by describing Indian languages and literatures as inadequate imposed English and British education on the Indian people.

This Company's policy served as a set-back to Indian languages and Literatures for many long decades.

8

Sir Philip Francis' Horrible Humiliation and Disgrace to England

When Warren Hastings served as the Governor-General in India, the senior-most officials of the East India Company were shamelessly involved in plundering India. Lost in corruptions and plunders of wealth, they did not mind displaying brazenfacedly their own greed, malice, jealousies, erudeness, obstinacy, and antagonisms. There was vulgar tug-of-war between the most-powerful, responsible and highest-paid officials of the Company. There were open confrontations, contentions, and contrariness. Opposition, rivalries and mad-race for power, position and prestige had become deadly and destructive.

The result of this kind of polarity resulted in misgovernment, in justices, and corruption in India and the downfall of many eminent individuals. Such hostilities, intolerance and disputes brought disgrace to the East India Company and to England.

Sir Philip Francis, who was violently opposed to Warren Hastings, reached Calcutta on October 19, 1774, as a member of the Supreme Council of India. He was one of the most powerful members of the Supreme Council, because he was regularly getting the wholehearted support of two other powerful members of the Council G. Monson and J. Clavering.

Sir Philip Francis made it impossible for Warren Hastings to implement his policies in India. He criticized and condemned Warren Hastings. He opposed his policies with regard to Governor-General's treatment of the Begums of Oudh, the arrest of Maharaja Chet Singh and the execution of Pandit Nandkumar.

Warren Hastings had hanged Pandit Nandkumar for 'forgery', on August 5, 1775, for exposition Warren Hastings corruptions.

The whole India and also England were thoroughly aware of Lord Warren Hastings—Sir Philip Francis blatant opposition to each other, their enemity, obstinacy and non-cooperation with each other.

Both took tremendous interest in humiliating and contradicting each other.

Sir Philip Francis had one great weakness. He was passionately in love with his dream-girl Catherine, a Danish beauty, residing in Calcutta. Catherine was his darling, his flame, and his Goddess of Love.

Sir Philip Francis was bewitched, and charmed by this Tranquebar tentalising temptation.

Sir Philip Francis was always in search of an opportunity to love the young, beautiful and graceful Catherine. Any love or romance with Catherine, however, was an impossibility. She was a married lady, living fully-protected with her newly-married Indian civil service official husband, George Francocis Grand. The marriage had taken place on July 10, 1777.

Sir Philip Francis was almost mad in his love. He developed a kind of abnormality or idolatry with regard to his heart-throb. He lost all self-restraint and behaved like an uncontrolled wild Romeo.

On December 8, 1778 night, he lost the balance of his mind. Wild with passion, he decided to make love with Catherine. He had full information that on that night she was completely alone in her Calcutta house, since the husband had gone out. There was absolutely no possibility of George Francosis Grand's return throughout the night.

Sir Philip Francis hatched a conspiracy in his mind. He was determined to make love with Catherine, the Queen of his heart.

Sir Philip Francis was a man of indomitable courage and

determination, with a robust will-power. He had made up his mind to capture Catherine and not to spare her under any circumstances. He was hopeful of conquering the great Venues or conquest.

His fascination, fancy and fondness had crossed all limits of human sentiments.

Like a brave soldier, with total self-confidence, and shrewdness, in the darkness of the night, Sir Philip Francis, made a bold entry into Catherine's premises, softly, silently, secretly, without any noise or sound, and completely overpowered the young, charming Danish beauty-queen.

It was Sir Philips Francis great success. It was his great triumph, and accomplishment.

A dream had come true.

It was the fulfilment of his long-cherised passion or desire. It was an unforgettable moment of his life.

Sir Philip Francis spent long hours with his beloved.

It is not known whether Catherine also enjoyed those moments. It is also not known whether she was also in love with the most powerful member of the Supreme Council of India.

No one knows, whether the romance was one-sided or the powerful fire was burning on both sides.

Astonishingly, Sir Philip Francis had performed a miracle. There was all silence throughout the night and no cries, no protestations and no calls to the security-guards for help. All this was mysterious.

Catherine's house was well-protected. There were security men all around.

After this great miracle, Sir Philip Francis wanted to return to his house hurriedly. He ran out of Catherine's house in total darkness without anyone's notice.

Suddenly, as a bolt from the blue, the security-guards, jumped at him and caught him red handed. He was moving out of Catherine's premises almost like an armed plunderer, after plundering the most precious, shining gem.

There was some confusion for some time.

Perhaps the security-guards recognized this most powerful Briton in India, after the great Governor General.

What happened is not known but tired, fully alive, frightened Sir Philip Francis reached his house, unharmed, unwounded.

The criminal conspiracy could not remain a secret in Calcutta or London. The news of this infatuating romance reached every part of India within no time. The news moved liked a wild-fire. Warren Hastings was informed about this horrible incident. Catherine's husband could not remain ignorant of the December 8, 1778 night the game-of-love.

It was beyond everyone's tolerance.

No one could believe that Sir Philip Francis would play such a noxious game of romance and hide and seek, at the dead of night.

The Company's Government in India was furious. Sir Philip Francis had brought disgrace to the administration. He had disgraced England.

Sir Philip Francis's romance proved disasterous to Catherine's and Warren Hastings. It was ruinous to Sir Philip Francis. Now the enemity and bitterness between the two most powerful Britons in India took a deadly turn. George Grand was furious. He was dejected, disappointed and wild at this unimaginable breach of trust and treason. He was not prepared even Catherine for this crime.

He approached the Supreme Court and the court looking at the gravity and enormity of the crime, fined a huge amount of money Rs. 50,000 as damages on the criminal conspirator. George Grand decided to severe his relations with Catherine, who had betrayed him and there was divorce between them in 1779.

Sir Philip Francis had still not learn a lesson. He did not control his wild infatuation for Catherine and kept her at Hughly under his close, intimate protection.

Sir Philip Francis was full of humiliation and extreme anger. He held Warren Hastings responsible for his judicial punishment and humiliation. He criticized and condemned the Governor-General.

Sir Philip Francis was not satisfied with attacks on Warren Hastings, he decided to challenge Warren Hastings for bloody duel.

Surprisingly Warren Hastings accepted the challenge and the great duel took place on August 17,1780.

It was a disgrace and dishonour to the East India Company's Government in India. It was a disgrace to England.

The duel was fierce and freightening. It was long and almost unending. Both the gladiators were under the panic of instant death. The blood was flowing on the ground. There were terrible, painful injuries and wounds. Warren Hastings had the upper hand. He could have cut Sir Philip Francis to pieces within moments. Tired and frustrated, in utter helplessness, with tremendous difficulty, Sir Philip Francis could save his life.

He survived despite his profuse bleeding and deep wounds.

Sir Philip Francis had no alternative but to ran away to England. He left India in December 1780.

Catherine also left for England immediately.

Sir Philip Francis had failed completely in India.

He wanted to destroy the peace and prosperity of his greatest rival Warren Hastings. With the help of Edmund Burke and Richard Sherid Can, he was successful in Warren Hastings' impeachment by the British Parliament in England. The impeachment ruined Warren Hastings, who had to spend about 70,000 in defending himself.

Warren Hastings died, after great deal of trouble on August, 22, 1818. He was followed by Sir Philip Francis, who died on December, 22, 1818.

Catherine died on December 10, 1835 in France.

Due to pressure from Napoleon Bonaparte, she had married Talleyr and on September 19, 1782, but got separation from him in 1815.

She died in Autehill, France.

Sir Philip Francis, thus, ruined at least three lives, including his own, due to romantic misadventures.

9

When Mughal Emperor Shah Alam Wept and Cried. Unlimited Tortures and Barbarianism in the Delhi Red Fort

Political weakness, like a powerful magnet, attracts, power and total weakness of Government structure attracts countless powers from every direction in a fast manner.

Immediately after the death of Emperor Aurangzeb, the great Mughal Empire, from Kabul to Cuttack, started crumbling down and its disintegration was extremely fast and painful. There was endless violence and bloodshed, in which even Mughal Emperors Jahandershah and Farukhsiyar were cut to pieces. Nadirshah rushed to India and invaded it. Countless people were mercilessly massacred. He was followed by Ahmadshah Abdali, who invaded and plundered India, time and again till he left India on December 12, 1762.

Shah Alam came to power in 1759 and in 1771, he was installed on the throne of Delhi in the Red Fort by the Marathas, who had emerged as a great power at that time. Earlier in 1765. Shah Alam had permitted Lord Clive to collect revenue from Bengal, Bihar and Orissa against a payment of an annual tributes of Rs. 26,00,000. But immediately after the installation of Shah Alam on the throne of Delhi, under the protection of the Marathas, the British Government decided to stop his 'tribute'.

The Mughal Emperor, unlike Aurangzeb, was not extremely sound financially to maintain a huge force for protection or administrative requirements. The whole world knew that Mughals were not a great military power. The result was endless violence and open bloodbath in the Red Fort.

Every power in India was attracted towards the Red Fort. They wanted to capture Delhi. The greatest ambition of Ghulam Qadir, the Rohilla chief, was the capture and plunder of Delhi. He wanted to take possession of the priceless Mughal diamonds, gold and silver. In the middle of 1788, he attacked and captured Delhi with his powerful, well-disciplined forces. After the capture, attempts were made to corrupt the Mughal forces through bribes etc. so that his mission could be accomplished without any resistance. The Rohilla chief plundered the people of Delhi to total satisfaction. He entered the Red Fort and plundered the members of royalty and aristocracy, day and night. He was extremely successful in his mission of plunder.

The Rohilla chief was extremely ambitious. His greed knew no bounds, and he always felt that he had not been able to collect all the invaluable treasures of the Great Mughals.

He therefore thought of a unique device. He started torturing the queen, princes and other members of the royalty and aristocracy. He wanted to collect every diamond every precious Mughal asset.

In a savage, inhuman manner, he asked the Mughal Emperor to provide more and more information about the 'hidden' invalables. Shah Alam was totally helpless. It was an impossibility for him to satisfy the greed of the Rohilla chief.

Ghulam Qadir Rohilla felt that the Mughal Emperor was not disclosing the secrets. He was hiding the vital information. At last, Ghulam Qadir took out his daggar in the Diwane Khas and mercilessly blinded the Mughal Emperor by plunging the daggar into Shah Alam's eyes.

The Rohilla chief was still not satisfied. He ordered hit solders to stab the Mughal Emperor, who fell on the floor and wept and cried. His pain was unbearable. There was blood all around, He had lost his capacity to see what was happening in the Red Fort. Countless other members of the royalty and aristocracy, who were also tortured, wept and cried.

It was a horrible scene. The Red Fort had neither seen such cruelty and inhumanity earlier. It was unprecedented and unparalleled.

The news of Ghulam Qadir's capture of Delhi spread like wild fire, and the Marathas from Poona, Indore and Gwalior immediately reached Delhi and within a short time the Mughal Emperor Shah Alam was once again put on the throne of Delhi.

The Maratha forces were successful in capturing Ghulam Qadir Rohilla in Meerut. He was taken to Mathura. He had committed the most shameless and unpardonable crimes. The Marathas were extremely angry. They wanted to teach him a lesson for his greed and cruelty, for his eavagary. By the orders of Mahadaji Sindhia he was bound with a strong rope and assaulted, for some time, and finally he was bound and placed on ajackass with his face towards tail and paraded through the streets. He was abused and insulted in every possible manner.

This punishment however, was not suitable in the eyes of the Marathas. They had full realization of the tortures inflicted by him on the Mughal Emperor. Noting less than death appeared to the Marathas as the most appropriate punishment to the plunderer.

The Marathas assaulted him again and when he wept and cried his tongue was torn away, and then his hands and feet were hackef off. There was blood everywhere. The Marathas were still unsatisfied and therefore his ears were hacked off, his face was blotted out, and finally a dahhar was thrust into his eyes. He was blinded.

The Marathas never wanted him to remain relive even for a single moment and soon he was hanged from a tree in the presence of countless people.

The Mughal Emperor Shah Alam was still undergoing a terrible pain and torture.

Within no time, the dead body of Ghulam Qadir Rohilla, which was in a horrible shape, was brought to the Red Fort, Delhi. It was placed in the Diwane Khas in front of the Mughal Emperor Shah Alam.

Perhaps, the Mughal Emperor felt some satisfaction but because of his blindness he could hardly see what had actually happened.

Mansur Ali, who was a traitor and who had assisted the Rohilla chief in Shah Alam's tortures and plunders, was tied to the leg of an elephant and dragged through the streets till his death, by the orders of Mahadaji Sindhia.

The British Government was watching the situation in Delhi in a calm and cautious manner. The greatest ambition of the British Government was the capture of the Red Fort and the downfall of the Mughal Empire.

They found the weakness of the Mughal Government as the finest opportunity to capture Delhi. Without any loss of time the Britain captured Delhi and reduced the Mughal Emperor to a pensioner of the East India Company.

Shah Alam died on November 10, 1806.

The last Mughal Emperor Bahadurshah Zafar had his own share of tortures. The time the tortures were inflicted by the British Crown under Lord Canning. He was arrested and tried for his participation the Great Indian Revolt of 1857. His sons, Mirza Mughal and Mirza Sultan were treaturously shot dead on September 22, 1887, by William Hodson. His grandson Khizer Khan met the same fate. Many other princes and members of aristocracy were mercilessly hanged and Bahadurshah Zafar was deported to Rangoon, where he died, cut off from the rest of the world, a painful death, on November 7, 1862.

10

Nawab Wazir Ali, The Fearless Tiger of Oudh, Who Massacred the British in Broad-day-light in Banaras, January 14, 1799

The East India Company ruled India for about 100 years and yet it failed to evolve a theory of government. A commercial concern, it was primarily interested in 'shaking the pagoda tree'. It adopted ways and means for minting money which had hardly any moral justification. It's favourite policy of grabbing money was to pressurize the Indian States. It received inestimable financial assistance from the State of Oudh for conducting its wars and for pursuing its other policies in India. But it was not satisfied. It's greed continued to mount up. In 1798, it invented a new political device to extract more and more money from Oudh, an extremely flourishing and prosperous Indian State. When Nawab Wazir Ali refused to satisfy its greed, the Company deposed him and put another person on the throne of Lucknow. He was charged in official documents for working against the interests of the British and organizing a league of Muslims, Marathas, Rajputs and Afghans, for the overthrow of the British power in India. The justification provided by the British for the removal of the ruler of Oudh was that he was adopted son of Nawab Safuddaullah and therefore not the legitimate claimant of the Crown. Earlier, the highest British officials had participated in his coronation and in his marriage, which they described as one of the most magnificent marriages ever recorded on the pages of history.

Wazir Ali, born in 1781, who become the Nawab of Oudh in September 1797, could not appreciate the administration of Indian territories by traders and merchants, who did not realize that even colonial rule must have a moral base—a moral justification. Inspite of tremendous pressure from the British, this Tiger of Oudh could never be tamed. He was not prepared to surrender even a single pie to the British from the State treasuries. Ultimately, the British dethroned him and ordered to leave his home, his family and his State and proceed to Calcutta.

The people of Oudh did not like the dethronement of their beloved ruler. Wazir Ali himself found no justification for British intervention in the internal affairs of Oudh. When the news of Wazir Ali's deposition reached different parts of India there was a cry of horror and the rulers of Indian sovereign States felt alarmed and insecure.

Wazir Ali's dethronement by Sir John Shore on January 21, 1798, created a discontent and anger far and wide, and when Wazir Ali was taken to Banaras on his way to Calcutta, by the British, many of his followers and friends could not remain in Lucknow, and reached Banaras. The fire of revenge was burning in their hearts. On January 14, 1799, losing all hopes of British justice, humanity and fairplay, they organized a revolt against the British Government and massacred the British officials in Banaras. British Political Agent, W. Cherry was murdered in the brond-day-light, on the streets. Samule Davis, British Judge at Banaras ran for his life. All the British, who could be found, were attacked. It was an open challenge to the British Government. It was an open massacre.

After directing the massacre, Wazir Ali went to Butwal, and from there he reached Jaipur. He had not the Oudh army at his command to face the British military power openly. He was bold, courageous, and extremely competent but had hardly any resources to fight the British outside Oudh. The British wanted to get rid of this rebel.

He was a thorn in their flesh. The British Governor-General, therefore, asked the ruler of Jaipur to hand over Wazir Ali to the British Government. Inspite of tremendous pressure and threats, the brave Rajput ruler of Jaipur, Maharajah Pratap Singh refused to comply with the British request.

It was a great political humiliation for the British. Lord Wellesley, the Governor-General, was told point blank that Wazir Ali was the honoured guest of the Rajput State and therefore the question of his surrender to him, did not arise. Under utter helplessness, humilation and ridicule, the British Government agreed that no harm would be done to the Sovereign, who massacred the British in broad daylight, if he was handed over to it.

Maharajah Paratap Singh had friendly consultations with the Great Rebel Sovereign, who agreed to accede to the British request. In December 1799, therefore, Wazir Ali went to Calcutta with the British guards, and he was put in Fort William, in confinement. Later, it was decided that Wazir Ali should be transferred to a place, built for Tipu Sultan's captive sons, in the Fort at Vellore. How far was he responsible along with Tipu's sons, for the Vellore Mutiny of 1806 in which Indian soldiers rose at the dead of night on July 10, 1806, slaughtered the sentries, killed the main-guard at the Fort, shot the British officers and hoisted an Indian flag over the ramparts—is not known.

What is however clear from the contemporary sources is that the British treatment of the Sovereign of Oudh, while in confinement, was hardly liberal or sympathetic. After remaining in total incarceration, the great Nawab—after 17 years, 3 months and 4 days' 'rigorous' confinement, died in May 1817.

The British had absolutely no justification for the dethronement of Wazir Ali. Their Oudh policy was condemned in the most severe terms even in England. Oudh was not only well-governed but also prosperous and friendly. It had already supported the British whenever there was any crisis. Dethronement was almost like stabbing in the back. It was treacherous, cruel and inhuman. The same policy continued to be followed by Wellesley's successors, too, till they were successful in annexing one of the richest states of India. No doubt this annexation improved the financial foundations of the British Empire, nevertheless, it also shook it to its base when there was a ghastly bloodbath during the Great Indian Revolt of 1857.

Young Wazir Ali was a great ruler. He was educated and had highly refined tastes. He maintained a large army and also paid 20,00,000 rupees on annual basis to the Company so that it could maintain its 'subsidiary forces'. Wazir Ali was fond of Jewels and he had one of the finest collections of Jewels in the whole world. The value of his Jewels was more than 320,000,000 rupees. His 'Heram' comprized more than 500 of the finest beauties of India. He lived amidst all the gorgeous splendour of magnificence. In order to encourage and patronize the Company he spent 800,000 rupees every year on European manufactures. In Lucknow, during his rule, there were more than 100 well-maintained gardens, 20, magnificent palaces, 1200 elephants, 3000 fine-saddle horses, 1500 double-barrel guns, 1700 superb lustres, 30,000 shades of various forms and colours, several hundred large beautiful mirrors, girandoles, and clocks, some of the latter were curious, richly set with jewels, having figures in continual movement and playing tunes every hours, two of these clocks cost him 12,000 rupees. He had acquired some of the most modern instruments and machines of every art and science, and some of the finest Indian and European paintings including the landscapes of Claude Lorriane.

His marriage provides an excellent idea of the property and affluence of Oudh during those times. The marriage, which was celebrated in 1795, was described as one of 'the most magnificent marriages of modern times.' At the time of marriage, his Highness was covered with jewels, to the amount of more than 80,000,000 rupees. The 'shamianas—some of them about 120 ft. long and 60 ft. high and 60 ft. broad, were richly decorated and illumined by 200 elegant girandoles, brought from Europe, particularly for the purpose, and 500 top female dancers of the country entertained the guests.

11

Tipu Sultan, The Tiger of Mysore and a Martyr to the Cause of Freedom

Tipu Sultan was a great fighter. He was prepared to sacrifice his life for the honour of the People. He was a Terror to the British, who had to endure great hardships and humiliations at the hands of this Tiger of Mysore, in the battlefields.

Tipu Sultan was a great military General. He captured Mangalore, Canara, Malabar, Coorg and Travancore. He wanted to oust the British from India and, therefore, he wrote to Arabia, Afghanistan, Turkey, France and Constantinople for cooperation and help. He also addressed letters to Indian sovereigns. The Great Napoleon Bonaparte of France was so much impressed by this fearless fighter that he immediately left France for India, with his large 'invincible' force to oust the British from India.

Tipu Sultan was not prepared to compromise with the British at any cost and during the Battle of Seringapatam, when the British requested him for peace, he boldly rejected their offer and died on the battlefield like a great soldier.

H.M. Parker describes Tipu Sultan a "Star of the Battle" and "The Sultan of the Brave" on the basis of a chorus, sung by the Mysore soldiers, in the battlefield, on Tipu Sultan's heroic sacrifice.

Tipu Sultan, 1753-99, as mentioned earlier, was a brave fighter. When he died, on May 4, 1799, in the Battle of Seringapatam, after having rejected the British terms for peace of paying £ 2,000,000 and surrendering about half of his state, his soldiers sang the songs of his valour and the supreme sacrifice. They said:

Light of the Faith, Thy flame is quench'd
In this deep night of blood.
When sabres flash'd; and volleys rung,
And quickest sped the parting breath
Thou, from a life of empire, sprung
To meet a soldier's death.

Star of the Battle! thou art set;
But thou didst not go down
As others who could Fame forget,
Before the tempest's frown;
As others who could meanly crave
The mercy of their haughty foes:
Better to perish with the brave,
Than live and reign with those.
Allah! 'tis better thus to die
With war-clouds hanging redly o'er us
Than live a life of infamy,
With years of grief and shame before us.

No! thou hast to thy battle led
Sunk like thy native sun,
Whose brightest, fiercest, rays are shed,
When his race is nearest done.
Where sabres flash'd and volleys rung,
And quickest sped the parting breath,
Thou, from a life of empire, sprung
To meet a soldier's death.
Allah! 'tis better thus to die
With war-clouds hanging redly o'er us,

Than live a life of infamy,
With years of grief and shame before us.

Tipu Sultan could have easily saved his life by accepting the British terms and conditions, but like a true soldier, he refused to surrender and sacrificed himself for the honour of his people. He did not stop fighting against the British forces, under the command of General Harris and Arthur Welliesley till the last breath of his life.

When Tipu Sultan died on the battlefield on May 4, 1799, there was tremendous satisfaction and rejoicing in the British camp. It was indeed a great victory for the British. The British succeeded in capturing countless weapons, gold and silver.

The British Generals immediately directed the British officials and soldiers to take up the search for the dead-body of Tipu Sultan. With great difficulty, with the help of the captured enemy-soldiers, the British could take hold of the body of the Mysore Tiger, who was lying in a pool of blood.

When the body was taken out, everyone was shocked beyond all expectations. Everyone was surprised that all the most precious jewels and matchless diamonds were missing from the body. Even his crown, his diamond-neclaces, his gold-rings, etc. had disappeared, within no time. Even his sword and other weapons of gold, studded with priceless diamonds, were not traceable.

It was shocking.

It was disheartening.

It was an open theaft. It was a magic of manupulation on the part of the British soldiers, who had killed the Mysore sovereign.

This kind of deceit, fraud and concealment was simply intolerable to the British Government.

The East India Company's soldiers and other employees, right from the days of Robert Clive, suffered from kleptomania. They were ordinary people, who were capable of playing all kinds of tricks and traps. Most of them were not liberal-minded or honest. They often suffered from the contraction of heart or miocardia, but the

Seringapattam robbery was beyond all tolerance. It was cunning, collusive and covinoue.

The searches proved futile.
The culprits could not be caught.

The matter was brought to the notice of Lord Wellesley. There was condemnation and criticism of the white-lie-wolfs in England. The Government threatened to take severe action against those who were responsible for this crime.

But the fraternity of fraud succeeded in picking up the Picklock Prize and the Trophy of Theaft.

The People in India were shocked.
The Parliament in England was shocked.

Priceless treasures were lost for ever. But the East India Company succeeded in creating endless, countless dens of docoits in India.

Such plunders and robberies continued in India throughout the Company's rule and even later.

12

'The Hindoostanee Intelligencer': A Unique Source of Investigation for the Study of Indian Powers and Indian Politics in the Beginning of the Nineteenth Century

During the darkest decades of the Press in India, when Lord Wellesley, had succeeded in completely paralyzing the newspapers and silencing, what he often described, "the tribe of editors', Thomas Hollingbery, a veteran journalist, succeeded in establishing a new quarterly, the Hindoostanee Intelligencer, at Calcutta, in 1801.

It was a rare journal, concentrating on Indian powers and Indian politics, based exclusively on Persian newsletters. Conflicts and clashes, intrigues and diplomacy, wars and peace, among the various Indian powers and their changing political attitudes and policies, due to the emergence of the British power in the subcontinent, occupied the wholehearted attention of the Hindoostanee Intelligencer. Unlike other contemporary journals, which took great interest in the Company's affairs—its administrative policies and measures; its Endeavour's in the field of education, religion and social reforms, the Hindoostanee Intelligencer, write excellent articles and editorials on suppression of violence in Delhi by Shah Nizamuddin's troops, A.H. Bhadur's preparations in the beginning of November 1799 for an expedition against Rewari Court intrigues and differences between Kasirao Holkar and the Peshwa, Zaman Shah's preparations for an invasion of India, establishment of authority by the son of Muhammad Shah at Peshawar. Jaswantrao Holkar's attack on Sindhia's battalions, commanded by Colonel George Hessing. Besides these chronicles of events, the journal published "original essays and political places." The Hindoostanee Intelligencer was among those journals in the country which for the first time published Hafiz and Sadiq and many other oriental poets in original Persian along with their English translations. The first issue of the journal, for example published the following poem of Hafiz. I reproduce only the English translation:

> Oh hide not our joys; them let the world see;
> That I drink is most true, whate'er is, it be,
> Loose the knots of grim care, nor reflect on fate's tide,
> That's the knot that no conjurer's art has untied.

The importance of this source lies in the fact that it shattered to pieces the Christian missionary propaganda about the primitive and savage character of the oriental life and literature, and establishment beyond doubt that the oriental philosophy, literature, and religion had at least some elements of profoundly, humanity and sublimity,

- It demolishes the still current notion that the newspapers in the beginning of the nineteenth century were completely Europeanized in character and had no interest in oriental and Indian ideas and institutions.
- It also establishes beyond doubt that contrary to the beliefs of certain historians and recent researches, oriental languages were being used in newspapers published almost two decades before the establishment of James Marshman's *Samachar Darpan* and Rammohun Roy's *Sambad Kaumudi* and *Miratul Akhbar*.

Now the question arises why, this rare sources of historical research has remained unutilized for over one hundred and eighty years? Why scholars concentrating on Indian powers and oriental studies have turned a blind eye to this unique treasure of information. Why Margrita Barns, J. Natarajan, Nadig Krishanmurti, C. Chhalapathi Rao, Salahuddin Ahmed and Ralpf Turner did not mention or discuss this journal in their studies on Press in India?

Besides, the non-availability of this journal in most of the archival repositories, museums and libraries in the world, the factors responsible for this neglect are:

- the source does not find a mention in the catalogues and indexes of newspapers published in Indian in the nineteenth century;
- it does not find a mention in the contemporary Indian newspapers and periodicals; and
- it was published when the press in India was under rigorous censorial control and therefore it's circulation must have been extremely limited, the journal existed only for two years.

Whatever the reasons for its neglect so far, it can hardly be denied that the newspaper is of great historical significance for three reasons:

The press remained under censorship from 1799 to 1818. Most of the newspapers were suppressed by the Company's government. Permission was refused to a large number of editors to establish new newspapers.

Editors were deported from India for their comments on Indian politics and the administration of the East India Company while about 30 newspapers came into existence before the imposition of censorship in India in 1799 and about 150 after the relaxation of control over the newspapers between 1818 to 1835, hardly any new newspaper could be established in Calcutta between 1799 and 1818. The importance therefore of Thomas Hollingbery's journal increases a thousand fold, because it became one of the most important non-official source of information for the period.

- it was the only newspaper established till that period in India which was based exclusively on Farsi Akhbars or Persian newspapers and which gave a lot of attention to the India Princes and Indian powers; and
- it was among the earliest newspapers in the country, which published an "Oriental Anthology" regularly, both in original and with translations in English. For the beauty of its English translations the journal would remain unforgettable for decades to come, for example, the journals published the following English translation of a poem in Persian by Hafiz:

> Veil'd is my soul in this corporeal clay;
> Blest be the hour that tears it away,
> Th' imprison'd bird in sadness pour her strains;
> So pines my soul to join her native plains.

Besides translations, Thomas Hollingbery also published originally poetry in the Hindoostanee Intelligencer.

In 1801, under the title lines written, and dedicated to Lietenant Colonel Kyd, it wrote:

> Now lightly beams the dewy star of morn
> And blushing tints the rising scene adorn;
> Rich with the rosy breath of opening flowers:
> The breeze sweeps softly thro the fragrance bow'rs.

Thus the Hindoostanee Intelligencer also occupies a unique place among the literary sources of the nineteenth century India. It may rewardingly be utilized for a study of the changing character of Engilsh poetry or literature in India during the British rule.

Now it would not be unprofitable to examine, the main contents and their character, of the Hindoostanee Intelligencer from 1801 to 1802. A few illustrations or excerpts from the journal would be sufficient for the purpose. About politics Delhi, the Hindoostanee Intelligencer wrote in its maiden issue in 1801.

> At the period of our last accounts, in the end of October 1799, it was stated that a new soobadar of Delhi had been appointed by Lukhawjee and that Shah Hizamoodeer was preparing for a journey to Poona. But that appointment never took effect and the Shah still remains in office.

Writing about the politics of Patiala and Amritsar, the journal observed:

> From 15 November 1799 to the 17 January 1800, Zuman Shah was at Peshawar, meditating the invasion of Hindoostanee. He had detached two chief Futtuh Khan and Hoshung Khan with any army against Bekaneer. But about the end of this period, commotion in his own obliged him to retreat into Kabool.

Under the title Juswunt Rao Holkar, the Hindoostanee Intelligencer published the following news items in 1801.

> On the 16th July attacked Sendheea's Battalions commanded by Col. George Hassing, within five kos of Oojun. The loss on both sides only amounted to about one hundred persons.

It is unfortunate that only four members of this journal of politics and literature are available. Though information about the founder editor, Thomas Hillingbery, who was earlier collected with the Bengal *Hurakaru* and the *Calcutta Chronicle* is available, among the government archives of the times, it is unfortunate that no information about this valuable source is available anywhere. The four members of this journal are also not available in this country.

References

1. Pearce, D. (ed), Lord Wellesley's Memoirs, Vol. I, pp. 278-79.
2. For details see Sankhdher, B.M., Development of the Press in India, 1780-1835, Ph.D. Thesis, University of Delhi, 1976, (in Press).
3. *The Hindoostanee Intelligencer*, Calcutta, 1801, No. I.
4. *Ibid.*, Nos. 1 to 4.
5. *Ibid.*
6. *Ibid.*, No. 1.

7. Authors of The Indian Press (London 1940, A history of the Press in India, (London, 1955), Indian Press (New Delhi),
Social Ideas and Social change in Bengal, (London, 1965), James Silk Buckhingam (London, 1934) respectively.
8. See Sankhdher, B.M., Fighter for Press Freedom: The story of Charles Maclean, Vidura, New Delhi, June 1978, pp. 173-175.
9. See Sankhdher, B.M., Development of the Press in India, *op. cit.*, pp. 17-220.
10. *The Hindoostanee Intelligencer*, Calcutta, 1801.
11. *Ibid.*
12. *Ibid.*
13. *Ibid.*
14. *Ibid.*

13

Begum Zebunissa Samru and Lord Lake's Unpardonable Crime

Begum Zebunissa Samru, who died on January 27,1836, was one of the most fascinating Kashmir princess warriors of the nineteenth century India. She was perhaps the sole prominent woman of her times, to establishes Roman Catholic Churches in India. She inspired countless people of Italy through her great services for the spread of Roman Catholicism in this part of the globe. She lived in Sardhana, Meerut, and helped countless Catholics through charities and other endeavours. She handed over a huge sum of money at that time Rs. 5000 to Lord Bishop of Calcutta for the promotion of Christian principles.

Begum Samru, a bewitching beauty was a great warrior and administrator. She had employed hundreds of people in Sardhana for her security, for participation in battles and for other administrative works.

She was in constant touch with the Mugal emperors, Marathas and other powers in India.

Begum Samru married Walter Reinhard, 1720, a sailor soldier from Salzburg and Strasburg, known as Samru, who served the Mugal emperor, the Nawabs of Oudh, the rulers of Bharatpur, Jaipur, etc. and who was responsible for the bloody massacre of about 150 British soldiers and officers in Patna. After Samru's death in 1778, Begum Samru married a man of arms from France Levassoult, who commanded her forces and after a mutiny of soldiers, committed suicide.

Many British administrators were full of admiration for Begum Samru. A day before leaving for England in 1835, in a letter to Begum Samru, the Governor General Lord William Bentinck poured tremendous praise on the great Lady of Sardhana, who had converted Sardhana into a little Indian Rome.

In 1803, Lord Lake defeated Ambaji in the battle of Lasari. Begum Samru of Sardhana, who was assisting Ambaji, was persuaded by Captain James Skinner to come to the Britishmilitary General Lord Lake's camp. The warrior princes was an extraordinary beauty. She was brilliant, young, smart and active. She wanted to come to terms with the British Government so that she could keep herself engaged in her socio-religious activities. She therefore, decided to meet Lord Lake at the earliest.

Begum Samru arrived at Lord Lake's camp in her grand, royal beautiful light-blue palanquin, decorated with yellow, golden satin draperies and escorted by her heavily armed bodyguards and other soldiers, on elephants, camels and horses. It was a huge procession.

Lord Lake know about this bewitching warrior-princess. When he heard the news of her arrival at the camp, like a mad militaryman, he rose hastily and ran out of the camp to greet Begum Samru, while she decended from her magnificent palanquin.

When Lord Lake saw this all-captivating, all-conquering unveiled Kashmir beauty, bedecked in gems and jewels, he lost all control over himself. He developed a kind of abnormality. He behaved in the most absured, stupid, mindless and blind manner. In the excitement of the moment, almost driven by madness, he held Begum Samru in her hands and then shifting his hands around her shoulders firmly, greeted her with a long, hearty, passionate kiss.

Hundreds of people saw this senseless, wild, inflammable, ludicurous act with total astonishment and wonder. They could not believe their eyes.

The scene was far beyond everyone's expectations. It was mindless, furious, eccentric, senseless and shameless.

It was a terrible moment.

Offended, boiling under extreme irritation and indignation, the escorts and bodyguards, with naked swords and other weapons were awaiting Begum Samru's signal. They would have cut Lord Lake to countless pieces within moments, even at the risk of their lives.

Begum Samru however was an extraordinarily brilliant lady. She was skilful, shroud and smart. She never wanted violence, massacre and bloodshed at that critical moment. Her discrimination, clear sightedness, and acute quick-wit came to her rescue and relief. She showed a brilliant presence of mind. Describing Lord Lake as a 'clergyman', with utmost self-confidence she turned towards her angry, furious-looking escorts and attendants and said with an all-capturing smile :

See, my friends, how the clergymen greet their children.

The storm was over.

Begum Samaru continued to rule over Sardhana for decades till her death on January 27, 1836.

Such an incident had never happened in the history of British rule till that time. Such absurdity and senseless occurence had never taken place under the Great Mughals or in the ancient times.

Lord Lake was not recalled by the East India Company but the echo of this incident had reached every part of India and even England. This was unparalleled and unprecedented.

14

Lord Lake's Defeat at Bharatpur, 1805

Lord Lake's defeat at Bharatpur in 1805 constitutes a dark chapter in the history of British conquests in India. It was humiliating, disasterous and complete. The British forces were forced to surrender, helplessly, after loosing their 3200 finest soldiers and officers.

The British were defeated a number of times even before 1805, but there was never such a great demoralization as provided by the crashing defeat at the hands of a small Indian state: Bharatpur.

The British had applied every possible military and diplomatic tactic but they failed disasterously to capture the Fort of Bharatpur. From December 12, 1804 to February 20, 1805 from the day Lord Lake took position before Deeg to the day his forces were cut to pieces the British used their finest and most sophisticated weapons; their best military talent, their most experienced Generals; they changed their military strategies and fighting tactics and devices but the Bharatpur forces, under Maharajah Ranjit Singh completely outclassed them.

There was never such a great siege in the military history off the country or of the British Empire. There was never such a demoralizing defeat for the British. Bharatpur Humiliation of the British remains unparalleled in the history of British conquests in India.

On December 10, 1804, Lord Lake received orders from the Governor-General Lord Wellesley to annex Bharatpur without any delay. The order had the approval of the Court of Directors and the highest Company's authorities in England. The Governor-General thought that annexation of Bharatpur was essential to destroy the rising power of the great Maratha leader Yashwantrao Holkar who had completely defeated the British forces under Brigadier Monson, forced him to in humiliating retreat and had captured all his guns, horses and ammunition. Yashwantrao Holkar was friendly to Bharatpur and the Maharaja of Bharatpur Ranjit Singh had provided him all help in his fights against the British.

When Lord Lake, who considered annexation of Bharatpur as indispensable for peace in the British dominions in India, pitched his tents around the Fort of Deeg on December 12, 1804, the ruler of Bharatpur was taken by surprise. He never expected the concentration of the entire British military talent around a small fort of Deeg without any warning or alarm. Maharajah Ranjit Singh had no time to make any preparations while on the other hand, Lord Lake, David Ochterlony, Willam Monson, Colonel Maitland, Captain Grant, Lt. Colonel Don—all had made elaborate preparations for the storming of the Fort. On December 23, 1805, at the dead of night, the 10,000 British soldiers effected a small breach in the magnificent strong Deeg Fort defended by a strong mud wall with bastions and a deep ditch all round, and stormed the Fort. Next morning, on December 2, 1804, David Ochter Lony sent an immediate communication to the Governor-General Lord Wellesey informing him about the capture of the Deeg Fort.

After the fall of Deeg, Lord Lake now planned a siege which has hardly many parallels in the history of Modern India. His plan was to repeat as the Deeg Strategy and make a breach in the Bharatpur Fort by artillery fire and then to capture the Fort by storm. His only fear was Moti Jheel, which could flood the entire area around Bharatpur and make digging of trenches and attack for the British an impossibility. The Fort of Bharatpur was considered as impregnable, because of its unique mud and stone walls, deep, ditces and the Moti Jheel which could turn the territories around Bharatpur into an unfathomable ocean. Moti Jheel was a strategy through which Bharatpur could drown the entire British military force without a fight without the use of guns of the heroism or valour of the great Jat soldiers.

Happy at the news of British victory over Deeg the Government immediately dispatched additional force to reinforce Lord Lake, who had approximately 15,000 soldiers including cavalry, infantry and artillery, at his command after the capture of Deeg by surprise. Even Ismail Beg, Yashwantrao Holkar's partisan, had also promised to join Lord Lake, with his 400 Horses.

Mahrajah of Bharatpur had his own limited resources. He was not aware that without any solid preparations, he would be required to face the mighty British forces under Lake, Ochterlony, Captain Walsh, Major Howkes, Colonel Maitland, Monson, Captain Grant, Lt. Colonel Don, Lt. Colonel Taylor and others. Negotiations with Lord Lake were impossible after the fall of Deeg—which had made the British over-ambitious and proud.

Maharaja Ranjit Singh had no alternative but to send the ladies of the royal household to Jodhpur and Jaipur for asylum and to seek the assistance of his two great friends Yashwantrao Holkar and Amir Khan. The ladies of the royal household however refused to leave and all the people of his Court assured him that they would fight for defending Bharatpur to the last drop of their blood. The Maharajah wanted to send the ladies because he was sure that the war would be long, tedious, exhausting with limited resources and a small, though brave, military force. The ladies put a new life into the Maharajah's courage—who assured all possible help by Yashwantrao Holkar, and Amir Khan, who had to be financially supported by the Maharajah to the tune of rupees six lacs so that he could immediately reach Bharatpur with his forces.

Lord Lake commenced his march to Bharatpur on December 28, 1804. He was joined by Major General of HM's and 5th Regiment and the whole army moved towards Bharatpur on January 1,1805. On January 2,1805 commenced the Great Seige. Lord Lake took a position about 2 to 3 miles away from the Fort, perhaps, the fear of Moti Jheel haunted his mind.

With huge preparations, on January 4,1805, it pounders were erected about 500 yards away from the fort wall and the next morning January 7,1805, commenced the heavy artillery fire battery of mortars commenced throwing shells into the town, from all sides, under command of Britain's finest military strategicians, and under the over all planning of Lord Lake who was sitting at a distance of 2 to 3 miles haunted by the fear of the blue waters of Moti Jheel. Heavy firing commander continued till January 9, when in the afternoon Colonel Ryan, Colonel Maitland and major Howkes with 150 select European soldiers and the huge Indian battalion were ordered to make a powerful assault on Bharatpur. The British forces were raining mortars and shells. But the British failed to make any impression on the Bharatpur forces, which killed about 45 European and 42 Indian officers and soldiers, including Colonel Maitland.

Moving out of the trenches, the British forces, who were raining mortar and fire-shells on Bharatpur, made an assault on January 10, but every attempt to cross the deep waters of the huge ditch around the city and the Fort, was foiled and the British forces had to retreat. On January 16, the British made a heavy assault and succeeded in wounding the brave son of the Maharajah, Randeer Singh, who was personally supervising the entire defence operation, after Bharatpur had formed a stockpade in a breach created by the British through heavy artillery fire. But the British had to retreat once again with heavy casualties.

Lord Lake wanted Bharatpur at any cost. He was not afraid of the British casualties. On January 18,1805, Major General Smith joined him from Agra with 3 Battalions. Ismail Beg who had promised all support to the British also joined with his 400 horses. The situation was turning for the ruler of Bharatpur, who was cut off from all sides and who had to remain content with his limited resources inside the Fort of Bharatpur. The only help which he was receiving during this time was from Lord Goverdhan, whose temple he would visit in disguise, at the dead of night, when he would come out of the Fort and distribute alms to the poor and return without the supreme British intelligence service ever coming to know of it. That was perhaps, also the way through which he would know the

British strength and plans of assault for the next day and foil them without great losses or casualties.

Yashwantrao Holkar, who was around, adopted his own tactics to help Bharatpur. He was always around Bharatpur and whenever the British tried reinforce Lord Lake he would attack the reinforcing forces. As a result, Lord Lake had to send his troops to Fatehpur Sikri, where he had pitched his tents. Lord Lake however failed to do anything against Yashwantrao Holkar who damaged the British reinforcements and troubled, the British forces every now and then. Amir Khan was not lagging for behind. He had also created a lot of anxiety for the British. On January 23, 1805, he reached Kumher with his forces and made it almost impossible for Captain Walsh to Join Lord Lake. Ammeer Khan not only defeated Captain Walsh Forces but also forced him to hide himself in some small village. Though Lord Lake reached Kumher and killed about 600 soldiers of Ammeer Khan on January 28, 1805, yet the British losses were extremely heavy.

The British Government directed the Bombay Division, to reach Bheratpur and Lt. Colonel Don, Captain Grant and others formed a great force to attack Bharatpur. Captain Grant was successful in capturing 11 Bharatpur Guns. But the plan was not properly worked out. Lt. Colonel Don reached late and Lt. Colonel had to suffer endleas humiliation and harassment at the hands of the Bharatpur Horses. The British forces were exposed to the most heavy and destructive fire from the Bharatpur Fort. The British ladders and other equipments were destroyed. The British defeat and casualties were indeed alarming.

Lord Lake however was not completely demoralized. Bharatpur had not yet used the most dangerous weapon in its hands against the British forces—the greatest fear of Lord Lake: Moti Jheel. He therefore ordered a final attack on Bharatpur on February 20, 1805 at 3 O'clock. The Bharatpur forces once again forced a crushing defeat on the British.

Thousands of British soldiers and officers met their doom. More than Three Thousand men lost their lives. The entire cream of British forces was lost. It was the greatest humiliation Lord Lake ever suffered in his life. It was the greatest humiliation of the British who were posing themselves as a Paramount Power in the country. It was a Great Humiliation to the British Scientific Knowledge and Inventions and the Military Strategy and Planning. A small Indian State had humiliated them and all their assaults had become completely ineffective and meaningless. The British had become a laughing stock for the European Military Powers. The French, the German, the Portuguese, and the Spanish. They had become a laughing stock for the Sikhs, the Marathas, the Rajputs, and the Afghans.

The world was laughing at the British humiliation.

Out of utter helplessness, nervousness, fear and anxiety, the British removed Lord Lake from the position of Commander-in-Chief. He returned to England in 1807 and died the next year. Monson was wounded and had no alternative but to return to England in 1806 and in December 1807, he also breathed his last.

The news of Bharatpur Defeat created endless sorrow in England. Thousands of families had lost their sons, fathers, uncles, nephews or others relations in the Bharatpur Massacre. Even Lord Lake's resort to treachery and bribe had not made any impression on the brave soldiers of Bharatpur. The Government immediately ordered the Governor-General Lord Wellesey to pack up and return to England the same year.

Bharatpur had thus shocked the entire world.

The British were no match to the Bharatpur forces—was writ large on every British Document. Bharatpur became a sources of endless humiliation to the rising British Power in India. It became a watch world of Terror in England for many decades.

15

India's Most Powerful War Song Against the British, Produced 58 Years Before Bankimchandra Chatterjee's 'Vandemataram'

Poetry played a significant role in India's struggle for freedom. Bankimchandra Chatterjee's soul-striving Sanskrit poem Vandematram created a stir in the whole country. After its production in 1882, there was hardly any corner of this vast sub-continent, where the people did not feel inspired by this unique, immortal literary creation. It was a superb expression of Indian nationalism. The whole freedom struggle, in fact, during the late nineteenth century and later revolved around this battle-cry.

Hundreds and thousands of soul-striving, inspiring poems were produced during the national struggle. Even if we concentrate only on the Hindi poetry, we find the unforgettable poems of Bhartendu Harishchandra, Sohanlal Dwivedi, Makhan Lal Chaturvedi, Nirala, Maithalisaran Gupta, Mahadevi Varma, Acharya Chatursen Shastri and Subhadra Kumari Chauhan. Who can forget Chatursen Shastri's inspring poem:

'झुक सकता है सूरज लेकिन दुर्गावती नहीं झुक सकती,

रूक सकती है जमना पर, रानी की तेग नहीं रूक सकती',

or

'वन्दना के इन स्वरों में एक स्वर मेरा मिला लो,
वन्दनी मां को न भूलो'।

by yet another poet.

Even about the terrible human disaster, the Bengal famine of 1943 in which countless people lost their lives due to sheer British criminal apathy, inhumanity and indifference, Dr. Harvanshrai Bachchan wrote :

'पड़ा बंगाले में काल
भरी कंगालों से धरती, भरी कंकालों से धरती'।

But perhaps not many could surpass Jaishankar Prasad's patriotic force and fire, when he wrote:

'हिमाद्रि तुंग श्रंग से,
प्रबुद्ध शुद्ध भारती
स्वंय प्रभा सभुज्वला
स्वतंत्रता पुकारती,
अमर्त्थ वीर पुत्र हो,
दृढ़ प्रतिज्ञा सोच लो,
प्रष्ठास्त पुन्य पंथ है
बढ़े चलो'।

Almost all the eminent authorities on Hindi Literature are unanimous in their opinion that before Bhartendu Harish Chandra, there was hardly any nationalistic poetry in Hindi during modern times. They are also unanimous that the real nationalistic fire could be seen only in the poems of Sohanlal Dwivedi, Nirala, Maithalisaran Gupta, Subhadrakumari Chauhan, Mahadevi Varma, etc.

Most of the scholars of Hindi trace the origin of nationalistic poetry to *Hind Kesari, Prabha, Madhuri, Chand, Kranti, Bharatmitra,*

Swadesh, Abhyudaya, Pratap, Karmavir; Saraswati and other such Hindi newspapers and periodicals. There is no doubt that the poems published in these papers did provide fire and thunder to India's struggle for freedom.

No historian would ever believe that even before Bankimchandra Chatterjee's ' Vandematram' or Bharatendu Harishchandra's poetical attacks on British colonialism, there were soul-stirring, inspiring nationalistic poems in Hindi. One such poem is available, not in India, but in England. It was indeed an immortal poem, which can challenge comparison with the finest nationalistic poems, produced in this country, during the national struggle.

It is unfortunate that the original has not been traced so far and only an English translation of the poem is available in the columns of a 1824 London newsmagazines. Even the name of the poet is not known to the world of archives and historical research. The catalogues of its British Museum, London and the India. Office Library and Records, London, do not make a mention of this great archival treasure.

It appears simply unbelievable that the poem was produced in 1824 or earlier.

There is a very interesting story about this great Brajbhasha ode. It was found from the dead body of a Pindari leader, who was killed, on the battlefield, in a fight against the British before 1824. It was found in the sash of the 'Pindari patriot'.

The Brajbhasha ode appealed to the people to march against the British and to hear the call of the nation. It appealed to the Hindus and to the Muslims to fight against the British, who had treacherously captured the power in this country and who had provided a rude shock to India's greatness and glory. It said :

Mount and away ! hark, the naqura's loud call,
Bids the serf quit his labour, the chieftain his hall.
Bright looks and sweet voices awhile must give way.
To the flash of the spear, and the war-conquerer's neigh.

The kaffers shall tremble, who view from afar

Our conquest-crown'd banner, like buchram's red star,
And fly to the ships, whence they trecherously came;
To rob us of glory, to clothe us in shame.

Would they track our bold march, let them look where on high
Cur war fire's reflection hangs red in the sky,
An iris of hope to the free and the brave,
A meteor of fear to the coward and slave.

The poet appealed to the Rajputs to hear the nation's call. He questioned if the Rajputs would not march towards the battlefield, when in the past, their ancestors made the most heroic sacrifices for the cause of the country. According to the poet, the Rajputs were the vanguards of valour and the guides of the bold.

Will the fiery Rajpoot hear the trumpet that rings,
With a nation's appeal to the off-springs of the kings,
Nor rush to the field, like his proud sires of old,
The vanguards of valour, and guide of the bold.

A similar appeal was made to the Muslims :

Let the musalman rise, with his old battle-cry,
For the glad hour of freedom and vengeance is nigh,
Let him think on the sceptre his forefathers swayed,
And the might of pastages rest on his blade.

The poem ended with a unique note:

Sound ! sound to horse! the loud clanging hoof
And the neigh of impatience gives gallant reproof,
March ! and the trump of our "durrahs" shall roll,
Like a fast coming storm on the infidal's soul.

The poem is remakable not only for its unique archival value and its great nationalistic content but it is also significant for a complete reinterpretation of certain historical theories and facts.

This ode compells us to re-examine if the Pindaris, as portrayed by some British bureaucrats, historians and critics, were solely mercenary soldiers, devoid of any sentiments for their motherland. Were they fighting against the British or other powers in an unprincipled manner? Were they a horde of indisciplined, disorganized soldiers with no finer sensibilities or values of life? Was the British policy of ruthless suppression of the Pindaris, even without proper identification sometimes in the name of law and order, wholly justifiable?

And it also directs our attention to the fundamental question; how immediately after the death of Aurangzeb, we lost, as depicted by some British, our everything, even our sense of unity and oneness.

If new states emerge does it necessarily mean the complete destruction of the social, political and cultural fibre of a nation? Were the British, through their rule, solely responsible for the creation of unity among the Indian people—which ultimately led to India's freedom and planned progress?

16

Thomas Macaulay : A Scholar or Swindler

Lord Thomas Babbington Macaulay wrote his famous Minute on Education in India in the beginning of 1835 and it was decided by the British Government that the medium of instruction in India should not be Hindi, Urdu, Gujrati, Marathi, Tamil, Sanskrit, Persian or Arabic but a foreign language English and all Government funds would be used for the encouragement of 'western science and literature'.

Thomas Macaulay had no understanding of Vedic Literature and science. He did not know Sanskrit, Hindi, Persian, Arabic and other oriental languages and literatures. He was a young man of 35 year. Without any study or research in the field of oriental literature, he remarked in his Minute of 1835.

'There are no books on any Subject which Deserve to be compared to our own... Medical Doctrines which would Disgrace an English Farrier, Astronomy which would move Laughter in the girls at an English Boarding School.'

He had not read Bhragu Samhita, Charak Samhita and other Sanskrit works on Ayurved or medical science.

Thomas Macaulay was completely ignorant about the Oriental Literature, but he did a lot of damage and disservice to India and its educational progress. The progress of education in Sankrit, Arabic, Persian, Hindi, etc. became slow.

On return to England, he became a member of the British Cabinet, but the Prime Minister of England Lord Melbourne did not like him. He once remarked that he would 'prefer to sit in a room with a chime of bells, ten parrots and Lady Westmoreland than with Macaulay. The London newspapers described Lord Macaulay as 'Cheat', 'Swindler' and 'Charlatan'.

Thomas Macaulay became extremely popular after the publication of his History of England in 4 volumes. The first 2 volumes of the History were published in 1848. The first edition of 3000 was sold in 10 days. By April 1850, 2200 copies were sold. The demand for his History of England was so great that 35000 copies of volume 3 and 4 had to be published in December 1855.

On December 28, 1859, Lord Macaulay died in his 'study', splendidly dressed from top to bottom, seated in his cosy chair, in all cheerfulness, with his most favourite countless books and publications all around him.

17

Rammohan Roy and the British Ignorance

Raja Rammohan Roy, May 22, 1772–September 27, 1833, a great social reformer and religious thinker, reached Liberpool from Calcutta on April 8, 1831. He had left Calcutta by ship on November 19, 1830.

He was known in England, France, Germany and many other parts of the world been before his reaching England. He was considered as a great genius by the western world. The people of Spain were so much impressed by this great Indian that they dedicated their model Constitution to this 'most liberal, wise and virtuous' leader.

An eminent American physician in Bristol, who provided medical treatment to Rammohan Roy in Bristol wrote in 1833:

> 'No one in past History or in the present time ever came before my judgement clothed in wisdom, grace and humanity'.

Summing up Rammohan Roy's achievements as a man massive scholarship and an individual who through enlightenment, wanted to purify social, political and religious life of the people all over the world, James Pattle remarked in Calcutta on April 5, 1834:

> 'If it had been the good fortune of Rammohun Roy to have

lived in ancient Rome or Grecian times, I say, the historian, the poet, the painter, the sculptor would have vied with each other in immortalizing his name.'

The Times, London and the *Standard*, London, however, immortalized Rammohan Roy, when they wrote on September 30, 1833:

'A more Remarkable man has not Distinguished Modern times and advance of opinion.'

Mary Carpenter, with whom, Rammohan Roy lived in Bristol in 1833, was full of admiration for this 'Light of India'. She wrote on October 27, 1833:

When from afar we saw thy burning light
Rise gloriously o'er India's darkened shore,
In spirit we rejoiced, and then still more
Rose high our admiration and delight.

And the Bristol Mirror, Bristol describing Rammohan Roy as a Bright, Serene, Unequalled Star, wrote in 1833:

And thou didst triumph, for by thee,
Were knowledge, truth, and freedom won,
And willing others to be free
'The precepts of Heaven's Holy One.'
That lamp whose luster lent thee light
Thou gav'st to Asia's dark night.

The Native East is rich in gems
Her diamonds yield unclouded light.
But O', not all the diadems,
Wherewith she ever charm'd the sight
May vie with thee, who shon'st afar
A bright, serene, unequalled star!

And thou art set-set in West
So do the stars of Heaven decline,
And hallow'd be the peaceful rest,
Of one who did so brightly shine,
If worth and talent claim a tear
Rammohun Roy! thou hast it here.

Rammohan Roy greatly enjoyed his visit to England and France, though he also died there on September 27, 1833 at Bristol. He met almost all the leading individuals in England, including the members of Parliament, and the great political thinker Jeremy Betham.

He met the King of England and on September 13, 1832, he sailed for Paris to meet the Emperor of France Louts Philippe.

Rammohan Roy greatly appreciated the wonderful warm reception accorded to him both by the Government and the People of England. Countless people stood on both sides of the road to greet this tall, well built, handsome, aristocratic scholar-reformer in his typical oriental embroidered long gown and attractive, shining turban.

Interestingly, huge crowds of men, women and children rushed to see him in Liberpool, Manchester, London, etc. The People cheered him saying :

"Long live king of Ingee.
Long Live Tippoo Saheb."

Rammohan Roy, the prophet of Indian Awakening, would have felt astonished at the way, the People of England greeted him. Rammohan Roy was not the king of India. He had nothing to do with the sovereignty of India or that of any Indian state.

And Tipu Sultan, the ruler of Mysore, had died three decades back on May 4, 1799.

18

Rammohan Roy and Politics in India

Rammohun Roy was one of the most enlightened individuals of the nineteenth century. *The Times*, London, the *Bristol Mirror and the Standard*, London described him as 'the most extraordinary individual in 1833. He was educated in the real sense of the term, well informed about international politics, conversant with almost all the religious doctrines of the world, and had a remarkable command over Persian, Arabic, Sanskrit, Hebreo, Latin, Greek, English and Bangali.

He was an intellectual prodigy. He went to Tibet at the age of 15 and studied Buddhism. In his 30s, he wrote his criticism of idolatory on the basis of Vedas.

He had a liberal frame of mind and had firm faith in social justice, religious tolerance and free thought. He was an internationalist and had a firm conviction that most of the problems of the world could be resolved through mutual exchange of ideas or through an International Congress.

A pioneer in the field of journalism, he was connected with a large number of newspapers and periodicals, as editor or proprietor, such as *Sambad Kaumudi*, *Miratul Akhbar*, *Brahmanica*, *Magazine*, *Bangadoot*, *Bengal Herald*, etc. He was also associated with James Buckingham's *Calcutta Journal*, David Richardson's *Bengal Chronicle*,

James Sutherland's *Calcutta Chronicle*, H.T. Prinsep's *India Gazette*, and James Marshmen's *Samachar Durpan* and the *Friend of India.*

He was among those few Indians who wrote for London News papers. He was such a staunch supporter of free thought that when the Company's Government imposed certain restriction on the Press in 1823, he organized a movement against such policies and as a protest closed down his *Miratul Akhbar*.

Almost for three long decades, he was an inseparable part of the media. Through his papers and other leading journals of the time, he wrote on almost every significant problem of the day, and demonstrated his meticulous care in dealing with some of the most complicated issues of the world in all their intricate details. He was concerned about movements for constitutional government in Spain, Italy's struggles against the Austrian yoke, agitation in Ireland for good government, politics in Naples, slavery in America, revolution in France and Reforms in England.

It is, however, astonishing to note that this enlightened leader did not utter even a single word about the Blackhole of Calcutta, suicide committed by Robert Clive in England. Warren Hasting's impeachment by the British Parliament. Lord Lakes' humiliating defeat at Bharatpur. British display of military power in Mysore, Philip Buton's murder in Assam. Heroism of Mahabandula, major General Robert Gillespie's murder or when Trimbackjee Danglia organized a revolt against the British, murdered Gangadhar Shastri, and burnt the British residency in Poona. Elphinstone had to run for his life.

It was among the most significance political developments of the time because the Marathas still wielded tremendous influence on Indian politics, and demanded "chauth" from the East India Company, from time to time. Rammohun Roy maintained a dead silence. He did not write either about the heroism of Trimbackjee Danglia or the great revolt. He however continued to speak and write whether God was singular or plural; whether idolatory was good or bad. Trimbackjee Danglia's revolt was debated both in the British Press and Parliament in England.

II

In 1826, the British looted Bharatpur. This loot was condemned by the British officials themselves, including Sir Charles Metcalfe. It was described as "disgraceful" in extreme. Men, women and children—all were plundered mercilessly and manhandled. Rammohun Roy, who was no more in the Company's service, could condemn such a "mad" plunder. But instead of exposing the highhandedness of the British, Rammohun Roy continued to translated his Bengali Grammar into English and concentrate on "Symbol of the Trinity".

III

The Barrackpore Muitiny attracted the attention of the British Parliament and the member of Parliament condemned it. The Governor-General, in the State of mental torture, tendered his resignation and returned to England. The question was inseparably connected with Indian social traditions and moral values. But Rammohun Roy did not take up the grievances of the Indian soldiers with the Government and preferred to remain silent.

IV

Around 1827, when the British violated its Treaty with Siam and attacked it, William Adam and James Sutherland could not remain silent. They openly condemned the British action. They wrote so critically that the British suppressed their paper, the *Calcutta Chronicle* and imposed a heavy penalty on them. Rammohun Roy, a friend of William Adam and James Sutherland was expected to support these great journalists on such a significant issue and condemn the Company's suppression of the *Calcutta Chronicle* but he decided to drop his voice.

V

The British Government banned public meetings in Calcutta in 1827. The newspapers challenged the British Government regarding the legality or constitutional validity of such a measure. In their opinion the Company had no legal authority to ban public meetings. The editors were punished for such bold criticism. The ulcer was burning, but Rammohun Roy maintained his cool.

There were many other such extremely important national issues on which the 'Maker of Modern India' could raise his voice, but for reasons best known to him, the Prophet of Indian Nationalism continued to pedal softly.

This was not the extreme. Around 1822, an aristocrat from Bengal, Pratap Narain Das was openly flogged to death by the Company. The incident created a cry of horror in Bengal and even outside. John Hayes, a Judge, at Comilla did not permit even his crimination according to Vedic rites. His dead body was not handed over to his family despite of endless requests. There was every possibility of an outbreak of Violence. The Company, therefore issued a notification announcing the death of Pratap Narain Dass due to 'cholera'. This was a white lie. The *Asiatic Journal*, London and the John Bull, Calcutta Condemned the Company. The people in Bengal were restless, but surprisingly Rammohun Roy's *Miratul Akhbar* brazen-facedly supported John Haye and the Company's inhuman action.

Had Rammohun Roy taken a bold stand on some of these extremely important questions and put forward his own objective assessment, it is certain he would have served the cause of India, the Indian people and the humanity at large, better. He was a distinguished journalist and an upholder of free expression and thought and also the author of the Press Petition—described as the Magna Carta of Indian Journalism and there was no reason why his voice would have gone unnoticed both by the Government and the People.

But Rammohun Roy whose voice had reached Europe and America much before he left for Liberpool on November 15, 1830 maintained his taciturnity and undertone.

An important reason for his low signing on these important issues seems to be his over-occupation with 'one God-three Gods'-'sakar and nirankar' and the most burning social problem of the time in India—widow-burning. His career as a servant of the EICO for almost a decade might have also influenced the soft attitude of this retired pensioner towards his ex-employers.

Perhaps the most important reason for his quite tone was his idol-worship of the East India Company or his firm faith in the "divine" character or the British rule or Indo-British Relations, a rule which had appeared to Burke, Sheridan, Hicky, Duane, Maclean, Stanhope and even Macaulay as the worst kind of tyranny and lastly Rammohun Roy's iconoclastic attitude, till the last day of his life, that the Indians who had administered India under Shahjahan and Shivaji, Akbar and Aurangzeb were still not "ripe" for self-government.

19

When Maharaja Ranjit Singh Played Holi with William Bentinck

Maharaja Ranjit Singh was one of the most powerful rulers of India in the first half of the nineteenth century. He ruled over a large state and possessed an excellent, most modern military force. Even the British Government was terribly afraid of him.

Maharaja Ranjeet Singh wanted to cultivate intimate, friendly relations with the British Government. He, therefore, invited the British Governor-General Lord William Bentinck to Punjab in 1831.

Lord William Bentinck immediately accepted the invitation and crossed the Satlaj to meet the Sikh sovereign.

He went to Lahore from Shimla via Ramgarh, Nalagarh, Rupur, not only with Lady William and countless other English women but also with a large number of senior British Officials, including H T Prinsep, General Ramsay, Major Benson, Captain Wade, Caldwell, Revanshaw and Major Lockett.

He was also accompanied by a large military force which comprised eight guns of horse artillery, two squadrons of the lancers, HM's 31st infantry and two squadrons of "Colonel Skinner's Horse."

Maharaja Ranjeet Singh and his sons and all the principal Rajas and Sardars and other high officials including C in C Khoshal Singh, Faqueer Azizuddin, Raja Kunwar Karak Singh, and Raja Dhion Singh gave a warm welcome to Lord William Bentinck and his wife. About the preparations made by philosopher Faqueer Azizuddin, a contemporary Calcutta newspaper the *Calcutta Government Gazette* wrote in 1831.

> "All the flowers and tropes of the poets of Asia, all the powers and beauties of nature and art were put in requisition by the Faqueer to express the feelings of delight. The showers of friendship had cooled the oppressive heat. And the balmy zephyrs of the Himalaya of mutual esteem had refreshed the hearts."

There was a lavish display of military power and an immense 'suwaree' of tall elephants, richly caparisoned and bearing on their gilded 'Howdas' all the principal Rajas and Sardars of the court, six battalions of infantry. The 'Ghorechuraha', were dressed in yellow silk, armed with beautiful spears, matchlocks, pistols and bows.

Soon Maharaja's horses, all splendidly caparisoned, were paraded before the distinguished guests.

According to a contemporary source, the His Highness's forces, with costly trappings of velvet and gold, were more than a match for any power, except the British, in the East. In marching and firing they were not excelled by any of the Company's troops and their discipline was highly creditable to the Maharaja.

On October 30, 1831 there was a fantastic Evening party in honour of Lord William Bentinek, Lady William and countless English women who had come to Punjab. They were greeted with finest music and Holi dances. Regiments of amazons, beautiful, armed with smiles, bows and arrows entertained the British Governor-General. Excellent Holi songs were sung by some of the most beautiful women of the state. This battalion of fair, good-looking women in yellow silk dresses represented 'vasant' or livery of spring-an emblem of joy. Even the Maharaja wore a yellow turban.

Hundreds and thousands of guests who had come from far off places bore yellow silk dresses.

The dancers and the Maharaja opened the Holi campaign by

pelting one another most vigorously with gold dust. The Maharaja embraced the Governor-General. He also played Holi with Lady William who was completely covered with gold dust. No one escaped and the engagement soon became general. The whole British party was covered from top to bottom with colours.

Sweets and wines were offered to all the guests in the most lavish and friendly manner. There was music and laughter all around. The countless dancers continued to entertain all those who had graced the occasion.

After the festival of music and colours, Maharaja Ranjit Singh took Lady Bentinck to an excellent exhibition of the most precious items of his royalty and the world. This included the world-famous Kohinoor!

Perhaps the display of Kohinoor was a mistake on the part of the Maharaja because the British could not forget the 'Kohinoor' and the moment there was an opportunity, after Punjab's annexation, it was perhaps immediately removed to England, along with other countless precious jewels.

On October 31, 1831, Maharaja Ranjit Singh, gave a grand farewell to the Company's Governor-General, who gave the Maharaja a "yaadast"—an offer of "perpetual friendship" signed by him, and Lady William presented to the great Maharaja some of the finest items of presents including a handsome Music Box.

Thus Holi had a wonderful effect. The British honoured their commitments and there was no violence or bloodshed in Punjab till the Maharaja breathed his last in 1839.

20

Why the British Government was Terribly Afraid of Maharaja Ranjit Singh of Punjab?

Maharaja Ranjit Singh (November 2, 1780-June 27, 1839), the ruler of Punjab was a Terror to the British Government. The highest British authorities in India, Lord William Bentinck, Sir Charles Metcalfe and Lord Auckland—all went to Punjab to meet this brave sovereign.

The British Government was always afraid to antagonize Maharaja Ranjit Singh or to interfere in his internal administration. He had a powerful army, trained by the Indian and the foreign Generals.

Maharaja Ranjit Singh died on June 27, 1839 due to paralysis at Lahore.

After the death, the question before the Punjab Council of Ministers was whether Ranjit Singh would be cremated alone or would some Maharanis also commit self-immolation with the dead body of the Great Maharaja.

The Sikh Maharanis, including Jindhan Kaur told the Council of Ministers clearly that they had absolutely no intension of self-immolation with the dead body of Maharaja Ranjit Singh. They advanced two reasons one that Lord William Bentinck had already declared sati or widow burning as a crime or as illegal since

1829 and two that the cruel custom had no religious sanction or validity.

The whole cabinet was disappointed.

It never wanted the Great Legendary Hero to be burnt alone.

Ultimately it was decided that all the non-Sikh Maharanis would immolate themselves on the funeral pyre of the Maharaja.

16 young and beautiful Maharanis, therefore, were burnt alive with the dead body of Maharaja Ranjit Singh.

Of-course, it was not without the prior consent of the bewitching beauties. Due do June summer-heat and the fierce flames, the Maharanis cried and wept. The foreign dignitaries and others present including the representatives of the British Government at the sad occasion also could not control their tears.

No one, however, had the guts to oppose.

No one could say that the burning alive of 16 young and beautiful Maharanis was cruel unethical, irrational or inhuman.

The British Government, though a paramount power, continued to be panic-stricken even when Ranjit Singh had breathed his last.

21

The Jaipur Revolt, 1835, when William Bentinck wanted to Annex Jaipur

During almost one hundred years of the East India Company's rule in India, a large majority of British officials, including the Governors-General, declared non-intervention in the internal matters of the India "sovereign" states as the cardinal principle of the British policy.

But whenever any new State was conquered or annexed, under the pretext of "misgovernment", "hostility, "disturbance", "intrigue" or "insanity of the ruler", or in the name of "progress", or "radical reforms", there was a universal jubilation in the British camp both in India as well as in England.

Such annexations provided the Company an opportunity to plunder. The Company's officials, including military-men, became "nobobs" overnight, through these conquests.

The Company's shareholders were happy because they got more dividend. The British Parliament was happy because the Government could charge more interest on its loans sanctioned to the Company. The priest was happy because after every new conquest the area of his operations widened. Lord William Bentinck had learnt a bitter lesson, of undue interference in 1806, in the Vellore Mutiny, after which he was recalled, disgracefully, and in which a large number of British officials were slaughtered.

He, therefore, made a declaration of non-intervention in the matters of the Indian States as the basic principle of his policy in India as Governor-General.

But the pressure of the employers, the shareholders, the militarymen, and the Christian missionary organizations continued to mount up and William Bentinck found it difficult to adhere to the policy of non-intervention.

Encouraged by the British reaction and response, both in Parliament and outside, William Bentinck decided to add one more feather to his cap. He deposed the ruler of Coorg and annexed it.

There was again a great rejoicing in the British camp.

The British were always afraid of the Marathas, the Jats, the Gorkhas, the Sikhs and the Rajputs. They had suffered endless defeats and humiliations.

William Bentinck now thought of extending the British influence in Rajputana, But to touch the Rajput States was no joke. It was almost like playing with fire. Bentinck, therefore, thought of some other device, some diplomatic moves some sophisticated steps through which the Rajput State could be brought under British power.

Through diplomacy the British had succeeded in capturing Bharatpur in 1826 and plundering its invaluable gems and pearls, gold and silver. Now Bentinek concentrated on nothing less than Jaipur, which was fabulously rich. He went to Ajmer and met the sovereigns of Jaipur, Jodhpur, Kota, Bundi, and Kishangarh on January 18, 1832. He also met the greatest terror of the time: Amir Khan of Tonk.

The British officials had already started playing their diplomatic game in these States. There was interference. There was intrigue, and an attempt to undermine the established authority.

At Jaipur, the diplomatic moves more subtile, more sophisticated and more camouflaged. But the Rajputs were quite sagacious. They had seen the fate of Mysore, Coorg, Jaintia and Kaachar. They had also seen how the British sequestrated from Baroda, territories yielding about 4,20,00,000 rupees every year, against the wishes of the people and how Nawab Nasirruddin Haider of Oudh was forced to grant a huge loan to the British Government.

When William Bentinck and his team discussed the various matters at Ajmer, the Jaipur representative, Sanghi Jodha Ram, therefore, told H.T. Prinsep absolutely frankly and clearly that the British were not just in demanding 8,00,000 rupees per annum from Jaipur as tribute. It was exorbitant and based on absolutely false information and miscalculations. The Jaipur representative, therefore, pleaded that the exhorbitant tribute must be immediately reduced.

The British Government, which was interested only in extending its influence and power, did not pay any heed to the Jaipur requests. On the contrary, it continued to promote intrigues and dissensions, with the help of rival chiefs.

The intrigues reached such a height that attempts were made to kill even the relations of the Jaipur representative and the Jaipur Government had to draw the British attention towards such intrigues.

There were cases of maltreatment, too, but the British remained cold and indifferent. William Bentinck refused to do anything even for the suppression of highway robberies in Shekhawati, when he met the Rajput sovereign in Ajmer.

The Jaipur royal family, the aristocracy and the people did not like the British attitudes and policies. There was unrest all around on the British refusal to reduce the tribute. Similar attitude and policy were adopted towards Mewar also.

British intrigues and support to the rival chiefs was a matter of disaffection and unrest for the people. The unrest started mounting up after Bentinck's return form Ajmer.

As a shock, the people heard in 1834, the news of British occupation of Sekawati, a part of Jaipur State. The same year Terawati was also occupied by the British, under Bentinck's direction.

The people felt bewildered.

The same year, the British took possession of the Jaipur portion of the Sambhar Salt Lake, and on January 27, 1835 even the Jodhpur part of the Lake could not remain uncaptured.

The people were simply surprised to the vulgar display of British military power. They had now no patience, the British were extending their influence and power without any justification. Their support to the rival groups was always increasing. The Jaipur Government protested but all in vain.

Bentinck wanted one more feather to his grand cap, after Mysore and Coorg.

Soon, an opportunity presented itself.

The young Maharajah of Jaipur Sawai Jai Singh died on February 5, 1835, after some serious illness.

Some people, perhaps at the instigation of the Jaipur rival chiefs, gave currency to the rumour that Maharajah Jai Singh had not died a natural death and he had been poisoned not by any one else but the sagacious, bold and wise Sanghi Jodha Ram, the Jaipur Minister and one of the most powerful diplomats of the time.

The British wanted to create a misunderstanding with the help of some rival chiefs. They wanted to implicate the popular diplomat, who was the most powerful opponent of British interference in Jaipur and other Rajput States.

The news of death came as a bolt from the blue. The people were in tears, but for Major Nathental Alves the Governor-General's agent for the States of Rajputana, it was a god-sent opportunity to play the trump-card. He immediately reached Jaipur and issued the most offensive proclamation that Jaipur Maharaja had died an unnatural death.

The people and the Government were shocked beyond measure. They saw a deep diplomatic design in the British Proclamation. Jodha Ram, at his own initiative suggested, an impartial Judicial inquiry by the British. He even volunteered to resign from his responsible position to enable the British to holds an impartial investigation.

William Bentinck, however, was not satisfied.

The British Government wanted to get rid of its greatest adversary. Jodha Ram was, adversary. Jodha Ram was, therefore, thrown out of Jaipur. He was locked up at Dausa.

Such highhanded treatment of the most distinguished leader was intolerable to the people. Jodha Ram had won the love and admiration of countless people through his bold and fearless advocacy of the Jaipur cause. He had opposed all British intervention, whether it was in Sekhawati or Terawati, whether it was in the Jaipur part of the Sambhar Lake or in the Jodhpur part.

Since the Maharaja had died a natural death, the British could not collect any evidence against the noble Minister, even the rival chiefs could not help the British in this shrewd venture.

The people were happy. They now awaited anxiously the release of the great hero. But instead of release, Nathenial Alves issued orders for the immediate expultration of Jodha Ram.

There was disappointment and anger every where.

Dewan Amarchand Saravagi, Hidyatullah, Shiv Lal Sahu, Manikchand Bhaosa, Hukumchand Sanghi—all felt deeply hurt or wounded.

With Jodha Ram in captivity, it was a golden chance for the British to dictate their own terms to the Government of Jaipur.

On June 4, 1835, Nathenial Alves, therefore, entered the Jaipur Palace with his escorts and a team of select officials to meet the Maharani. The news of Nathenial Alves entry into the Palace spread like a wild fire and when high level consultations were in progress, hundreds and thousands of people had gathered on the streets to hear the final verdict. There was unrest and anger. The crowd was restless and in a great fury. This kind of intervention and pressure was beyond their tolerance.

As soon as the British team and armed force came out of the Place, the crowd became uncontrolable.

22

The Poet who Wrote About India's Freedom in the First-Half of the Nineteenth Century

When Rammohan Roy and Dwarkanath Tagore were talking about social reform and social reconstration, when Dr. Krishna Mohan Banerji was praising the Christian religion; when Mirza Ghalib was writing odes on Sir Charles Metcalfe, William Bentick and Lord Auckland, a poet from Kashipur condemned the British rule and wrote about India's freedom. The poet was Lokratna Pant Gumani.

Unfortunately historians social scientists have not done any justice to him. His contribution has not been properly evaluated even by scholars of Indian Literature.

Lokratna Pant Gumani, 1791-1846, was an outstanding poet of Hindi, Sanskrit, Nepali and Kumauni. He was born in Kashipur. His father was Devnidhi Pant and mother Devmanjari. He was greatly assisted in his studies in philosophy, religion and literature by Ramkrishna Pant and Haridutt. He married twice. It is unfortunate that his correspondence, memoirs, diaries, etc. are not traceable. He remains almost unknown till today to world of politics and literature. He travelled to various parts of the country: Allahabad.

Hardwar, Rudraprayag, etc. and produced some excellent poetry. A contemporary of Rammohan Roy, Thomas Macanlay, Dwarkanath Tagore, Justice Radhakant Dev, Charles Trevelyan, Mirza Galib, Yugalkishore Shukla, Henry Derozio, Bhawanicharan Banerjee, David Richardson, Ishwarchand Gupta, Jameshedji Jijabhai, Jyotirao Phule, Savitri Phule, Prasannakumar Tagore and Balshastri Jambhekar. Lokratna Pant attacked the British rule and wrote about India's freedom. Lokratna Pant Gumani, about a decade before the Indian Revolt of 1857, was the first Hindi poet to talk about India's Independence or Liberation from the British Colonial yoke. It was more than 50 years before Bankimchand Chauerjee's 'Vandemataram'. It was more than 30 years before Bhartendu Harishchandra wrote about the sad plight of the Indian people. It was more than 45 years before the foundation of the Indian National Congress by W.C. Banerjee, A.O. Hume, William Wedderbum, Pherozeshah Mehta, Dadabhai Naoroji and Budruddin Tyabji. Lokratna Pant Gumani was ahead of Swami Dayanand Saraswati and Helena Blavastsky and Henry Olcott, who established the Arya Samaj and Theosophical Society respectively.

Like Dadabhai Naoroji, Romeshchandra Dutt and Mahadeogovind Ranade, he drew the attention of the government and the people towards droughts, famines and scarcities of food. He was among those few intellectuals, who analyzed deeply how and why the British could establish their hegemony in India.

He was among those few political analyists who could predict-100 years before Mahatma Gandhi's Quit India Movement (August 8, 1942), when the British would quit India.

Influenced deeply by the Vedic Literature Mahabharat and Ramcharitmanas and many Indian philosophical and scientific works, a worshipper of Ram, Lokratna Pant Gumani wanted to spiritualize human life. He wrote how money had become a paramount power. He wrote about the miserable state of the Indian widows and about prostitution. He wrote about the socio-economic condition of Kashipur. He was an outstanding critic of the British rule. He wrote how the British were lucky to have a sway over India and how the British would ultimately quit India:

The day when the multitude of clouds swoop down on earth with a violent shake from above, verify on that day shall the British leave and return to England

जा दिन सेतुन तें नदिया सब रेतिन के बटकारा घिरेगी
जा दिन नाद समान बनी कहुंभारि शिला जलपाय तरंबी
जा दिन मेघ घटा धरती पर ऊपर में बतखाय गिरंगी
ता दिन जान गुमानी कहै इत छोड़ि विलायत जाय फिरंगी।

He didn't like that there was not even a single brave man who could challenge the British and demonstrate the real valour of the country.

Lokratna Pant Gumani was a remarkable conscience keeper. He tried through his poetry in Sanskrit, Hindi, Nepali and Kumauni to teach righteousness to the people. He was not influenced by Christianity or the British rule. His method of preaching the people was highly effective. He took ideas from the Indian Literature and put them to the people in the most simple and comprehensive style. He was a great advocate of education. He felt that had there been proper expansion or development of education and unity among the Indian soverigns or rulers, the British rule in India would have been a total impossibility.

Vidya ki jo badhti hoti, foot na hoti rajan mein
Hindustan asambhav hota vash karna lakh varshan mein
Kahe Gumani angrezan se kar lo chaho jo mann mein
Dharti mein nahin veer, veerata tumhe dikhata jo ran mein.

Lokratna Pant produced *Ramnampanch Panchashika, Ram Mahima, Gangashatak, Jagannathastak, Krishnastak, Ram Sahasta Ran Dandak, Chitra Padyavali, Kalikastak, Tatva Vidyotini, Punch Panchashika, Ram Vinay Vigyapati Saar, Need Shatak, Shatopadesh, Gain Bhaishajya.*

His remarkable characteristics was his total clarity. He knew the goals, he knew the routes and he knew how to move.

He writes against the British colonial exploitation and autocratic ways. He did not like the destruction of Temples and Palaces by the British. Through his writings he wanted the people to leave the narrow slippery cowpaths of obscurity and move on the majestic highways of social reconstruction and enlightenment. He wanted to destroy the social barriers and creates new bridges of love and tolerence. He wanted to establish the triumph of truth through righteousness. His words glittered and glowed and to some extent they were indeed capable of creating thunder and fire.

Like Henry Wilson, Miss Emma Roberts and David Richardson, he was a worshipper of Ganga. In his Hymn to Ganga, he wrote:

Blessed was Lord Shiva, who bore thy impact on his head
Blessed was Bhagirath, who brought thee down
Blessed the earth that carried thee on her bosom
And blessed the ocean that clasped thee in sweet embrace
A single drop of thy waters, sweeter than nectar,
Makes a creature immortal.

Lokratan Pant did not write like Rammohan Roy's *The precepts of Jesus Christ: The Road to true Happiness* or like Dr. Krishanmohan Banerjee embraced Christianity. But found complete solace, delight or 'anand' in the worship of Ram. In a poem on Ram he wrote:

Oh Son of Dashrath I offer my prayer unto thee
I hold thy lotus feet
Like a vast ocean this world frightens me awfully
Delay not, my lord, guide my vessel to steer clear of all Obstacles
All across the turbulent seas.

His poetry was simple, superb. He was an excellent craftsman of words and phrases. He created musical and magical effect through his poems. The arrangement of letters was so systematic that it matched beautifully with the beating of drums. It was a kind of ornamentation, a fantastic prosodic fancy, which has been quoted by Charuchand Pande. He selected his words in such a manner that it looked as if the magical reverberating drumbeats emanating from some sacred procession at night descending down the majestic hills had got mingled with sweet-soft rhythm of enchanting meter-bound vedic poetry to evoke the grace of God.

Dharanidhar danujbhar har har
Daman par par shaman saṛ
Narakhar har Hridaya chaṛ char
Muni visar sar madhi vihar

Dharani-dhar-dhanujbhar-har-har
Daman-par-par-, shaman-sar
Dhinak-dhin-dhin, Ghinak-ghin-ghin
Tinak-tin-tin-, Ta-ghin-ghin.

23

British Vulgarity: Maharani Jind Kaur's Humiliation

The British Government did not demonstrate much respect of the Indian rulers during the East India Company's rule in India. Countless Indian rulers had to undergo great torture and humiliation from time to time. Sometimes the British officials indulged in worst kind of vulgarity, indecency, and lack of civilized behaviour. Their actions brought disgrace and humiliation not merely to the East India Company but also to the British nation.

Some of the Company's officials, mad with power, behaved in the most uncultured, savage and beastly manner.

Maharaja Ranjit Singh, the sovereign of Panjab, was a Terror to the British Government. The Company's Government was terribly afraid of the Sikhs. But after the death of Maharaja Ranjit Singh, 1839 everything underwent a radical change.

After the Sikh Wars, Maharani Jhindhan Kaur decided to leave Panjab for some time and live in Nepal, for a change. She asked the British Government for permission to leave Lahore. After a great deal of effort, she succeeded in obtaining the Company's permission.

However, in granting the permission, the British Government did not show any politeness, large-heartedness or courtesy. On the contrary, the British Government tried to blackmail or exploit the great Panjab Queen. She was ordered to surrender all her precious possessions, gems and jewels, before leaving for Kathmandu.

Due to utter helplessness, the bewitching Sikh beauty surrendered her countless invaluable assests, gold and diamonds.

This was highly disturbing, distressing and disrespectful. The British, flouting all etiquette and manners, resorted to such a mad policy which was totally unfriendly and offensive.

Maharani Jindan Kaur was full of sorrow. She never expected the British Government to behave in such an uncivilized manner.

But the greatest humiliation was yet to come. The British Government had yet to demonstrate to what extent it could sink or fall.

With all preparations, the brave Maharani left her palace and embarked on her journey to Nepal. She was escorted by some Sikh soldiers. When the Maharani was about to cross the Panjab border, she was stopped abruptly by a huge team of British soldiers and officials. She was told that she would be required to undergo a search before leaving the country.

The fearless Maharani told the British soldiers that any search at that time was an impossibility. She had already surrendered her countless gems and jewels to the Government.

The Maharani was furious. She felt threat the British Government wanted to insult the Queen of Panjab. She told the British officials that she would not grant any permission for search.

In the most unpleasant, brutish, tactless and vulgar manner the British officials asked the Queen of Panjab to take off her clothes. Unashamedly, they bodily searched the Maharani, for quite some time before permitting her to move.

That was completely unflattering. The search was rude, crude and disrespectful. Never in the history of British India, a queen was subjected to so much torture and vulgarity. Maharani Jindan Kaur had never faced such discourtsey and indecencey in her life.

The British search was condemnable. It was impolite,

uncultured and uncivilized, even in the history of the entire human race, such vulgarity and obscenity, is rare with regard to the great queens.

> It was a shame and a slur.
> It was insanity or madness.
> No gems or jewels were found in this body search.

24

British Governor-General Lord Dalhousie and the Shameless Auction of Nagpur Royal Precious Jewels

Lord Dalhousie, the Governor-General of India, January 12, 1848–February 20, 1856, was responsible for violence, bloodshed and tremendous unrest in India. His autocratic, expansionist and aggressive policies displeased and disappointed all—the people and the sovereigns. His unbridled ambitions and military-spirit resulted in the downfall of the East India Company, after the Great Indian Revolt of 1857.

British India, under Lord Dalhousie, was constantly under a state of hostility, militancy and war.

Immediately after his appointment as Governor-General on January 12, 1848, he threw India into the horrible, bloody Sikh War. He was defeated by the Sikhs at Chillianwala, but succeeded in colouring Punjab 'red' on the map of India and soon in annexing Panjab.

In the most obnoxious, absurd and hostile manner, Lord Dalhousie plundered countless guns, rifles, swords, spears, daggers and battle-axes from Lahore and Peshwar and disarmed the people.

It was notorious, shady, shabby and shocking.

Soon, Lord Dalhousie reached Burma and fought a terrible war there. He succeeded in capturing the valley from Prome to Rangoon.

Son of a Commander-in-Chief George Dalhousie, Lord James Dalhousie, followed an extremely ignoble, despicable policy for acquiring more and more territory. He displeased the people and the sovereign? through his policy of stupid 'Doctrine of lapse'. This policy demonstrated Lord Dalhousie's total bankruptsy of ideas and a complete lack of ethical attitude. In a disreputable manner, he annexed Satara, Jhansi, Oudh and Nagpur.

Lord Dalhousie had completely broken his health. Since his appointment in India, he was suffering from unbearable pain. Every day, his life-blood was being drawn away, drop by drop. He had become invalid, croppled, lame and dumb, and yet he was unable to put a check on his ambitions and stupidity.

His wife died of sea-sickness, while about to reach to England in 1853.

After the annexation of Nagpur, Lord Dalhousie behaved in a beggarly manner. He adopted an extremely despicable attitude towards Nagpur. He stooped low and shocked the entire country and even England by plundering the Nagpur palaces. He plundered the most precious ornaments of the Maharanis of Nagpur.

Lord Dalhousie was not satisfied with plunder alone. He demonstrated to what extant the British Government could sink.

Brzenfaredly, Lord Dalhousie passed on the rare, precious items to 'Hamilton and Company' for immediate auction.

This was shameless and degrading. This had never happened in the history of Nagpur. This had never happened in the history of Indian states or in any part of British India or the British Empire or perhaps the entire world.

This looked unpardonable and condemnable to the people. It deserved Lord Dalhousie's impeachment by the British Parliament. It was a humiliation to the Nagpur royal family. It was a crime. The precious ornaments of the Kings and queens in India were always given to the people by the royalty as rewards, as a token of appreciation for meritorious services. Royal ornaments were never sold. This did not happen under the Great Mughals. It did not happen earlier under Emperor Ashok and Chandragupta Maurya.

Lord Dalhousie retired on February 20, 1856. The auction took place in December 1857.

The Indians were full of anger and even the British felt greatly humiliated by this act of shame, stupidity and lack of humanity or decorum.

An English correspondent of '*the Morning Star*', Calcutta, was full of shame and disappointment. On December 25, 1857, after the auction, he wrote to '*the Morning Star*': "I felt ashamed that I was an Englishman."

25

Outstanding Journalist James Buckingham and the Great India Revolt of 1857

The Great Indian Revolt of 1857 was proceeded by a powerful revolution in the realm of ideas. The East India Company followed countless such explosive, unimaginative and absurd policies in India that it became impossible for the people to sympathesize with it or to tolerate its absurdities. It continued to commit countless blunders, year after year, which brought endless humiliation and disgrace to England.

Lord Clive had to cut his own throat with a sharp knife on November 22, 1774, in England, because the British Parliament, the British Press and the people in England were not prepared to pardon him for his obnoxious frauds, intrigues, bribes, and acts of plunder and violence in India. Warren Hastings destroyed the whole impression of England, and its sublime culture, when he fought a bloody duel with Sir Philip Francis—guilty of criminal assault on Catherine Grand—a beauty queen—in Calcutta, on August 17, 1780. He had to be impeached by the Parliament in England for hanging, mercilessly, Maharaja Nand Kumar, and the maltreatment of the returns of Oudh. Lord Wellesley had to be recalled, disgracefully, for his absurd expansionist policies and the horrible British defeats in Bharatpur. Lord Auckland completely humiliated

England, when 16000 British soldiers and officers were massacred in the 'Afghan Disaster of 1842'. Lord Hardinge, like a petty shopkeeper, sold out Kashmir for a few lacs of pounds, and James Dalhousie broke all records of tyranny and torture, when in a wild, dictatorial manner, he tried to annex every independent Indian state, under some pretext or the other, including the most ridiculous, uncivilized and insensible policy of 'doctrine of lapse.'

The Indian people, including the most formidable intellectual elite, was simply amazed at the mad demonstration of military power by a commercial concern. From time to time outstanding writers, poets, journalists, social reformers and other enlightened individuals, such as Justice Padhakant Dev, Rammohan Roy, Bhawanicharan Bannerji, Lokratna Pant, Jamsetji Jijabhai, Jagganath Shankar Seth, Rajab Ali Beg 'Sarur', Yugalkishore Shukla, Dwarkanath Tagore, Prassannakumar Tagore, Dr. Krishna Mohan Bannerji, Kasiprasad Ghosh, Ishwarchandra Gupta, Ramgopal Ghosh, Rassikkrishna Mallick, Madhavchandra Mallick, and Balshastri Jambhekar tried to impress upon the British Government the need to adopt a rational, humanistic attitude towards the needs and aspirations of the Indian people. Nevertheless, many British officials had to part with their lives due to their arrogance, pride, tyranny and torture.

The British intellectuals in England and in India were also not lagging far behind. William Bolts, James Hicky, William Duane, Charles Maclean, William Robinson, Miss Emma Roberts, Leicester Stanhope, William Adamand even Thomas Macaulay and Sir Charles Trevelyan had drawn the attention of the Company towards its absurd policies and blunders.

David Richardson had even published poems in his Calcutta Literary Gazette, Calcutta, about India's freedom in 1834.

Another British poet wrote in 1833:

"My country 'tis the crisis of thy doom,
Thy morn of brightness or thy eve of gloom
The leaf of fortune quivers in the gale,
Oh 'seize it e'er the darker side prevail.
'Tis thine to see the noble fabric fall,
Or gird its weakness with an iron wall."

But the outstanding British writer, editor, Parliamentarian and social-reformer, who made it impossible for the East India Company to breathe, for countless years, before its downfall, after the Great Indian Revolt of 1857, was James Buckingham. He was bold and courageous, and he was prepared to sacrifice his life for freedom of thought and expression, and for the welfare of the people of India. Born in England on August 25, 1786, he reached Calcutta in 1815. Inspired by the noblest ideas of mankind, he made it impossible for the Company to indulge in corruption, injustice, inhumanity, tyranny or torture.

James Buckingham was the editor of one of the most powerful newspapers of India, the *Calcutta Journal*, which he established in 1818. It became a daily next year, on July 1, 1819. James Buckingham, for the first time in India, made arrangements for securing latest information for his paper, not merely from Bombay, Madras, Malabar and Coromandal coast, but also from Rome, Paris, London, Colombo and Peking. The *Calcutta Journal*, was sent to various parts of the world including America and its articles and editorials were frequently reproduced by newspapers and magazines published from England etc.

James Buckingham was intimately connected with many other newspapers. He wrote about education, social transformation, women, crimes and many other burning problems of the day, including widow-burning. His attacks on the Company's maladministration, injustice and Corruptions were extraordinarily bold. It became an impossibility for the Company to tolerate his criticism of the British policies.

James Buckingham was warned and ultimately thrown out of India. He had to leave Calcutta in April 1823. He was tortured and humiliated. The Company's Government always tried to impose strict censorship over the Press in India. It never wanted the criticism of its policies to reach England or to come to the notice of the Court of Directors, the British Parliament and the British Crown.

On reaching England, James Buckingham emerged as a loin-hearted champion of the rights and liberties of the people of India. He attacked the Company in such a powerful manner that it became an impossibility for the Company to survive. James Buckingham served as a towering stalwert and inspirer of the Great Indian Revolt of 1857. Through his speeches and writings, he was digging, day by day, the graves of the Company, and preparing the ground for a great uprising against the British colonialism in India. He established the *Oriental Herald and Colonial Review* in London.

The articles and comments which he published in his journal and other newspapers in England were full of fire and thunder. Such a criticism of the Company's maladministration and injustice was beyond every imagination.

James Buckingham attacked the British Government in India, exactly in the same manner as Sir Surendranath Bannerjee, Lokmanya Balgangadhar Tilak, Veer Damodar Savarkar, Bhikaji Cama, Dr. Annie Besant, Chandra Shekhar Azad, Shaheed Bhagat Singh, Netaji Subhaschandra Bose, Jawaharlal Nehru and Mahatma Gandhi did, in later years during India's heroic struggle for Independence.

James Buckingham rained bombs and bullets on the Company when he wrote countless brilliant articles for the newspapers published in England, particularly the *Parliamentary Review,* London, such as:

1. Bribes given by the Company to men in power.
2. Force and fraud the only modes by which the territorial conquests of the Company have been achieved.
3. Lord Clive's account of a fictitious Treaty with a native, named Omichund, for the purpose of fomenting a rebellion against Meer Jafar.
4. Reward bestowed on Vansittart by Company for his treacherous conduct.
5. Cruelties practised on the natives of India and plunder of their sovereigns.
6. Official despatch of Colonel Munro, describing his own cruelties.
7. Debt of 2,00,000 and fall of India Stock to 20 per cent discount.

8. Anomalous and shortsighted policy of Great Britain towards her East India Dependencies.
9. On the evils inflicted on India and England by the monopoly of salt.
10. British despotism and avarice in the East.

Soon after reaching England he had become an outspoken member of Parliament. In the Parliament, he condemned and criticized the Company's unethical policies in India. He was extremely bold and fearless and it seems, his greatest mission in life was the welfare and happiness of the people of India.

James Buckingham was not satisfied with his activities in the British Parliament and his contributions to the British newspapers and periodicals, alone. He wanted to touch the heighest peaks of life. He, therefore went around countless countries of the world, for enlightening the people about various problems, which confronted them. He wrote and spoke on a large variety of subjects and produced scholarly works on '*Arabia*' '*Mesopotamia*', '*Assyria*' and '*Media*'.

Another wonderful achievement of James Buckingham was the establishment of a grand, excellent British and Foreign Institute in London. Through this great institute he continued to inspire India and the rest of the world, in a most dynamic manner, till the termination of his life on June 30, 1855. Less than 2 years prior to Mangal Pandey's execution on April 8, 1867 and the commencement of the Great Indian Revolt of 1857, on May 10, 1857.

It is surprizing that James Buckingham continued to concentrate on India upto his last moments. When the whole of England was concentrating on the British administration and policies in India, the brightest diadem, James Buckingham shocked everyone through his profound ideas and brilliance. He demonstrated his genius when he published in 1853, from London, 'A Plan for the Future Government of India'.

It was an outstanding work.

It was based on decades of experience, study and expertise. It was a pioneering work, completely unprecedented and unparalleled. It was a creation of a liberal, humanitarian and noble mind. It laid

India under his perpetual debt. It was a memorable accomplishment by every yardstick.

James Buckingham recommended the complete transformation of British administrative mechanism in India. He pleaded for administrative reforms and the restructuring of the entire Indian Civil Service.

With the welfare of India in mind, James Buckingham made a startling recommendation. He recommended the immediate abolition of the Court of Directors and the establishment of a 'responsible Elected Legislature in India'.

James Buckingham was, indeed a powerful champion of the cause of the people of India. He was also a unique inspirer of the Great Indian Revolt of 1857.

26

How India Saved the Life of Dr. Schntz, an Outstanding Sanskrit Scholar of Germany, in 1857? Raja Radhakant Dev's Unique Gesture

Raja Radhakant Dev was among the greatest Sanskrti scholars of the nineteenth century. He was the author of an outstanding Sanskrit work—*Sabdakalpudram*—which he produced after a hard work of about 3 decades. Radhakant Dev won 'Queen Victoria Medal' for his scholarly achievements in the field of Sanskrit Literature.

Raja Radhakant Dev wanted to promote the study of Sanskrit Literature all over the world. He helped countless scholars in their Sanskrit studies. The Government of the East India Company in India was so much impressed by his scholarship and works for the upliftment of the people that it appointed him the Justice of Peace in 1939. He was the first Indian to be made a Justice of Peace in the whole country. It was an extraordinary achievement because he lived in the age of Rammohan Roy, Henry Deroz 10, Bhawanicharan Banerji, Dwarkanath Tagore, Prassanakumar Tagore, Rev. Krishnamohan Banerji, Balshastri Gangadhar Jambhekar, Jamshedji Jijabhai, Jagganath Shankarseth, Russikkrishna Mallick, Yugalkishore

Shukla, Mirza Chaleb, Nirathan Haldar, David Lester Richardson, M.M. Wilson, H.T. Prinsep, Miss Emma Roberts, James Buckingham, James Sutherland Thomas, Macaulay, Charles Trevelyan, Alexander Duff, Feroze Mullah, and Kasiprasad Ghosh.

To receive any honour in that age of outstanding scholars, poets and political leaders was not an easy task.

Radhakant Dev spent his savings on British India Association of which he was the President. He spent a lot of money on Dharma Sabha of which he was the founder member. He spent a lot of money on the Hindu College, Calcutta of which he was the founder president. He spent a great deal on Agricultural Society which was established with his active cooperation. He financially supported many educational institutions and was the patron of certain newspapers published from Calcutta and elsewhere.

In 1855 he had to establish the Hindu Dharma Raksha Sabha because the Christian Missions and the Company's Government had made it impossible for him to breathe. They had suffocated the entire Indian society. Through all kinds of ways, they were forcing or persuading Indians to become Christians. The number of Christians had touched an all time record till that time of 100000 individuals Radhakant Dev worked day-and-night to counteract this planned scheme of Conversions.

There was a total unrest in the country, around 1857. The policy of Doctrine of Lapse, etc. had made the people violent. The Government had granted Indians Converted to Christianity a right to inheritance. Such encouragements and subtle ways of encouraging Christianity to destroy Hinduism in India was resented by Radhakant Dev. He spent a major parts of savings to defend India against this tremendous onslaught.

In 1857, there was a tremendous scarcity of foodgrains in Calcutta. Radhakant Dev organized famine relief measures. He donated money and material. He requested the government to provide relief. But the Government showed total indifference and the people starved.

The Government rejected Radhakant Dev's excellent proposal to stop exporting food grains during the Famine. But the

Government was arrogant, adamant and unkind. It rejected Radhakant Dev's proposals and continued to export even when people were starving in Calcutta etc.

Radhakant Dev looked at these tyrannical ways of the Government. To what extent the government could be wooden in its responsibilities towards the people.

It was a cruelty and the crime. Radhakant Dev spent his savings to rescue the people. He had practically no funds to offer creater relief and save human lives.

At such a critical juncture in 1857, when the Revolt had started Radhakant Dev received an extraordinary information how a great Sanskrit scholar of Germany Dr. L. Schntz was on the brink of total ruin. How he was starving because of bankruptcy.

This great German scholar was about to sell off his rare, invaluable 30 years old collection of rare Sanskrit books and manuscripts in order to survive. There was no hope of any assistance to him from any quarter. The whole precious collection could hardly provide him sufficient amount to survive bankruptcy even for a couple of years.

Radhakant Dev took a pledge to save Dr. L. Schntz, and the invaluable Sanskrit collection. He immediately sent him a huge donation. The Sanskrit scholar in Germany survived for countless years and so was his precious collection of scholarly gems. Dr. L. Schntz wrote to Radhakant Dev on October 21, 1857. "Your kind relief came in at a time when it had become nearly imperatively necessary to part from my dear Sanskrit books, acquired in a period of 30 years." The Sanskrit scholar from Germany concluded: "Words cannot express the feelings by which I was overwhelmed. If I could transport myself to India, my eyes would tell you more of heartfelt gratitude than words are able."

27

Glorious Victory of Indian Revolutionaries over Delhi, and the Great Indian Revolt of 1857

Countless people in England were full of admiration for the great and glorious Indian Revolt of 1857. They did not like the maladminstration, injustice and corruption of the East India Company in India. Joseph Hume, James Buckingham and many other British intellectuals wanted administrative reforms in India and the representation of Indians in the British Parliament. Some scholars condemned the Company's rule in India because it was based on colonial exploitation and blackmail. The sole concern of the mercantile Company, according to some Britons was trading monopoly and profits through every possible ways. An eminent British statesman and at one time the Prime Minister of England Lord Disrael's described the powerful, heroic and widespread Revolt of 1857 as the 'national Revolution'.

The exploitative and inhuman policies of the East India Company had created tremendous unrest in the country. Lord Clive's greed, mischief, plunder and frauds brought about tremendous disgrace to England and the East India Company resulting in the greatest humiliation of Lord Clive and his ignoble cutting of his own throat. Warren Hastings's arrest of Maharaja Chet Singh of Banaras, execution of Pandit Nand Kumar, cruel and inhuman treatment of the Begums of Oudh—all led to his impeachment in England and attacks on his policies by the greatest British parliamentaries and scholars, such as Edmund Burke.

The Revolt of 1857 was extremely fierce and disasterous for the British. Countless Britishers were massacred by the Indian Revolutionaries. They were tired of British corruptions, injustice, plunder, blackmail, exploitation and expantionist policies. The revolutionaries were angry and furious. Countless revolutionaries had come to Delhi from far-off places. They were determined to throw the British out of India even at the cost of their own lives.

The result was Flames, Fire and cries of freedom everywhere in Delhi. Among the earliest victims in Delhi were George Benesford, his wife and 5 young daughters. They were all massacred at the Delhi Bank House on May 11, 1857.

The five daughters fought heroically with the revolutionaries on the roof of an outhouse and did not surrender till they were alive.

The family was not prepared to run away or escape. That was indeed brave and heroic. That was indeed great and glorious.

Countless British soldiers tried to save the British honour. They were, however, massacred by the Indian revolutionaies. Brigadier General J. Nicholson, Colonel C. Chester, Captain C.W. Russell, Captain J.W. Delamain, Lt. W.H. Mountsteven, W.H. Napier, Captain F. Andrews, Lt.J.H. Bradshaw, W.R. Webb, Lt. W.W. Pogson, Lt. Col. R.A. Yule, Dr. S. Moore, E. Briscoe, A. Harrison, Lt. J.R.S. Fitzgerald, Capt. E.W.J. Knox, S.B. Elkington Lt. T. Cabbett, E. Phillips and Lt. M.A. Humphrys—all had to part with their lives within no time.

There were great confrontations and clashes at Hindon, Kashmere Gate, Najafgarh and Badli etc. The revolutionaries did not spare even Capt G.C. McBarnett, Major G.O. Jacob, Lt. W. Crozier, Lt. C.F. Cambier, Lt. D.F. Sherriff, Lt. S. Jackson, Lt. E. Speke, Lt. J. Brown. Because of absured expasionist and unimaginative policies of the Company, E.C. Wheatley, O.C. Walter, C. Bannerman, A. Murray, Lt. Q. Battye, Lt. R.P. Homfray, Lt. Col. W.H. Lumsden had to sacrifice their lives.

The East India Company misbehaved with the Mughal Emperor Shah Alam. The British Governor-General Lord Amherst was charged for his vulgar misbehaviour with the Oudh queens. In the eyes of the Indian people the British display of poser and annexation of Carnatic, Surat, Tanjore, etc. were completely unjustified and indefensible.

Lord Lake's defeat and humilation in Bharatpur in 1805 and Colonel Monson's defeat in Kota had destroyed the British military prestige, and the British Newspapers condemned the Company's military policies in India.

The British were treating Indian soldiers as cannon fodder. They were exploiting and blackmailing the Indian soldiers in their employment. They were against Indian soldiers performing their religious ceremonies. In Vellore there was the massacre of some Britons, who had ordered the Indian soldiers to remove their 'Tilaks' from the foreheads, etc. The Mutiny at Barrakpore was a result of maltreatment of soldiers, their lack of promotional avenues and poor, low, dishonourable salaries and allowances. Without any rewards or monetary incentives, the Indian soldiers were required to sacrifice themselves in far-off places and even outside India for British victories.

Like a petty mercantile firm, the East India Company had sold Kashmir for a 10,00,000 and the Afghan soldiers had completely defeated and humiliated the British forces in the famous 1842 Afghan Disaster!

Most of the Governor-Generals were extremely unqualified, ignorant, and stupid individuals. They had no administrative competence, calibre or capacity. Their policies resulted in the massacre of countless innocent Britons and in disgrace to England.

On August 16, 1834, the English editor of the *Bombay Gazette*, published a poem on British rule in India. It was an anonymous poem written by a "young civilian" of Bengal—an Englishman :

We live among them like a walking blight,
Our very name the watchword of affrigh,
No sympathy, no pity, no remorse,
Our end is profit; and our means are force.

The poet felt that the time had come when the people of India would revolt against the British superstructure. They would "rise to life and light" and humble the British power :

Year after year augments the dreadful sum
Of rankling anguish ominously dumb;
There needs but one superior to the rest,
To rule the chords that are in every breast;
There needs some surpassing act of wrong
To break the patience that has bent so long:
There needs but some short sudden burst of fire
May chance to set the general thought on fire;
There needs but some fair prospect of relief,
Enough to seize the general belief;
Some holy juggle, some absurd caprice,
To raise one common struggle for release,
And like a sleeper starting from his dream,
Who sees the phantoms vanish at his scream,
The nation shall rise to life and light,
And scarcely find a foe to brave its might.

The savage massacre of the British continued with increasing brutality throughout May, June, July, August and September 1857. Flags of freedom were flying everywhere in Delhi and its neighbourhood. Countless British soldiers and civilians, including women and children, had to run away from Delhi, under terrible panic.

The Indian victory was complete or total. The British Generals had been completely outclassed, outmanouvered and outmatched. The revolt was well-organized and well-directed. Even the Mughal Emperor Bahadurshah Zafar had openly participated in the great revolt. The Mughal princes and countless other revolutionaries from neighbouring and far-off places had created an unprecedented hovoc in Delhi and had made it impossible for the British to breathe.

There were rejoicings and celebrations all around. The Mughal Emperor moved around the whole city in a grand procession comprizing elephants and horses. The Mughal Emperor boldly addressed the revolutionaries from Meerut etc. at Begum-Gate on May 12, 1857.

The British had suffered a humiliating defeat. It was axiomatic that the British Generals were no match to the Indian revolutionaries in heroism, bravery and determination. The British Governor-General Lord Canning looked helpless, disappointed and in tears. The Company's government was completely broken and frustrated. It was demoralized. Delhi had gained its freedom. It was completely independent of the British colonial administration.

The news of Indian victory in Delhi spread like a fire. The flames of revolution could be seen now in Kanpur, Allahabad, Bareilly, Moradabad, Sambhal, Jhansi, Gwalior, Mathura, Etawah, Jaunpur, Mandsor, Kota, Ajmer, Neemuch, Jodhpur, Lucknow, Dharwar, Nargund, Nasirabad, Sardhana, Bulandshahar, Aligarh, Patna, Bagpat, Hissar, Rewwri, Shahjahanpur, Amroha, Bijnor, Rampur and countless other places in India.

The revolutionaries all over the country were in intimate, fast contact with the greatest leaders of the Revolt such as Nana Saheb, Tautiya Tope, Maharani Lakshmibai, Begum Hazat Mahal, Bakt Khan, etc.

For creating unrest and discontent in the country against the British exploitation even the new-papers had played a significant role. The ideas of Justice Radhakant Dev, Ishwarchandra Gupta, Lokratna Pant, Balshastri Jambhekar, Prassannakumar Tagore, Rassikkrishna Mallick, James Buckingham, David Richardson, James Sutherland, etc. had served as an inspiration to the revolutionaries.

Henry Derozio provided a great inspiration to Indians when he wrote 'The Harp of India':

> Why hang'st thou lonely on yon wither'd bough ?
> Unstrung, for ever, must thou there remain ?
> Thy music once was sweet —who hears it now ?
> Silence hath bound thee with her fatal chain;
> Neglected, mute, and desolate art thou,
> Like ruin'd monument on desert plain,

O ! many a hand more worthy far than mine,
Once thy harmonious chords to sweetness gave,
And many a wreath for them did fame entwine,
Of flowers still blooming on the minstrel's grave :
Those hands are cold; but if thy notes divine,
May be by mortal waken'd once again,
Harp of my country ! let me strike the strain.

In another poem "To India: My Native Land", Henry Derozio wrote :

My country ! in thy day of glory past
A beauteous halo circled round thy brow,
And worshiped as a dicty thou wast.
Where is that glory, where that reverence now ?

The Calcutta Literary Gazette, the Calcutta Gazette, the Bengal Annual, the Bombay Literary Gazette, the Oriental Star, etc. published from time to time articles and poems which were remarkable for their expression of Indian patriotic instinct. In February 1834, D.L. Richardson's the Calcutta Literary Gazette denounced the oppressive measures of the British government in India, under which according to this paper, the "sun of liberty had set." It questioned:

Will India once again be free?
And will she dare to break her chain,
And drive the oppressor o'er the sea?

It felt that the time was not far off when the Indian people would fight for their "rights and liberties" against the British imperialism. It wrote:

The East proclaims the coming morn,
That glorious time is not so far
When India and her sons shall rise."

On March 31, 1834, The Madras Male Asylum Herlad, wrote:

> Oh, doubt it not, it will come at last,
> The day—the wished for day be born
> E'en now the midnight hour is past
> The East proclaims the coming morn
> That glorious time is not so far
> When India and her sons shall rise.

The great, glorious Delhi victory of the revolutionaries thus provided a deathless inspiration to Indians all over the country. It was a great success and a brilliant accomplishment.

The Revolt of 1857 was a tremendous breakthrough, a total triumph and a masterpiece of planning. The East India Company fell like a huge castle of sand. It was impossible to count the number of those British who lost their lives. The Queen of England had to apologize for the Company's misdeeds and blunders.

The Revolt of 1857 was violent and widespread. It was as significant as the American War of Independence and the glorious French Revolution of 1789.

28

Maharaja Bhaskar Rao Nargundkar and the Massacre of British Forces during the Great Indian Revolt of 1857

The Great Indian Revolt of 1857 was extremely violent, widespread and fierce. It was both a powerful thunderbolt and the eruption of a huge volcano. It proved deadly, dreadfully disasterous and destructive to the East India Company's Government in India. Because of colonial, ill-conceived, explosive British policies, countless innocent Britons had to part with their lives. Even women and children had to undergo unbearable tortures before their deaths.

Governor-General Lord Dalhousie was greatly responsible for Indian anger, hatred and violence during that great uprising. People from all over the country, the Marathas, Sikhs, Pathans, Jats, Gorkhas, Rajputs—all were mad with anger. Lord Dalhousie had lost his balance of mind and due to his greed and unbearable pressures from the employers in England, he continued to commit blunders till the termination of his maladministration in India in 1856. He invented a unique device of colonial blackmail of annexing, plundering and conquering more and more territories under the facade of his inhuman and absurd 'doctrine of lapse'.

Flames, fire and open demonstrations of freedom could be seen in different parts of the country. People were hostile even in Kabul,

Kathmandu and Rangoon. The result was that the East India Company's castle of colonial corruption and injustice fell like a huge heap of sand.

The Revolt of 1857 was a miracle of marvellous management. It was unprecedented and unparalleled. People thousands of miles away from each other received in an excellent, swift, secret and sophisticated manner, newsletters and messages of Maharani Lakshmibai, Nana Saheb, Tautiya Tope, Maulvi Azimullah Khan, Bahadurshah Zafar, Mirza Mughal, Mirza Sultan, Bakht Khan, Begum Hazrat Mahal, Kunwar Singh, Rao Tula Ram, etc. It is simply astonishing that from Barrackpore, Behrampore, Meerut, Delhi, Kanpur, Lucknow, Bareilly, to far off places like Nagpur, Satara, Patna, Lahore, Kota, Rewari, Jhajjhar, Gwalior, the uncontrollable flames of freedom were visible even in Jabalpur, Sagar, Belgoan, Roorkee, Bulandshahr, Ambala, Moradabad, Narsingpur, Amroha, Bijnor, Gorakhpur, Mathura, Jhansi, Hosingabad, Gonda, Rampur, Sambhalpur, Aligarh, Bagpat, Jaunpur, Mandsor, Etawah, Neemuch, Sardhana, Nasirabad, Jodhpur, Sambhal, Allahabad, Rewa, Azamgarh, Dharwar, Nargund and countless other places.

How a revolt of fantastic dimensions and such a grand magnitude and on such a large scale could be organized, with the involvement of millions of people, despite British tyranny and torture, is simply bewildering.

Out of extreme panic and nervousness, the British Government had already imposed a ruthless censorship on the Indian Press, and countless newspapers such as 'the Doorbeen' and 'the Bengal Hurkaru' were prosecuted or punished.

Even after the treacherous broad-day-light murder of the Mughal princes Mirza Mughal, Mirza Sultan in Delhi and the obnoxious capture of the Mughal Emperor Bahadurshah Zafar, the Great Indian Revolt of 1857 did not come to an end. In Nargund, Maharaja Bhaskar Rao Nargundkar emerged as one of the most fearless and inspiring heroes of the great uprising.

The Revolt in Dharwar, with its centre in Nargund, took place on May 16, 1958. The East India Company wanted to annex Nargund under its ambitious policy of 'doctrine of lapse'. Maharaja

Bhaskar Rao Nargundkar was extremely brave and courageous. He was not prepared to compromise with the expansionist colonial policy of the East India Company—which had sunk below all norms of decency, justice and fairplay. Mad with increasing power, it wanted to conquer or annex every Indian state or territory, because such a policy of blackmail and plunder had resulted in unimaginable colossal economic gains both to the Company and its thoroughly corrupt officials.

Bhaskar Rao Nargundkar had made it absolutely clear to the British Government that he would prefer death to a slavish life. He never wanted Nargund to be a part of the British Empire.

The East India Company was wild with anger. It was furious. It never imagined that Bhaskar Rao Nargundkar would challenge its power. Therefore, the Political agent and Commissioner of the region, Charles Manson was ordered to march towards Nargund and capture it immediately. Charles Manson obeyed the orders and reached Nargund without any delay and surrounded the Nargund forces.

Bhaskar Rao Nargundkar was fully prepared for such a terrible attack. On May 26, 1858, at the dead of night, the Maharaja ordered his forces to march. There was a bloody, fierce fighting around Nargund at the dead of night. Charles Manson was taken by surprise. He never expected that Bhaskar Rao was so much alert and would not wait even for a moment and would attack the British forces while they were almost asleep. The British forces were cut to pieces and Charles Manson met the same fate.

It was a grand victory. It was a result of the bravery, fearlessness and farsightedness of the Maharaja—who had emerged as a great hero and an inspiration to the people. Earlier, Bhaskar Rao had also captured Ramdurg. There were great rejoicings and celebrations all around. People danced with joy at the defeat of the mighty British: forces.

It was, a great humiliation for the Governor General Lord Canning, and the East India Company. It was shocking and painful for the British administration. Wild with extacy, the People of Nargund hanged Captain Charles Manson's head at the Nargund Gate.

Captain Charles Manson's forces massacre at Nargund proves beyond doubt that the people were deadly against the British expansionists policies throughout the country, and the Revolt of 1853 was not confined to Meerut, Delhi, Kanpur and Lucknow. It would also be unfair to presume that the uprising was not well-planned. The great British statesman and once the Prime Minister of England Lord Disraeli was absolutely right when he described the Great Indian Revolt of 1857 as a National Revolution.

29

When Delhi Princes were Shot Dead in Broad Daylight by Captain William Hodson

On September 22, 1857, a magnificent royal procession started in Delhi, from Humayun Tomb to Red Fort. It was the procession of the most important individual of the British Empire—the Moghul Emperor Bahadurshah Zafar, and his family—which included the Moghul princes.

It was after the Great Indian Revolt of 1857, which started at Meerut on May 10, 1857 and which resulted in the large-scale massacre of the British in different parts of the country. Indian flags flew in different parts of the country, including Delhi, after the British defeat. The finest soldiers, and officers of the East India Company were cut to pieces and it became almost impossible for the British to remain in India. The British tried all kinds of strategies. They wanted to capture Bahadurshah Zafar at any cost. British Forces fought with the Indian revolutionaries and ultimately William Hodson, a cavalryman, was entrusted with the task of negotiating with the Moghul Emperor.

The British Government promised every kind of help and protection to Bahadurshah Zafar and his family—who were staying in September 1857 in the Humayun Tomb. William Hodson, after

According to some soldiers, Bahadurshah Zafar, had reached the Red Fort,earlier.

all kinds of assurances requested the Moghul Emperor to leave the Humayun Tomb and stay in his Palace in the Red Fort. The Moghul procession started on September 22, 1857 from the Humayun Tomb escorted by the British Forces, headed by the Cambridge graduate William Hodson.

Hundreds and thousands of people joined the huge procession. It was marching towards the Red Fort. Hundred and thousands of people, standing on both sides of the road, joined the procession, as it came near them. Soon the procession had turned into a sea of humanity. William Hodson when he saw the procession turning into a sea of humanity became wild. He felt terribly insecure. He thought that the Indian people would become wild and violent. They would cut him and all the British soldiers to pieces within no time. He was in a horrible panic. He was upset and did not know what to do: how to save himself and the British soldiers from imminent death.

All of a sudden, a devilish idea flashed in his mind. Loving his balance of mind, in sheer madness and anger he ordered the procession to stop and the Mughal prince Mirza Mughal, Mirza Sultan and the grandson of Bahadurshah Zafar—Khizr Khan, to take off their clothes immediately.

William Hodson, mercilessly, shot them down to death. This was cruel and devilish. This was unethical and without any moral justification. This was a treachery treason and an open betrayal.

Luckily, the Mughal Emperor Bahadurshah Zafar, according to some soldiers, had already reached the Red Fort.

Willaim Hodson felt happy and relieved. He thought that the Brisish Governor General Lord Canning would honour him and appreciate or admire his boldness, courage or heroism.

Lord Canning, however, did not praise him. He felt extremely sad and dejected because the Mughal Emperor Bahadurshah Zafar a great danger to the British existence in India, was still alive and William Hodson had committed a great blunder—a folly, and had not shot him dead, anytime.

30

Mirza Ghalib and the Revolt of 1857

Mirza Ghalib was the greatest Urdu poet of the first-half of nineteenth century. He was born at a time when there was a tremendous social transformation in India due to the advent of the British. He was bom on December 27, 1797 in an enlightened family of Akbarabad near Agra. His grandfather and father had served the great Moghals. His father also worked under the rulers of Lucknow, Hyderabad, Alwar, etc. During his youth, Mirza Ghalib witnessed a great politico-social change due to the movements launched by Rammnohan Roy, Bhawanicharan Banerji, Radhakant Dev, Ressikkrishna Malik, Prasannakumar Tagore, Balshastri Jambhekar, Jagannath Shankarseth, Jameshedji Jijabhai and Yugalkishore Shukla. A large number of organizations such as the British India Association, the Bethune Society, the Brahmo Samaj, the Dharam Samaj, the Academic Association, had created a stir in Indian Society. The Asiastic Society, Calcutta and Bombay and the Fort St. George Collage and Fort William Collage had demonstrated a deep interest in the enrichment of Indian Literature.

Mirza Ghalib was married to Umrao Jan Begum, the daughter of Nawab of Delhi at an early age. After the marriage Ghalib decided to settle permanently in Delhi. Quite early in his age, he started writing poetry. He also tried to obtain the post of a Persian teacher in the Delhi College.

Ghalib was surrounded in Delhi by some of the greatest literary masterminds. The Mughal Emperor Bahadurshah Zafar who was himself a great Urdu poet patronized Mirza Ghalib and asked him to write the History of the Great Mughals.

Mirza Ghalib produced a large number of works in his life-time. The Revolt of 1857 proved disasterous to Mirza Ghalib. A large number of his friends and relatives were cut to pieces or hanged and Ghalib wrote that the world had become 'dark'. The suppression of the Revolt of 1857 was so inhuman that even his sister's son Mirza Asoor Beg and her grandson could not escape British torture and death. Mirza Ghalib suffered incalculable financial loss due to the Revolt of 1857. The financial assistance which he was getting from the Mughal Emperor Bahadurshah Zafar, was abruptly stopped. He was getting some pension from the East India Company too, but due to his closeness to the Mughal Emperor Bahadurshah Zafar, it was also stopped. He had practically no means of livelihood. He had to suffer the horrors of poverty and starvation. He was, it seems, terribly afraid of the massacre and bloodbath that was taking place in every part of Delhi. The people were being hanged on mere suspicion. They were being shot dead without proper judicial investigation or trial. His worse suffering came when his younger brother Mirza Yusuf died and Mirza Ghalib's wife's ornaments were plundered by the British soldiers. Due to bloodbath and total anarchy in Delhi, Mirza Ghalib could not attend Mirza Yusuf's funeral.

The Press was under pressure and was gagged under the Press Act of 1857. It was therefore impossible for Mirza Ghalib to write fearlessly about the Great Mughals or the Revolt of 1857. The last days of Mirza Ghalib were indeed extremely sad. He was ill and bedridden most of the time. His movements were completely restricted. He wrote a letter full of tears to Nawab Allauddin Khan of Loharu around 1869, when he was 73 years of age.

Don't ask me about my well-being. In a day or two ask it from my neighbours. These words were almost prophetic. He died on February 15, 1869.

Ghalib produced a large number of literary works during his lifetime. The *Diwane Ghalib* in Urdu, produced in 1841 become extremely popular and a large number of editions had to be published in quick succession from Delhi, Agra and Kanpur. *'Nigaristan-e-shukhan* was a work in Persian. Apart from these *Dastarnboo, Panj-Ahang, Mehare-a-Nemroz, Kulliyate-a-Nasra Ghalib, Quait-Burhan, Durfish, Kaibiyani, Oode-Hindi* were all published during his life. He also wrote poems on William Bentinck, Sir Charles Metcalfc, Lord Auckland and Queen Victoria.

Mirza Ghalib was a literary genious of highest culture, sofistication and refinement. He had a love for the entire humanity. The beauty and freshness of his poetry can be understood through the following lines :

'Artless, artfull, aware, unaware
The closed eyes of beauty are my despair.'

His frankness was indeed admirable. He wrote:

'I have man's nature,
I am born of man,
And proud that I
commit the sins I can,
My worship of vein,
I'll ne'er abandon,
In stormly whirlpool,
I shall always dive.'

His philosophy of life can be summed up in the following words:

'God is one, that Is our faith
All rituals we abjure,
'Tis only when religions vanish'
That belief Is pure.'

Towards end of his life, Mirza Ghalib's sole desire was to be left completely alone and he wrote:

'My wish Is to go to the place
Where no one will be there,
No one who would speak to me
No one who could hear me.'

But there was indeed hardly any cause for disappointment or dispair, Dadabhai Naoroji, Bankimchandra Chatterji, Michael Madhusudhan Dutt, Dayananda Saraswati, Keshavchandra Sen, Sir Syed Ahmed Khan, Ramakrishna Paramhansa, Sir Surendranath Bannerji had already started their work for freedom, equality and justice.

The reason why Mirza Ghalib could not condemn the British colonial policies or write frankly about the revolt of 1857 was the prevalent atmosphere of inhuman tortures and cruel bloodbath. In the Revolt of 1857 a large number of British officials and militarymen had to part with their lives. These included Sir John Nicholson, General Havelock, General Cooper, Captain Jenkins, Colonel Ripley, Alexander Harward, Steward, Pingle, Birch, Inns, Sergent Hogsoo and Munro.

There was a tremendous anger in England and in India in the British camp. The British wanted to take a revenge. A British poet wrote :

Destroy these traitor legions,
Hang every pariah hound,
And hunt them down to death,
In all the hills and cities round.'

The suppression of the Revolt was without any considerations of morality or ethics. Mirza Ghalib was completely perturbed. He was in a great panic because the Muslims were being cremated and Hindus buried alive after lot of torture by the British including forced eating of pork and beef. The torture and tyranny continued unabaked for more than two decades. Bahadurshah Zafar's grandson Mirza Abu Bakr was shot dead by Captain Hudson on his way from Humayun Tomb to Red Fort on September 22, 1857 and Bahadurshah Zafar, was exiled to Rangoon where he died a tortuous death in December 1862.

Professor Imam Baksh Sabhai, who was teaching Persian in Delhi College, was shot dead in September 1857 along with his two sons and their dead bodies were mercilessly thrown into the Yamuna. Tatya Tope was hanged in Shirpuri on April 18, 1859. Even women were not spared. Young Shobha Devi was hanged along with eleven other women in 1857 in Muzaffarnagar. The total number of women who lost their lives during Revolt of 1857 was no less than 250. On March 20, 1860 more than 250 revolutionaries were hanged to death from a single tree in Bareilly. Lal Sham Shah Khamaria was stoned to death at Budwa. Hukumchand Jain of Hansi was hanged on January 19, 1858 and his body was not cremated but buried and Mirza Muneer Beg's body was not buried but cremated on June 19, 1858.

In such circumstances it was almost impossible for Mirza Ghalib to attack the British Government in India in poetry or prose.

31

Humour and 'Ode to Queen Victoria' Saved Mirza Ghalib from Death in 1857

The Indian Revolt of 1857, which brought to an end the East India Company's rule in India, proved disasterous to Mirza Ghalib, the greatest Urdu Poet of the Nineteenth Century India. Countless Indians lost their lives in the Revolt and during the suppression—which was without any considerations of morality or ethics.

Mirza Ghalib's house was wrecked and his wife Umraojan Begum's gold ornaments and other valuable were digged out and plundered by the British.

The house of his brother Mirza Yusuf was wrecked, Mirza Ghalib's sister Khanam's son, Mirza Ashoor Beg was shot dead. His sister's grandson could also not escape the bloodbath.

Bahadurshah Zafar's sons and grandsons, who were Mirza Ghalib's disciples, were mercilessly shot dead by Captain Hodson—while on their way from Humayun Tomb to Red Fort.

It was a terrible time, Indians were being killed without any investigation or trial on mere suspicion or even without it.

There was inhuman suppression and bloodbath all around and in Chandni Chowk, countless Indian revolutionaries were being hanged or shot dead day after day and night after night. Mirza Ghalib wrote:

Now every English Soldiers that bears arms
Is sovereign and free to work his will
Men does not venture out into the street
And Terror chills their hearts within them still
Their homes enclose them as in prisonwalls
And in the 'Chowk' the victors hang and kill
The city is a thirst for Muslim blood
And every grain of dust must drink us fill.

Mirza Ghalib was almost certain of his death. He had served the most prominent leader of the Revolt of 1857—the Mughal Empire Bahadurshsh Zafar. In March 1857, he had felicitated Bahadurshsh Zafar in the Diwane-Am, Red Fort, in the presence of hundreds of distinguished guests, including the British, members of the royalty and aristocracy, on his birthday.

Mirza Ghalib had intimate relations with countless other Indian Revolutionaries. How could he prove his innocence or his total alongness from the Revolt. He had shown his displeasure of the British annexation of Oudh in 1856 in his private correspondence.

In England, some poets and writers wanted the British Government in India to take revenge against the Indian Revolutionaries, who were responsible for the massacre of hundreds of British officials, soldiers, civilians—and for the downfall of the East India Company. The British Government was put to endless anxiety, fear and humiliation

England had lost its finest officials and militarymen including Sir John Nicholson, General Havelock, General Cooper, Captain Jenkins, Colonel Ripley, Alexander Harward Steward, Pingle, Birch, Inns, Sergent Hogson and Munro during the Revolt.

One British poet wrote :

"Destroy these traitor legions,
Hang every pariah hound,
And hunt them down to death,
In all the hills and cities round"

And that horrible day ultimately dawned on October 5, 1857, when as apprehended, Mirza Ghalib was to be hanged or shot dead in Chandni Chowk, Delhi.

As a bolt from the blue, without any notice or warning, at midday, countless British soldiers entered the lane in which Mirza Ghalib was residing—secretly, silently. They climbed on to a roof and then jumped down in front of Mirza Ghalib's house. They went straight to Mirza Ghalib and rounded up more than half a dozen other people too, without much violence, hardness or resistence:

The British soldiers brought them to Chandni Chowk. Mirza Ghalib and all others were terribly afraid. They knew that after a short interogation, they would be hanged or shot dead, 1,50,000 people had died in Oudh alone.

The British Government had also murdered Professor Imam Baksh Subhai, who was teaching Persian in the Delhi College and his 2 sons, and had mercilessly thrown their dead-bodies into the Yamuna in September 1857.

But a miracle took place and Mirza Ghalib was not shot dead but released after a thorough interogation. It was, perhaps Mirza Ghalib's extraordinary wit or humour which saved him.

Colonel Burn asked Mirza Ghalib, in broken Urdu, whether he was a Muslim, Mirza Ghalib, wearing his Turkish head-dress, replied, with an all-capturing smile; "HALF" Laughing. Colonel Burn asked what did 'Half' mean?

Mirza Ghalib replied : "Well, I drink Wine but 1 don't eat Pork." There was a burst of laughter.

Colonel Burn asked a serious, frightening question to Mirza Ghalib:

> "After the victory of the Government forces why did you not present yourself at the Ridge ?"

It seems, Mirza Ghalib once again tried his humour. He told Colonel Burn with a smile; "Sir, My rank required that I should have four palanquin-beatess, but all four of them ran away and left me, so I could not come."

Mirza Ghalib was still not sure of his escaping death. He knew that Colonel Burn still considered him a traitor, a conspirator and disloyal to the British Government. The British Government always felt that he must have conspired—along with Bahadurshah Zatar and other Indian Revolutionaries for the overthrow of the British Rule in India. The British Government had already stopped his pension since May 1857. There was hardly any convincing proof of his loyalty towards the British Government.

Mirza Ghalib, therefore, came forward with his most powerful trump-card his strongest support—his unfailing proof of loyalty to the British Government.

He placed before Colonel Burn, an acknowledgement of his letter to Queen Victoria of England—in which he had sent an Ode to the British Queen, in December 1856, through Lord Canning—appreciating her achievements and virtues.

Mirza Ghalib was set free. Though his brother Mirza Yusuf's house was plundered and Mirza Yusuf died after 11 days, yet Mirza Ghalib remained alive for almost one decade,

He died of illness on February 15, 1869.

32

The Great Indian Revolt of 1857 when England Shed Tears of Utter Helplessness and Ridicule

The Ruthless Massacre of British officers, soldiers and innocent civilians during the Great Indian Revolt of 1857 created Tearful Cries of suffering and sorrow among the people all over England. After May 10, 1857, the newspapers in England started receiving countless sub-stories or tales of woe from India. Britons were dying day after day and night after night in India. Charles Manson, Captain Russell, F. Andrews, Lt. S. Jackson, James Neill, William Hudson and countless other Britons had to part with their precious lives. More than 550 British men, women and children were tortured, humiliated and massacred in Kanpur alone.

The Revolt of 1857 had created tremendous fear, anxiety and regret in England. Some people were so much disappointed and disheartened that they condemned and criticized the East India Company for its absurd, tactless policies and blunders. Those who had lost their relations in bloodbath in India wanted the Company to immediately pack up and allow its employees to return to England and to save the invaluable lives from merciless slaughter. India appeared to them as nothing less than a deathtrap. They did not want the Company to continue to play with fire.

The Great Indian Revolt of 1857 was destroying England, it was financially disastrous and politically destructive. England was loosing its prestige as a military power. The population of England was extremely small and therefore every region was feeling the loss of its own people.

The queen of England Victoria was unhappy about the violence in india. The British Prime Minister, the British Cabinet, the British Parliament, the court of directors—all were nervous. It was a great defeat and humiliation. The British members of Parliament wanted immediate action and did not appreciate the Company's apathy or unconcern.

The capture of Delhi by the Indian revolutionaries, and the Mughal Emperor Bahadurshah Zafar's address to the revolutionaries, the hoisting of Indian flags in different parts of India, the royal victory-proccession through the streets of Delhi, the 21 gun salute twice on May 12, 1857, brought tears to the eyes of grieving Britons. Some intellectuals in England wanted the immediate termination of the court of directors and the establishment of elected representative institutions in India. The flow of blood in Meerut, Bareilly, Lucknow, Allahabad, Dharwar, Hyderabad, Indore, Ambala, Hissar, Arrah, Peshawar, Sialkote, etc. had compelled the people in England to spend tear, jerking, sleepless nights.

The number of revolutionaries was so large and disproportionate to the British military strength that England looked helpless and pathetic. The British Government in India was completely helpless because it had become an impossibility to depend on the Indian soldiers under its employment. Most of the Indian soldiers looked, hostile, violent, and defiant. Countless dead-bodies had collected inside the British Residency in Lucknow. The number of Indian revolutionaries was swelling menacingly for the British.

The British Government was also disturbed because of indiscipline, defiance and lack of bravery among some of its officers and soldiers. They had shown unimaginable panic and cowardice. There were cases of retreats and running away from the scenes of revolution.

The British Crown and the British Parliament wanted an immediate solution of the problem of violence in India.

Even after some successes, in India, it was becoming extremely difficult for the government of England to recruit soldiers for fighting, in England. The revolt was so fierce, violent and widespread that a huge British force of some one lac British soldiers were immediately needed to suppress the rebellion and to save the British honour.

Sir Charles Windham bravely offered his services and reached India for the suppression of the revolt but he was defeated by the Indian revolutionaries in Kanpur and he had to be transferred to Punjab.

The patriotic sentiment was so powerful in India that even women and teenagers came out of their houses to participate in the uprising and to slaughter the 'malechchs' and 'firangis'. In England, many people were demanding punishment to the rebels. The cry was 'Blood for blood'.

Some poet in England burst out:

Destroy, these traitor-legions,
Hang every pariah-hound,
And hunt them down to death,
In all the hills and cities round.

It is surprising that England could not despatch its forces to India, in June, July and August 1857. With tremendous difficulty it sent only 214 troops to India in September 1857. Despite repeated requests from India, less than 10,000 troops reached India in October 1857. It was indeed ridiculous, disturbing because these troops were sent in small numbers on October 1, October 15, October 17, October 20, October 30, 1857. Why the British Government was behaving in such an absurd manner is best known to it. In November 1857, again less than 15,000 soldiers were sent, in four lots.

India required a huge British force but even in December 1857 less than 10,000 soldiers were sent.

The number was inadequate and ridiculous for covering the whole of India. The panic and nevervousness of the British

Government was clearly demonstrative when it sent small forces on December 1, December 5, December 10, December 14, December 15, December 20 and December 25, 1857.

Throughout 1857, England failed to dispatch an adequate number of troops to India. Perhaps the total number of troops sent did not exceed 25000; why England was so unplanned was beyond understanding. The result was endless violence and massacre. In England, because of such preposterous policies, every morning meant mute mourning or tearful eyes.

The Revolt of 1857 continued even after the Queen's Proclamation of November 1858.

33

Indian Queen Begum Hazrat Mahal's Powerful Attack on Queen Victoria of England

In 1857, during the Great Indian Revolt, Begum Hazrat Mahal completely defeated the British forces in Awadh, Hundreds of British officials were massacred. It included some of the finest Generals and officials known to British Empire and History. The number of British soldiers who were cut to pieces in Lucknow was countless. Indian flags were hoisted on all the important private and government buildings. People sang and danced over India's victory.

Begum Hazrat Mahal maintained her cool and even in that atmosphere, surcharged with hatred and violence when she could have easily succeeded in a total holocaust of the British Residency in Lucknow, she did not attempt to set it on fire. Countless British women and children escaped the flames due to Lucknow's liberality or magnanimity.

Ultimately the British succeeded in capturing Lucknow, in 1858. More than 150,000 people were done to death. There was a cruel suppression and reign of terror.

England had however, realized its blunder. Queen Victoria issued a Proclamation on November 1, 1858. It was almost an open surrender, and an acceptance of England's guilt.

The Queen's Proclamation said that England would never interfere in the internal matters of the Indian states; it would never discriminate; it would never interfere with the religious sentiments of the people. It would never violate treaties and commitments.

'The Queen's Proclamation was the greatest apology ever submitted by the British Crown to the people of India. It was an open acceptance of all its sins. It was a confession of its maladministration, tyranny, highhandedness, racism, injustice and ill-conceived policies in India.

Begum Hazrat Mahal, however was not prepared to accept or honour the Queen Victoria's Proclamation. She knew well that it was nothing more than a Trick and a Trap. It was to her mind, an attempt to befool the People of India. It was an open lie. It was a falsehood and a deceit. Hazrat Mahal, therefore produced an excellent critique of the Queen's Proclamation. It was the most powerful attack on the British Empire. It was the most powerful warning to the Indian People. Hazrat Mahal got it circulated among the Indian People. She asked them to continue their struggle against the British Tyranny and Injustice. She warned them not to be misled by Queen Victoria.

No Indian scholar, leader or newspaper of the time could provide a better answer to the Queen of England.

PROCLAMATION BY THE BEGUM OF OUDH

The royal declaration was followed by a rejoinder to Queen Victoria by the Begum of Oudh. The Begum proclaimed:

1. "At this time certain weak-minded, foolish people have spread a report that the English have forgiven the faults and crimes of the people of Hindostan; this appears very astonishing, for it is the unvarying custom of the English never do forgive a fault, be it great or small; so much so that if a small offence be committed through ignorance or negligence they never forgive it.

   "The Proclamation of the 1st November 1858, which has come before us, is perfectly clear, and as some foolish people, not understanding the real object of the Proclamation, have been carried away, therefore we, the ever-abiding government, parents of the people of Oude, with great consideration, put forth the present Proclamation, in order that the real object of the chief points may be exposed, and our subjects be placed on their guard.

"It is written in the proclamation, that the country of Hindostan, which was held in trust by the Company has been resumed by the Queen, and that for the future, the Queen's laws shall be obeyed. This is not to be trusted by our religious subjects, for the laws of the Company, the settlement of the Company, the English servants of the Company, the Governor-General and the judicial administration of the Company, are all unchanged. What, then, is there now which can benefit the people, or on which they can rely."

2. "In the Proclamation it is written, that all contracts and agreements entered into by the Company will be accepted by the Queen. Let the people carefully observe this artifice. The Company has seized the whole of Hindostan, and, if this arrangement be accepted, what is there new in it? The Company professed to treat the Chief of Bhurtpore as a son, and then took his territory; the Chief of Lahore was carried-off to London, and it has not fallen to his lot to return; the Nawab Shumshoodeen Khan, on one side, they hanged, and, on the other side, they *salaamed** (Saluted) to him; the Peshwa they expelled from Poona, Sitara, and imprisoned for life in Bithoor, their breach of faith with Sultan Tippoo is well-known; the Rajah of Benaras they imprisoned in Agra. Under pretence of administering the country of the Chief of Gwalior, they introduced English customs; they have left no means or traces or the Chiefs of Behar, Orissa, and Bengal; they gave the Rao of Furrackabad a small monthly allowance, and took his

*Foreign Political Consultations, Dec. 17, 1858, Ms. 250-54.

territory. Shahjahanpore, Bareilly, Azimgurh, Jounpore, Goruckpore, Etawah, Allahabad, Futtehpore, etc.—our ancient possessions they took from us on pretence of distributing pay; and in the 7th article of the treaty, they wrote, on oath, that they would take no more forums. If, then, the arrangements made by the Company are to be accepted, what is the difference between the former and the present state of things? These are old affairs; but recently, in defiance of treaties and oaths, and, notwithstanding, that they owed us millions of rupees, without reason, and on the pretence of the misgovernment and discontent of our people, they took our country and property, worth millions of rupees. If our people were discontented with our royal predecessor, Wajid Ali Shah, how comes it they are content with us? And no ruler ever experienced such loyalty, and devotion of life and goods as we have done.

What, then, is wanting that they do not restore our country? Further, it is written in the Proclamation, that they want no increase of territory, but yet they cannot refrain from annexation. If the Queen has assumed the Government, why does Her Majesty not restore our country to us when our people wish it? It is well-known that no king or queen ever punished a whole army and people for rebellion, all were forgiven; and the wise cannot approve of punishing the whole army and people of Hindostan; for so long as the word "punishment" remains the disturbance will not be suppressed. There is a well known proverb—"A dying man is desperate" (*murta kya na karta*). It is impossible that a thousand should attack a million, and thousand escape:

3. In the proclamation it is written, that the Christian religion is true, but that no other creed will suffer oppression, and that the laws will be observed towards all. What has the administration of justice to do with the truth or falsehood of a religion? That religion is true which acknowledges one

God, and one knows to other. Where there are three Gods in a religion, neither Mussulmans nor Hindoos—nay, not even Jews, Sun-worshippers, or Fire-worshippers can believe it true. To eat pigs, and drink wine, to bite greased cartridges, and to mix pig's fat with flour and sweetmeats, to destroy Hindoo and Mussulman temples on pretence of making roads, to build churches, to send cleargymen into the streets and alleys to preach the Christian religion, to institute English schools and to pay people a monthly stipend for learning the English sciences, while the places of worship of Hindoos and Mussulmans are to this day entirely neglected; with all this, how can the people believe that religion will not be interfered with? The rebellion began with religion, and, for it, millions of men have been killed. Let not our subjects be deceived; thousands were deprived of their religion in the North-West, and thousands were hanged rather than abandon their religion.

4. "It is written in the proclamation, that they who harboured rebels, or who were leaders of rebels, or who caused men to rebel, shall have their lives, but that punishment shall be awarded after deliberation, and that murderers and abettors or murders shall have no mercy shown them, while all others shall be forgiven. Any foolish person can see, that under this Proclamation, no one, be he guilty or innocent, can escape. Everything is written, and yet nothing is written; but they have clearly written that they will not left off any one implicated; and in whatever village or estate the army may have halted. The inhabitants of that place cannot escape. We are deeply concerned for the condition of our people on reading this Proclamation, which palpably teems with enmity. We now issue a distinct order, and, one that may be trusted, that all subjects who may have foolishly presented themselves as heads of villages to the English, shall, before the 1st of January next, present themselves in our camp. Without doubt their faults shall be forgiven then, and they shall be treated according to

their merits. To believe in this proclamation, it is only necessary to remember that Hindostanee rulers are altogether kind and merciful. Thousands have seen this, millions have heard it. No one has ever seen in a dream that the English forgave all offence.

5. "In this Proclamation it is written, that when peace is restored, public works, such as roads and canals, will be made in order to improve the condition of the people. It is worthy of a little reflection, that they have promised no better employment for Hindostanees than making roads and digging canals. If people cannot see clearly what this means, there is no help for them. Let no subject be deceived by the Proclamation"!

34

The Mystery of Maharani Lakshmibai of Jhansi's Death: June 20, 1858

Lakshmibai was one of the greatest leaders of the Revolt of 1857. She was fearless, bold and courageous. Riding on a horse, with sword in her hand, she fought pitched battles against the British.

Countless poems were written about her bravery and courage and also about her deep love for her motherland. Some poet wrote annonymously:

No jewels to adore her but only patriotism, That' glowed so brightly, her only ornament! The whole world saw, Lakshmibai in eighteen-fifty-seven. The whole world saw her in her only ornament!

Fate had ordained her to be a fighter in her adolescence. No child she had to play in her lap and wipe away her tears. A son she adopted at last in eighteen-fifty-seven, the whole world saw her in her only ornament!

The mandates of the English she poohpooped with heroic defiance. And greeted with glee the tidings of revolt and rebellion. Whispered in her ear by Tatya in eighteen fifty-seven. The whole world saw her in her only ornament!

Enriched by English battalions Jhansi under fire. When like an enraged lioness for vengeance, in male attire. Fearless for battle left Lakshmibai in eighteen fifty-seven. The whole world saw her in her only ornament!

The British wanted her immediate capture. She was a Terror to the British. She had succeeded in hoisting Indian flags everywhere.

'The British, ultimately succeeded in defeating the Jhansi forces. But they could neither capture her nor obtain her dead body. Without any concrete evidence, after 3 days, they declared that Maharani Lakshmibai had been killed.

In some remote temple, some ashes were shown to them. Some of her belongings were also captured by them.

The British knew that a large number of Indian leaders had escaped to Nepal and "neighbouring regions, so that they could fight against the British later. Begum Hazrat Mahal, Nana Saheb and many of others had escaped to various places. Even Tatiya Tope remained in hiding for a long period."

The British; however, wanted to take the credit of Maharani Lakshmibai's death. Without any evidence, therefore, they made a declaration, after the defeat of the Jhansi forces, the third day: "Maharani Lakshmibai is no more".

Till today, the mystery of Maharani Lakshmibai's death has not been solved.

Why the Maharani could not have escaped in three days remains to be examined.

35

England's Prime Minister's Son's Heroic Sacrifice: The Great Indian Revolt of 1857

The Great Indian revolt of 1857 created a terrible commotion in England. Waves of sorrow and disappointment were visible everywhere. Countless well-known senior British Officials, militarymen, innocent women and infants were mercilessly cut to pieces during the Great Indian Revolt of 1857. This wholesale, widesphered bloody massacre and violence created a tearful atmosphere of disappointment, sorrow, agony, humiliation and defeat in the whole of the British Empire. The people in England felt that the downfall of the East India Company and the British power in India was imminent and certain. There was condemnation and criticism of the mercantile company's absurd, unimaginative, ambitious and fatal policies in India.

In the unprecedented and unparalleled bloodshed in 1857, even British Prime Minister Sir Robert Peel (1788-1860)'s brave and fearless son Sir William Peel, (November 2, 1824–April 17, 1858) had to sacrifice his precious life. Sir William Peel was an excellent officer in England's 'Royal Navy' and he was honoured with 'VICTORIA CROSS' and 'CB' for his outstanding accomplishments. After serving in various parts of the world including China, America, West Indies, etc., he hurriedly reached India during the 1857

Rebellion. He commanded a powerful 'Naval Brigade' quite successfully. For the immediate suppression of the Great Indian Revolt and to save the lives of countless British men, women and children, he had to involve himself in endless bloody fights in Lucknow. The Indian revolutionaries, however, fought bravely and defeated the British forces. On March 12, 1858, they were successful in killing the notorious William Hodson, who had treacherously murdered the Mughal Emperor Bahadurshah Zafar's sons, Mirza Mughal and Mirza Sultan in Delhi, while they were returning, in a huge procession, from Humayun Tomb to Red Fort.

Sir William Peel could save his life but he was severely, almost fatally, wounded in March 1858 at Lucknow. He immediately rushed to Kanpur from Lucknow, where he fell severely ill and died within no time, on April 17, 1858. He was less than 35 years of age.

In recognition of his bravery and heroism and the supreme sacrifice, the British Government installed the statue of Sir William Peel in Calcutta. His loss was mourned in England.

36

Mysterious Death of a Young Rajput Revolutionary Amar Singh and the Great Indian Revolt of 1857

The Great Indian Revolt, which started on May 10, 1857, was extremely destructive, brutal, fierce and widespread. It spread, menacingly, in different parts of India, like a wild fire. The British Government turned into a portrait of utter frustration, sorrow, helplessness and ridicule. There were terrible differences of opinion among the top civil and military officials of the East India Company, and there were occasions, when, out of total bafflement, they wanted to eliminate or shot-down their own responsible officers. The British Parliament, Press and the people were totally stunned. It became an impossibility for the Company to survive. James Nicholson, John Wedderbum, Sir H.M. Wheeler, James Neill, William Hodson, Charles Hanson, C.W. Russell, W.H. Napier, Captain Knox, Col. R.A. Yule and countless other men, women and children had to part with their lives.

The British Government in India was in tears. It was totally helpless. The brave Indian Rajputs, Sikhs, Marathas, Pathans, Jats and Gorakhas, in the British forces, who had covered the Company with highest greatness and glory, and showered unimaginable wealth on the Company through their sacrifices and victories, looked completely disloyal, unreliable, furious and totally undependable. The Indian soldiers were greatly responsible for the British victories in Oudh, Punjab, Sind, Nagpur, Satara, Jhansi, Gwalior, Burma etc. The Company had demonstrated complete apathy, unconcern and disregard for their religious sentiments, great traditional moral values, needs and aspirations. The Company had stabbed them in the back.

The British were playing with fire in India. The Company did not mind even dishonouring, exploiting and blackmailing the great Indian fighters under its employment.

Even after Queen Victoria's apology to the Indian people in November 1858, through her well-known Proclamation, Lord Canning did not show any 'clemancy'. He did not demonstrate any sympathy with the Indian revolutionaries or liability and broadmindedness. He did not introduce any radical reforms in the administration for the fast progress or betterment of the people of India. Countless people continued to be hanged or shot dead, under suspicion or even without it. There was unprecedented and unparalleled savagery, brutality and total lack of humanity, when some revolutionaries and their top leaders were tortured and killed in prisons.

A remarkable characteristic of the Great Indian Revolt of 1857 was its superb management. Not merely most confidential and secret messages, directions, proclamations and newsletters were reaching near and far-off places, like a freightening lightening, but the Indian revolutionaries, in disguise and some times openly, with finest equipments for fighting or guns and ammunitions, were moving at a supersonic speed from one part of the country to the other. The top leaders of the rebellion had planned every possible strategy to its minutest details. Many Indian rulers, though bound by treaties etc. with the British, were full of patriotic sentiments and they did not hesitate to provide all possible encouragement and support to the fighters of India's freedom from foreign tyranny and torture. The Mughal prince Mirza Qwaish had reached Udaipur from Humayun Tomb in Delhi, befooling the British forces, under William Hodson, who had treacherously shot dead Mirza Mughal, Mirza Sultan and

Khizr Khan in Delhi on September 23, 1857. Nana Saheb and Tatiya Tope had long meetings with Maharani Lakshmibai, Begum Hazrat Mahal and many other revolutionaries, prior to the outbreak of the uprising. Raghoji and Maulvi Azimullah had many meetings in England before the revolt. Azimullah had also visited France, Turkey, etc. Rao Tula Ram had reached Delhi to meet the Mughal Emperor Bahadurshah Zafar for necessary directions, and he provided a lot of assistance and money to the great revolutionary. Rao Tula Ram also went to Jodhpur, Bikaner, Jaipur, Jaisalmer, Kota and Bundi, and met their rulers. He even want to Iran, Afghanistan and Russia to seek the cooperation of the foreign powers in the destruction and demolition of British colonial superstructure in India.

The Rajput revolutionaries in Bihar, with their large trusted followings, were not lagging far behind. Extremely bold and courageous, an outstanding revolutionary-leader Kunwar Singh moved with his forces from Jagdishpur, Arrah to Gwalior, Jhansi, Kanpur, Lucknow, etc. to assist Nana Saheb, Azimullah Khan, Tatiya Tope, Maharani Lakshmibai, etc. during the great Revolt. Kunwar Singh had defeated the British forces at a number of places including Arrah and Dinapur on July 25, 1857. In his fights against Captain Le Grand, he was seriously wounded. He died on April 25, 1858.

After Kunwar Singh's great, glorious sacrifice, his younger brother Amar Singh emerged as the greatest revolutionary leader of the region. He was young, full of tremendous energy and courage and moved from one place to another at a remarkable speed, secretly. The British Government was terribly afraid of this great Rajput-fighter because he was an expert in 'gorrilla-warfare' and used the fortests of the region, to baffle and create panic and uncertainty in the British forces.

He commanded a solid force of 4500 revolutionaries, who were prepared to sacrifice their utmost for the destruction and demolition of British power in India, and it became an impossibility for the British to check or control his swift, secret movements. The Government was all the more disturbed because he was operating, in the most violent manner, quite near to the British seat of power, the British capital Calcutta.

In total bafflement, and frustration, Lord Canning's Government announced a reward of Rs. 5000 on his capture. It was not at all an easy task to eliminate him from the political scene because of his dynamism and indomitable courage.

In December 1859, after endless fear and violence, the British Government succeeded in capturing Amar Singh in Nepal. Soon, he was brought to Gorakhpur, in chains.

The British Government under Clemancy Canning, which had become notorious for its inhuman, savage tortures—including canning, whipping and flogging, and also for hanging and shooting-down Indians, under one pretext or the other, threw the brave, young, strong, well built Parmar hero Amar Singh into a sponging-house or a prison in Gorakhpur.

For quite some time the greatest ambition of the British Government was the total extinction of this great Rajput fighter from the political horizon. Under tremendous nervousness, panic and anger, most of the British officials never wanted this great inspiration and an unconquerable warrior to return to his home or Jagdishpur, even for a mock trial.

It is not known how the British treated this flame of revolt or terror within the thick prison-walls. Lord Canning looked completely helpless since he had lost all control over his subordinates, who without bothering to obtain the necessary orders from Calcutta, were mercilessly torturing and executing countless revolutionaries, all over the country.

Amar Singh's followers, sympathesizers, friends and countless other Indians were soon thunderstruck. They were startled, shocked and stunned. Their disappointment and sorrow knew no bounds, when the British Government, within less than 65 days made a tragic, heart breaking announcement.

The announcement said that Amar Singh had died in the prison on February 5, 1860 due to 'sickness'.

The unexpected tragic news brought tears to the eyes of the people. It was, nevertheless, not completely unpredictable in view of the British anxiety, restlessness and mad anger, after the Queen's Proclamation of November 1858. The British had maltreated and tortured the Mughal Emperor Bahadurshah Zafar in their captivity, against all norms of decency and justice, prior to his exile in Rangoon. Similar tragedies had taken place earlier in Meerut, Lucknow, Kanpur, Shahjahanpur, Gwalior, Bareilly, Peshawar, Sialkote, Delhi and countless other places in India, during the suppression of the Great Indian Revolt of 1857.

37

When the Great Education Thinker of the nineteenth century India was kicked out of the British Government. Humiliation of Sir Charles Trevelyan, by the British Viceroy Lord Canning

Sir Charles Trevelyan, born on April 2, 1807 in England and educated in Haileybury, was one of the greatest education-thinkers of the nineteenth century India. He wrote 'On the Education of the People of India' and 'The Application of Roman Alphabets to all the Oriental Languages.' He came to India in 1826, in the service of the East India Company and became, along with Thomas Macaulay and Alexander Duff, an outstanding founder of the British Educational System in India. He was among the foremost advocates of English Education in this country. He wanted the rapid spread of education among the Indian people.

The British Government was deeply impressed by his ideas and his tremendous administrative capacity and competence. He held some of the most important positions in the British Government, including Assistant Commissionership of Delhi.

The British Government was so much impressed by the originality of his thought and administrative talent that immediately after the Great Indian Revolt of 1857, he was appointed the Governor of Madras in 1859.

Lord Canning, who had served as Governor-General in India since February 29, 1856 and a Viceroy from November 1, 1858 to March 18, 1862 had extremely serious differences of opinion with the great educationist and financial expert. Lord Charles Canning was partly responsible for the Revolt of 1857 and countless people in England condemned and criticized him for his failure to appreciate adequately the grave symptoms and the extents of the 1857 Uprising. He had created a lot of discontent and unrest in India through his shameless confiscation of huge lands in many parts of the country. Though described by some British historians as 'clemancy Canning', he was responsible for the massacre of countless Indians during the suppression of the Revolt of 1857. He also wanted the complete elemination of the Mughal Emperor Bahadurshah Zafar from the political scene.

Lord Canning was confronted with another great challenge too. After the Revolt the Government had become completely bankrupt. It had suffered enormous financial losses. For all practical purposes the Government was at the existence-level or financial starvation. Lord Canning wanted to earn through all kinds of ways traps and tricks, the distinction of converting the Government deficit into a surplus.

Sir Charles Trevelyan did not want any hasty, ill-conceived action or a suicidal course. To him the British existence in India was paramount. It was more significant that Lord Canning's praise or admiration in England.

Lord Canning, however, was not prepared to follow inexplosive policies. He hurriedly decided to reduce drastically the Government expenditure on civil and military administration. Without bothering about the consequences, he decided to tax the people of India heavily. He decided to raise the Income Tax, in an autocratic manner.

Sir Charles Trevelyan, who had witnessed the wild, fierce flames of the Revolt of 1857, and who knew that the serious wounds of the rebellion were still fresh, criticized fearlessly the Government's unwise and fatal policies. He tried all kinds of persuasions and pressures, but the British Government was adament. It was not prepared to yield, compromise or see the reason. It did not pay any heed to the most brilliant ideas of Sir Charles Travelyan. Sir Charles Trevalyan tried, endlessly, to point out how such dangerous policies could be disasterous for the existence of the British Empire.

Sir Charles Trevelyan, out of total helplessness, decided to publish in 1860, his criticism of the Financial Policies of Lord Canning.

Lord Canning was furious.

Mad with his power and position, he was not prepared to tolerate such bold, brilliant and scathing criticism of his own policies by his subordinate.

He decided to punish Sir Charles Trevelyan mercilessly. He wanted to humiliate the great educationist and thinker. Sir Charles Trevelyan was also writing to the *India Gazette*, Calcutta, the *Calcutta Monthly Journal*, Calcutta and *The Times*, London, in his own name and also anonymously under the psydonym 'Indophilus' and 'CET'.

Sir Charles Trevelyan was kicked out of the Government. He was dismissed and totally uprooted in 1860. He was thrown out of India.

Dejected, disappointed and disturbed, Sir Charles Trevelyan had to spend some time in distress.

It was only after Lord Canning's retirement on March 18, 1862 and his death after a few months on June 17, 1862, that Sir Charles Trevelyan was once again appointed in the Government in 1863 as Financial Member of the Supreme Council. He died on June 19, 1886, with full honour.

38

Maharani Jind Kaur of Punjab: An Uncontrollable Flame of Terror and the Great Indian Revolt of 1857

After the death of Maharaja Ranjit Singh on June 27, 1839, the greatest ambition of the British Government in India was the conquest of Panjab, a peaceful, prosperous and powerful sovereign state, with a most outstanding, disciplined, well-organized and fully-equipped military force, trained by Italian and Indian Generals. The Sikh force was a terror to the British Government.

The greatest ambition of the British Government after the great Sikh wars and the annexation of Panjab in 1849, was to control and isolate the young, brave Maharani Jind Kaur, who was capable of inspiring an armed revolt for the complete downfall and destruction of the British power in India much before the Great Indian Revolt of 1857. Despite violence, bloodshed and intrigues in that state, she weilded tremendous influence on the people, not only in Lahore, Ludhiana, Amritsar, Kashmir, Multan and Peshawar but also in many other parts of India. Under Maharaja Ranjit Singh, his sovereign state had friendly relations with many Indian states.

The British Government was always afraid of the Sikhs. Lord Hardinge, Lord Dalhousie and Lord Canning—all dreamt of demolishing the Sikh power and to uproot, isolate and politically suffocate Maharani Jind Kaur, who was dynamic and daring. She was an uncontrollable flame, capable of creating endless havoe and panic in the British administration.

The British Government was greatly offended when an attempt was made to assassinate Sir Henry Lawrence in Lahore, when Sir George Lawrence was tortured and imprisoned by the Sikhs in October 1848, and when Patrick Vans Agnew and Lt. Anderson were treacherously attacked and killed in Multan on April 20, 1848.

The British Parliament in England and the British Government in India was stunned when Sir Hugh Gough was defeated, Brigadier General Charles Cureton was killed and when in less than 10 hours the Sikhs had massacred more than 2330 British soldiers.

To strike, smash and shatter the Sikh Maharani was not at all an easy task. Without dismantling, damolishing and destroying the influence and power of the great Maharani; it was an impossibility for the British Government to achieve the rack and ruin of the Sikh power. Maharani Jind Kaur was deadly hostile or antagoniastic towards the British interference in the administration of Panjab.

After the annexation of Panjab, the British had not merely plundered the people, but they had also disbanded the Sikh forces. They had disarmed the people and finally they decided to uproot the Maharani by throwing her out and putting her in confinement in Sheikhpura and Banaras. They did not honour their commitments, assurances and promises and completely reduced her pension or allowances. Her priceless ornaments, gold and diamonds and assets worth crores of rupees were taken away and kept under British control.

The Maharani was tortured, haraased and humiliated. Her son Maharaja Dilip Singh was mercilessly separated from her. He was converted to Christianity in 1853 and thrown out of India in 1854. He was kept in England so that there was no further trouble or a risk of armed rebellion in India.

Maharani Jind Kaur always appeared to the British Government as a great threat or terror. Before 1857, she was completely isolated. Her appeals against injustice and torture were ignored. The British attitude, policies and endless humiliations of the Maharani was creating heart-burning among the people. There was so much deep-rooted disappointment, dejection and anger in Panjab that an armed rebellion could break out any moment. The people had become wild and uncontrollable.

The British Government was apprehensive and in utter panic it decided to throw the Maharani out of India. Sha was sent to Nepal. It was an attempt to completely bulldoze her influence on the people. A complete check was kept on her communications, meetings and other activities. Even the British officials such as Sir John Login, were not allowed to communicate with her, directly, when she was in Kathmandu.

When the Great Indian Revolt of 1857 took place, even Maharaja Dilip Singh was not allowed to come to India from England and meet her.

What was the role of Maharani Jind Kaur in the Revolt of 1857 is still a mystry. It is not known whether she was in touch with Begum Hazarat Mahal, Maharani Lakshmibai, Nana Saheb, Tatiya Tope or Bahadurshah Zafar and countless other Indian revolutionaries in India or Nepal, daring the Revolt or after.

After the ruthless suppression of the Great Indian Revolt of 1857, and the death of Maharani Lakshmibai, Kunwar Singh, and countless other Indian revolutionaries, the British Government thought it completely safe to grant permission to Maharaja Dilip Singh to return to India and meet his mother. However, the moment he landed in Calcutta, the people recognized him and he was greeted most warmly with thunderous slogans. That was in January 1861. The British Government was totally stunned and in utter panic it put him on another ship for immediate departure to England. He could not meet his mother or visit Panjab.

The British Government still considered itself as unfortified or unprotected due to Maharani Jind Kaur's stay in Nepal. It never wanted to skate on thin ice and wanted to blow out her influence and power. To tear her influence to bits, it was decided to throw her out of that region. She was deported to England and in London surprisingly, she was put separately from her son, Maharaja Dilip Singh, now a Christian.

The British Government thus succeeded in totally destroying the influence of the Sikh Maharani, who considered the British, after her great tortures and humiliations, as untrustworthy 'firangis' and unprincipled 'malechchs'. For quite some time, she had started advocating the immediate liberation of the people from British tyranny, torture and injustice.

Uprooted, friendless, lonely, politically suffocated, the Sikh Maharani could not breathe in a strage atmosphere and she died in complete isolation, on August 1, 1863.

The great threat to the British Empire had suddenly vanished. The Sikh Maharani had melted into thin air—unknown, unwept and unheard.

39

Ruthless Suppression of the Great Indian Revolt of 1857 and the British Viceroy Lord Elgin's Mysterious Death

The Great Indian Revolt of 1857, which resulted in the most devastating downfall of the East India Company's Government in India, was astonishingly preceded and followed by endless hatred, terrible violence and widespread bloodshed in different parts of India and even outside. Inhumanity, torture and senseless massacre of innocent men, women and children was indeed dreadful and beyond all human endurance.

Countless innocent Britons had to part with their lives because the administration of the Company was not prepared to abandon its explosive colonial expansionist policies and even after the assumption of power in India by the British Crown, there was hardly any end to British blatant blunders. Queen Victoria's well-known Proclamation of November 1858 or the Act for the Better Government of India could not bring any peace or smile or satisfy the Indian revolutionaries, who had gone underground to escape execution or other severe punishments.

Some Indians had already declared openly that the Queen's Proclamation was a political trick and a trap. To them it was based on falsehood and deceit. It was yet another instrument of imperial blackmail. Begum Hazrat Mahal warned the people not to be misled or befooled by the false British promises. In her brilliant and scathing condemnation of the Proclamation, she boldly questioned the British integrity and asked why the British Crown had failed to restore the sovereignty of Oudh to the Indian people.

In her devastating criticism, she pointed out how the British Government had deceived or betrayed the Indians in Bharatpur, Satara, Gwalior, Poona, Bihar, Bengal, Orissa, Panjab, etc. and had indulged in a worst kind of political and military blackmail.

The People of India were extremely furious at the conversion of Maharaja Dilip Singh to Christianity, and the merciless deportation of Maharani Jind Kaur to England, after endless humiliation and plunder.

Panjab was burning with so much discontent and anger that even before the Great Indian Revolt of 1857, an attempt was made to assassinate Sir Henry Lawarence in Lahore in February 1847.

The People were full of extreme anger and displeasure in Oudh, because they did not find any justification whatsoever for the British annexation of Oudh, in 1856—which was well-governed, peaceful, prosperous and progressive.

The people did not like the British interference in Sambhalpur, Jaitpur, Jhansi, Nagpur, Gwalior, Satara, Sind, Burma, Nepal and Afghanistan. They were boiling with anger.

The people did not like the execution or killing of the Mughal princes, by the British, their indecent behaviour towards the Mughal queens and ladies of respectability, and the savage trial and treatment of the Mughal Emperor Bahadurshah Zafar and his forced deportation to Rangoon.

Lord Canning looked a pathetic figure, weeping, helpless and completely frustrated. He was totally unsuccessful in practicing his so-called 'clemency' or in exercising his authority. The British civil officials and soldiers were defiant and executing or shooting down the Indians, without trial, on mere suspicion or even without it. Disappointed, dejected and disturbed, shattered in health, Lord Canning looked a portrait of utter incompetence and ridicule.

The British officials and soldiers wanted to kill-all those Indians who were responsible for the downfall of the East India Company and the deaths of Sir Henry Lawrence, James Nicholson, Sir H.M. Wheeler, John Wedderburn, James Neill, Captain F. Andrews, Charles Manson, W.H. Napier, S. Jackson and countless other Britons during the Revolt.

Lord Canning's frustration and sorrow knew no bounds when all of a sudden his wife died in November 1861. On March 18, 1862, he hurriedly left India, but he could not overcome the terrible shocks, which he had received in India, and died immediately on reaching England, on June 17, 1862.

The British Crown decided to send an experienced diplomat to win over the people of India and to restore peace and tranquillity. Millions of underground revolutionaries and the Marathas, Jats, Pathans, Sikhs, Gorkhas and Rajputs, however, were beyond every control. Even the people in Burma, Nepal, Sikkim, Sind, and Afghanistan had developed a tremendous hatred for the British Empire, after the Revolt. The Kukas and Wahabis were wild with extreme anger and heart-burning.

Lord Elgin reached Calcutta as the Viceroy and Governor-General of British India in March 1862. He was extremely experienced and had served as a member of the British Parliament in England, as Governor of Jamaica, and as Governor-General of Canada. He had also been sent to China as a 'special envoy'.

The people of China did not like him because out of extreme anger and frustration, he had destroyed the magnificent Summer Palace, there. He was also not liked in England because he had befooled the British forces by ordering them to march towards China and finally betrayed them by diverting them to India in 1857, when India was in a fearful grip of a bloody revolution and the massacre of every Briton. He was also not liked by many Indian revolutionaries because he had come in the way of India's Independence by bringing large British forces from England for the suppression of the Great Indian Revolt of 1857.

For his role in the suppression of the Revolt, he had been picked up by the British Crown for the coveted position of Viceroy and Governor-General of India, after Lord Canning's departure.

Lord Elgin was hostile towards the Afghans, the Sikhs and the Wahabis and there was an uncontrollable wild anger and hatred towards the British repression almost everywhere in India. Elgin was fully aware of the Indian unrest and disaffection, which were spreading like a wild fire. Lord Elgin played a trick. In order to extinguish the fire of definance and hostality in India, he held grand, magnificent British Durbars-not at Calcutta, Madras or Bombay, but at Banaras, Kanpur, Agra and Ambala. The Indian people, however, were not impressed. They considered these splendid shows as an illustration of Government's criminal extravaganza. These could not pacify the people.

It seems, Lord Elgin always felt nervous and afraid. He was always in panic. He did not stay in Calcutta and it seems he considered the British metropolis as completely unsafe. He, therefore, preferred to remain always on the move. Even during winters, he spent a good deal of time far away from Calcutta, even in Simla. He was afraid of any radical change and, therefore, he did not introduce any reforms or improvements in the administration.

On November 7, 1862, the news of the Mughal Emperor Bahadurshah Zafar's tragic, tortous death in Rangoon, created a fire of discontent among the Indian people. On June 9, 1863, the whole country was shocked when it heard the news of a great Indian revolutionary Rao Tula Ram's death in Kabul. He had to go to Afghanistan to save his life during the suppression of the Great Indian Revolt of 1857. The news was heart-rendering, for the fighters for India's freedom. Earlier, the British Government had hanged mercilessly the Nawab of Jhajjar Abdur Rahman and Raja Nahar Singh of Ballabhgarh along with their more than 335 followers.

The Indian people were always in search of an appropriate opportunity to get rid of the British tyranny and to take revenge for the ruthless, illegal executions and other inhuman punishments of the revolutionaries.

On November 20, 1863, the British Government shocked the whole country. It made a most tragic announcement, which looked completely mysterious, unbelievable or false to the people. It was beyond everyone's wildest imagination. The announcement said that the Viceroy Lord Elgin had died at Dharamsala. The reasons mentioned in the announcements for death were 'over-exertion', 'fall from a horse-back' and 'heart-trouble'. Lord Elgin was a youngman of 52, and it became an impossibility to trust the seemingly contradictory reasons for Lord Elgin's death.

Lord Elgin's untimely, sudden, mysterious death and quick burial, not at Calcutta but in Dharamsala itself, was followed by Sir Ashley Eden's endless humiliation and kidnapping in Bhutan, the British Viceroy and Governor-General of India Lord Mayo's merciless assassination in Port Blair, Sir Robert Phayre's poisoning in Baroda, the bloody, inhuman massacre of British forces along with Sir Louis Cavagnari in Kabul and countless other such acts of revenge, violence and brutality.

40

Eminent Scholar Michael Madhusudan Dutt and his Love for the French Beauty Emelia Sophia

Michael Madhusudan Dutt was the greatest Bengali poet of the nineteenth century India. He was no less notable than Bankimchandra Chatterjee and Gurudev Rabindranath Tagore, in the field of literature. He inspired countless Indians through his poems "rolling in stream of music."

Michael Madhusudan Dutt was born at Sagardari in Jessore on the banks of Kapotaksha, and was educated at the Bishop College, Calcutta. He learnt Greek, Latin, Sanskrit, Italian, English, Bengali, and many other languages. On February 9, 1843 he embraced Christianity and married a Christian in Madras Rebeca Meetavys.

Michael Madhusudan Dutt was deeply interested in writing. He therefore, jointed the *Madras Chronicle*, the *Atheacum*, the *Spectator*, etc. and contributed articles and poems for these and many other journals.

He also served as a teacher in Madras from 1852 onwards. In 1856, he left Rebeca Meetavys and Madras and settled in Calcutta after marrying a young French Italy, Emilia Henrietta Sophia. In 1862, he joined the *Hindoo Partiot*, Calcutta.

Michael Madhusudan Dutt was a prolific writer. He wrote *Sharmistha* in 1859, *Padmavati* in 1860, *Krishnakumari* in 1861, *Mavakanan* in 1873, *Budo, Shaliker Ghade Ron* in 1860, *Ekel ke Bale Sabhyate* in 1860, *Mehaghnad Badh* in 1861, *Brajangana* in 1861, *Firangankavya* in 1862, etc. He translated *Dionabandhu Mitra's Nil Darpan* into English with the help of Rev. James Long. His *Tilottama*, which he wrote in Miltonic blank-verse, created a stir in the realm of Bengali poetry. He became extremely popular among the people because of his great literary contributions. He also wrote some poems in English he could not however, complete his two great dramas *Vishma Dhanurgan* and *Rizia* in Bengali and English respectively.

In June 1862, he left for London. He remained in Versailers for some years. While at Versailes, he received Rs. 8000 from Ishwarchandra Vidyasagar (1820-1891) as fincial help. In France he wrote Sonnets in Bengali, including *Choturdaspadi Kabitabali*, published in 1866. In 1866, he returned to India and served as an advocate in the Calcutta High Court. In 1871, he wrote *Hector Badh*. He lived like a prince, and despite his great earnings as a legal adviser to Panchkot state and as a Barrister, he had to leave for Hugli, and in acute financial crisis, he and his wife died in 1873.

Sri Aurobindo had great admiration for Michael Madhusudan Dutt. He described his great literary genius as the "voice of love". He wrote:

Poet, who first with skill inspired did teach
Greatness to our divine Bengali speech,
Divine, but rather with delightful moan
Spring's golden mother makes when twin-alone
She lies with golden Love and heaven's birds
Call hymeneal with enchanting words
Over their passionate faces, rather these
Than with the calm and grandiose melodies
(Such calm as consciousness of godhead owns)
The high gods speak upon their ivory thrones
Silting in council high,—till taught by thee
Fragrance and noise of the world-shaking sea.

Thus do they praise thee who amazed espy
Thy winged epic and hear the arrows cry
And journeyings of alarmed gods; and clue
The praise, since with great verse and numbers new
Thou mad'st her godlike who was only fair.
And yet my heart more perfectly ensnare
Thy soft impassioned flutes and more thy Muse
To wander in the honied months doth choose
Than courts of kings, with Sita in the grove
Of happy blossoms, (O musical voice of love
Murmuring sweet words with sweeter sobs between!),
With Shoorpa in the Vindhyan forests green
Laying her wonderful heart upon the sod
Made holy by the well-loved feet that trod
Its vocal shades; and more unearthly bright
Thy jewelled songs made of relucent light
Wherein the birds of spring and summer and all flowers
And murmuring waters flow, her widowed hours
Making melodious who divinely loved.

No human hands such notes ambrosial moved;
These accents are not of the imperfect earth;
Rather the god was voiceful in their birth,
The god himself of the enchanting flute,
The god himself took up thy pen and wrote.

Michael Madhueudan Dutt's greatest inspiration in literary pursuits was his tender, captivating, irrestible Goddess of Love from France : Emilia. Like a dream-girl, she stired and charmed him. She was his flame, his sweet-heart and the heart-throb. Michael Madhusudan Dutt loved her so deeply that it became an impossibility for him to live without this Venus. Emilia too loved him immensely.

All of a sudden a tragedy occured. As a bolt from the blue, the lovable Emilia died on June 26.

Michael Madhusudan Dutt was in tears. He had never imagined that such a tragic event would ever occur in his life. He had always felt that he and his bewitching Emilia were inseperable. It was simply impossible to bear the pain and sorrow of this loss.

And within no time, something extraordinary happened. The moment, Michael Madhusudan Dutt received the news of Emilia's socking, tragic death, he recited 'Tomorrow and Tomorrow' from William Shakespeare's 'Macbeth' and breathed his last.

That was within less than 75 hours of the great tragedy on June 29, 1873.

41

The Great Indian Barefoot Mahatma Booth Tucker

As a result of the establishment of the British rule, countless Christian Missions established their centres of operations in India. The missionaries mostly came from England, France, Germany, Denmark, Sweden, Portugal, Spain and America. They spent a lot of money for spreading Christianity among the people.

Their contribution was indeed admirable. They opened schools, colleges, hostels, dispensaries, hospitals, shelter-houses, churches, etc. throughout the country. They helped the people during draughts, floods, famines and other calamities.

They gave free education to the poor and free medical assistance, free literature, monetary incentives and employment to countless people.

They employed Indians in printing and publishing work, in translation of Bible and other religious works, in education, or teaching and countless other lucrative endeavours.

They even established separate schools for girls or women. They worked for social reforms. They tried to educate the people with regard to rights and privileges, etc.

Their only weakness was conversion. They wanted to spread Christianity in India through all kinds of ways, fair and foul.

This interest in the promotion of Christianity in this part of the globe provided a lot of 'respectability' to the British Empire in the western world.

It also led to violence and bloodshed. Even before the Great Indian Revolt of 1857 in which countless Christians, including those who were converts, had to part with their lives, there was bloodshed and violence in the country. Many Christian missionaries had to face the criticism and condemnation of the people. Indians were not prepared to accept that Srimad Bhagvad Gita, Ramayan, Upanishads, or the immortal Vedas were less profound or deep, less inspiring or instructive than the teachings of Jesus Christ, who did not exist even at the time of Alexander the Great.

Quite a large number of Christian missionaries, belonging to the ruling class, adopted a dogmatic and unsympathetic attitude towards the Indians. They were far from being polite, compassionate or forgiving. They attacked in Indian philosophy, religion and literature. Some of the missionaries did not mind attacking, condemning and criticizing 'Mahabharat', 'Ramayan', 'Srimad Bhagvad Gita', "Upanishads' and the 'Vedas'. Their greatest unpardonable blunder was to assert that culture and civilization were their sole monopoly.

Many of them in total stupidity, attacked Indians as uncivilized, uncultured and in need of enlightenment through Christianity. This kind of total bankruptcy of mind narrow-mindedness or lack of liberality and understanding created a lot of discontent, disaffection and disappointment among the people.

William Carey, who had once harangued a large gathering of people and attacked an Indian religion was attacked by the people. The attack would have proved fatal but for the timely intervention of security-guards.

John Chamberlain was attacked with sticks by the people in 1807 for canning a Brahmin; William Ward was also violently assaulted and abused for his rigidities, oddidities and endless irrational religious assertions; Josua Marshman, was attacked by the people and some of his tracts, criticizing Indian religions were stolen from his pockets.

Unimaginative, senseless and ridiculous assertions of superiority of one religion over another led to unnecessary, futile debates, disputes and displeasure.

There was violent furious opposition in some parts of India when the Government and the Christian Missions tried to make Bible compulsory in educational institutions and some Christian institutions were boycotted by the Indians towards the middle of the nineteenth century when the Christian Missions tried to convert some, innocent young men to Christianity.

In 1881, British Commissioner Booth Tucker decided to perform a miracle. He surprised the Government and the people. His paramount concern was the spread of the finest principles of Christianity among the people. He wanted that the flag of Lord Jesus Christ flew from one end on India to the other.

He completely transformed himself. It was a kind of metamorphosis. Like a Yogi, he lived a simple, inostentatious life, full of love and tenderness.

He seems to be inspired by the Vedic wisdom:

सर्वे भवन्तु सुखिनः सर्वे सन्तु निरामयाः ।
सर्वे भद्राणि पश्यन्तु मा कश्चित् दुःख भागभवेत ।।

May All Humanity Be Happy
May all be without disease
May all witness auspicious sights
May none have to undergo suffering

Booth Trucker changed his name as 'Fakir'. In order to completely overwhelm and impress the Indians, he discarded his luxurious western cloths and wore the saffron robes of a great Yogi, Mahatma or Sannyasi and led a simple life of purity, prayer and politeness. Full of tremendous enthusiasm, devoted, dedicated and inspired by the highest principles of human life, he tried to lift himself above all rigidities and narrowness and led a life of 'paropkar', 'parmartha' and 'paramanand'.

He was not satisfied even with all this. Astonishingly, the British

Commissioner, like an outstanding spiritual-genius, an otherworldly individual or a mystic, moved from street to street, lane to lane, door to door, in all humility and cheerfulness, to collect his daily bread or 'bhiksha'.

This great embodiment of nobility, remained totally barefoot, all the time, while moving around to spread the noble, immortal message of Christianity.

This was unique, unprecedented and unparalleled. Throughout the nineteenth century no Christian missionary ever converted himself into a great Indian Yogi to spread the brilliant light of Lord Jesus Christ in India or anywhere else in the world.

42

British Racism and Pandit Ishwarchandra Vidyasagar, an Outstanding Educationist

Pandit Ishwarchandra Vidyasagar was one of the greatest educationists of the nineteenth century India. In the most selfless and inspiring manner, he dedicated his entire life to the cause of education of the people of India and for social reform and reconstruction. He was deeply interested in mass education and also in the education of Indian girls and women, who had remained neglected for quite some time. He wanted to encourage both English education as well as the study of Vedic literature through the medium of Indian languages. He wanted the Indian scholars, well versed in Sanskrit studies, to learn English so that they could contribute enormously in the making of modern India.

Ishwarchandra Vidyasagar prepared excellent plans for the spread of national education throughout the country. His ideas served as a revolution in the realm of ideas. He was traditionist to the core but wanted to modernize the whole society in view of new ideas from the western world. He was deadly against superstitions and blind-beliefs and his utmost concern was to provide a rational foundation to India's social ideas and institutions.

Ishwarchandra Vidyasagar wanted to create enlightenment in India. He, therefore, served a large number of educational institutions, such as Fort William College, Calcutta Sanskrit College and the John Bethune Girls College, etc. He wrote excellent books and he was intimately connected with a large number of newspapers and periodicals. Thousands of scholars felt inspired by his ideas and his radical, revolutionary approach to the problems confronting the nation. Top education-experts of the British Government were profoundly impressed by his outstanding genius, his extraordinary understanding of Indian philosophy and literature and his wonderful talent to transform his dreams into reality. Almost at the beginning of his academic career, a fraternity of top Sanskrit scholars conferred on him the superb title of "Vidyasagar".

The education planners of England were totally puzzled in the first half of the nineteenth century because Indian women of honour or respectability were not prepared to join the British educational system. They were keeping themselves completely aloof both from the British Christian institutions and the institutions financially supported by the East India Company. Countless Indians always felt that the Christian mission institutions wanted to convert the Indian people, including women to Christianity. John Drinkwater Bethune came to India and established an institution meant exclusively for Indian women of high castes and respectability. The whole scheme of John Bethune failed disastrously in 1849, when not even 2 dozen students, including the children and relations of the newly appointed three teachers—Ramgopal Ghosh, Dakshinaranjan Mukherjee and Madanmohan Tarkalankar, could join the institution. John Bethune was in tears. He had spent a lot of money on the project. He had even the support and patronage of the Governor-General Lord Dalhousie. Some of the Bethune school enthusiasts were physically assaulted by the people and Raja Radhakant Dev was so much suspicious of the whole scheme that he established immediately in 1849 itself a parallel educational institution for the education of Indian girls and women.

Ishwarchandra Vidyasagar came to the rescue of the British Government and through some kind of 'sanjivani' saved the institution from sinking.

It was a great accomplishment of Ishwarchandra Vidyasagar. The

British Government was indeed grateful to Ishwarchandra Vidyasagar because in years to come the Bethune institution produced some of the finest women intellectuals of the country.

Ishwarchandra Vidyasagar performed miracles as Professor of Literature at the Calcutta Sanskrit College. He became the Principal in 1851. He made tremendous efforts to reform and revigorate the entire system of education. The British Government was full of admiration for his great scholarship and competence.

Ishwarchandra Vidyasagar had a hollistic idea about education and social transformation. His powerful movement for widow marriage was extremely successful. He had the support of countless Indians and some British intellectuals. He submitted a petition to the Government in favour of widow remarriage on March 17, 1856, which was signed by more than 35000 Indians, resulting in the passing of the Widow Remarriage Act on July 26, 1856. That was indeed a great social reform and a praiseworthy achievement.

Ishwarchandra Vidyasagar wanted to establish a rational, enlightened and progressive society. He wanted to put an end to every social evil. On December 27, 1855, he submitted to the Company's Government a petition against polygamy. Astonishingly it was signed by more than 25000 Indians. He was not satisfied even by this wonderful initiative and in 1866, he submitted another petition to the British Viceroy. It contained more than 20,000 signatures. Throughout his life, this great Sanskrit scholar, educationist and social reconstructor continued his powerful movements for completely transforming the society and government. His success was indeed outstanding. The British scholars and members of the British Government were full of praise for this simple man, born in Hugly on September 26, 1820.

His greatest miracle was the establishment of countless model schools in Madia, Burdwan, 24 Parganas, Hugli, Midnapore and 15 other rural areas. He also established at the direction of the Government and at his own initiative 35 girls' schools. He always pleaded for the spread of education among the poor and downtrodden and he wanted that there should be a restriction on school-fees so that education remained accessible to the people.

Some of the most prominent British educationists and officials, who considered Ishwarchandra Vidyasagar as an outstanding intellect keeping in mind the highest attainments of this Sanskrit genius, strongly recommended to the British Government for the appointment of Ishwarchandra Vidyasagar as Director of some educational programmes. That was before the Great Indian Revolt of 1857, in which the Company's Government fell ingloriously like a castle of sand. That was in 1855.

The people expected that the Government would honour itself by offering Ishwarchandra Vidyasagar some highest position in the domain of education. But it seemed that the highest Government positions were meant only for the British-reserved exclusively for Colin Browning, W. Holroyd and Henry Woodrow. The British racism, hypocracy and deceipt came in the way.

And the entire intellectual elite of the country was shocked beyond every measure. The British action produced fierce flames of fury. There was discontent, disaffection, distrust, and diasterous disappointment all around before the Great Indian Revolt of 1857.

The Great Indian educationist Ishwarchandra Vidyasagar got his great appointment in May 1855. He was not appointed as Director of Public Instruction or as deputy Director or as Assistant Director but to everyone total surprise as Assistant Inspector of Schools.

The British Government realized its blunder after some decades and about a year before his death on July 29, 1891, honoured him with CIE on January 1, 1890.

43

Patriotism and Rationalism of Bankimchandra Chatterjee

Bankimchandra Chatterjee, 1838-1894, was one of the most outstanding patriots and fighters of India's freedom from British colonial yoke, in the nineteenth century. He wanted the freedom of his motherland at the earliest. He wrote his world-famous 'Vandematram'

Mother 'I bow to thee!
Rich with thy hurrying streams,
Bright with thy orchard gleams,
Cool with thy winds of delight,
Dark fields waving, mother of might,
Mother free,
Mother, I bow to thee.

It was indeed a unique, heart stirring expression of Indian nationalism. Within no time it became not only the 'sliankhnad' of the struggle for freedom but also a movement. Though banned by the government, it inspired countless people during India's struggle for freedom and even today, it continues to be a perennial source of deathless inspiration.

Sri Aurobindo was a great admirer of Bankimchandra Chatterjee. He wrote:

O plains, O hills, O rivers of sweet Bengal,
O land of love and flowers, The spring-bird's call
And southern winds are sweet among your trees:
Your poet's worlds are sweeter far than these.
Your heart was this iman's heart. Subtly he knew
The beauty and divinity in you.
His nature kingly was and as a god
In large serenity and light he trod
His daily way, Yet beauty, Like soft flowers.
Wreathing a hero's sword, Ruled all his hours.

Thus moving in these iron times and drear,
Darren of bliss and robbed of golden cheer.
The sowed the desert with ruddy-hearted rose,
The sweetest voice that ever spoke in prose.

Aurobindo Ghosh described Bankimchandra Chatterjee as an "immortal" whose "fragrance and light" had divinity around them:

The tears fall fast, O mother, on its bloom.
O white-armed mother, like honey fall thy tears;
Yet even their sweetness can no more relume
The golden light, the fragrance heaven rears,
The fragrance and the light for ever shed
Upon his lips immortal who is dead.

Gurudev Rabindranath Tagore, writing about Bankimchandra Chatterjee remarked:

O master of delicious words! the bloom
Of chompuk and the breath of king-perfume,
Have made each musical sentence with the noise
Of women's ornaments and sweet household joys
And laughter tender as the voice of leaves

Playing with vernal winds. The eye receives
That reads these lines an image of delight,
A world with shapes of spring and summer, noon and night;
All nature in a page, no pleasing show
But men more real than the friends we know.
O plains, O hills, O rivers of sweet Bengal,
O land of love and flowers, the spring-bird's call
And southern winds are sweet among your trees:
Your poet's words are sweeter far than these.
Your heart was this man's heart. Subtly he knew
The beauty and divinity in you.
His nature kingly was and as a god
In large serenity and light he trod
His daily way, yet beauty, like soft flowers
Wreathing a hero's sword, ruled all his hours.
Thus moving in these iron times and drear,
Barren of bliss and robbed of golden cheer,
He sowed the desert with ruddy-hearted rose,
The sweetest voice that ever spoke in prose.

Bankimchandra Chatterjee was out and out a patriot and a nationalist. But his nationalism was not narrow or limited. It was based on rationalism.

Bankimchandra Chatterjee had his own concept of cold rationalism. At a time when the whole country was seriously debating whether Sanskrit should be the medium of instruction or the English; whether Vedic studies should be promoted in India or it would be worthwhile scrutinizing the ideas of Socrates, Artistotle, Plato and Jeremy Bentham, whether Indian Science and Technology should give place to Science and Technology, which developed gradually after the Industrial Revolution in England, Bankimchandra Chatterjee came out with his remarkable, bold and fearless interpretation of what was good for India and Indians. He said:

"We are not going to accept ancient Indian philosophy simply because it is our own; nor are we going to reject it because it happens to be indegenous. On the other hand, modern science is not to be acclaimed or denounced on the ground that it is foreign and not our own. We shall accept only what is true and reasonable and we shall not care if for our belief we are dubbed fools or infidels. And finally for determining what is true and what is false, we shall defend on our own power of reasonsing and not on the verdict given by others."

44

Savitri Phule's Extraordinary Courage, Enlightenment and Social Transformation in India

Savitri Phule was one of the most outstanding pioneers of enlightenment and social transformation in nineteenth century India. She was an inspiring educationist and a social revolutionary. Her greatest concern was the upliftment of the 'untouchables' and other down-trodden individuals of the Indian society. She worked day and night and tried to provide all possible opportunities for the physical, mental and moral advancement of the women. She wanted an immediate end of all kinds of superstitions, blind-beliefs, caste-rigidities, class-distinctions, and socio-religious oddities and absurdities, which served as a stumbling block in the progress of the country.

Along with her great husband, Mahatma Jotirao Phule, she opened countless schools for the most oppressed and neglected individuals in India's social super-structure. She was against poverty, illiteracy, ignorance, unemployment, and prejudice. She opened hostels and night-shelters, for outcastes, orphans and women, and provided them all security, education, free-literature, monetary-incentives and medical-care.

She was fully aware of the pitiable condition of the widows in India, she, therefore, started separate educational institutions for the widows. Her night-schools and adult-education centres became quite popular among the poor, handicapped, ill-equipped women and girls, including the outcastes.

Born in Satara in 1831, Savitri Phule received her education and training in teaching etc. from her husband, Mahatma Jotirao Phule.

With a lot of difficulty, and lack of financial resources, Savitri Phule continued her great, glorious work and created a lot of enlightenment among the people. She received a lot of cooperation of some newspapers in propogating her ideas and programmes. With the help of her husband, she succeeded in writing some books for her educational institutions.

It was a time when many Indian women had not taken great initiatives for creating political-consciousness or socio-economic upliftment in the country. Her endeavours in the field of social reforms, therefore, deserve utmost praise and admiration.

Much before the establishment of Swami Dayanand Saraswati's Arya Samaj, or Henry Olcott and Helena Blatvasky's 'Theosophical Society' of Swami Vivekananda's 'Ramakrishna Mission' or even the foundation of the Indian National Congress in 1885, Savitri Phule remained totally involved in her multifarious activities of enlightenment, social-transformation, and removal of illiteracy etc. day and night with the help of Satyashodhak Samaj, established by Jotirao Phule in 1874. Savitri Phule and her husband also received the cooperation and help of Lokmanya Balgangadhar Tilak, A.G. Agarkar, Sukhram Paranjpye, Moro Walvekar, Sadashiv Govande, Rev. Murray Mitchell and countless other members of the Scottish Christian Mission. Even the British Government was so much impressed by the Phule couple that it allotted a huge land for the construction of some educational institutions. Maharaja Sayajitene provided a lot of generous help and patronage to these social revolutionaries.

The couple drew its inspiration from George Washington, Chatrapatti Shivaji and countless other heroes of world history. Savitri

Phule advocated free, compulsory elementary education for all. She wanted to encourage women's education, adult education, and the education of the orphans, outcastes and 'untouchables'. During floods and famines, Savitri Phule organized relief-work for the unfortunate victims.

Savitri Phule was deadly against widow-burning, maltreatment of women, infant-marriages, social discrimination, unemployment and lack of medical care. She was also concerned about the miserable plight of the poor agriculturists and mill-workers.

She assisted Mahatma Jotirao Phule in the production of manuscripts for publication on slavery, discrimination, etc. including 'Satsar' and 'Satyadharma.'

She was in favour of western education and encouragement to Indian studies, including technical education. Her greatest concern was the establishment of countless rural schools, particularly for the education of the downtrodden, women, girls and orphans. She tried to provide free literature, health care, and shelter to the underprivileged individuals of the society.

Some anti-social and mischivous elements could not appreciate her missionary zeal, determination, inspiring activities and her endeavours to realize the great glorious dreams of social-justice, social-amelioration and attempts to provide adequate opportunities to all for mental, physical and moral growth and development.

Many criminal-minded individuals not merely criticized and condemned her great endeavours but they also tried to create endless hurdles in her way.

Savitri Phule was extremely courageous and full of high spirits. She did not pay any heed to her opposition. She continued to perform her duties without the least interruption.

An extremely interesting story is often told about Savitri Phule's long teaching career. On one dark, horrible night, while returning home, from her teaching assignments, all of a sudden, like a bolt from the blue, she was confronted with the most breath-taking, dreadful or freightening challenge of her life. She had never faced such a terrible problem till that time. She was totally non-plused and did not know what to do. Some wild, misled, stupid, anti-social elements shouted at her in the most uncivilized manner and stopped her abruptly at a completely lonely spot. Mad with boiling anger and adopting a most furious attitude, they threatened her and told her shamelessly that the path she had adopted was disasterous and dangerous in extreme and in case she did not put an immediate stop to her obnoxious activities, it would be impossible for her to save herself and her honour. She would be cut to pieces. She was told repeatedly to put an end to her mad, intolerable activities.

Savitri Phule was well aware of an attempt to assassinate her husband, Mahatma Jotirao Phule in 1856 by some misled, misinformed obscurantists, for whose betterment and enlightenment, he was working day and night, like a crusader, in the most selfless and dedicated manner. Savitri Phule knew full well the fatal consequences of opposing, offending or antagonising the dim-witted, stupid, criminal-minded idiots, who had blocked her way like a granite rock.

Savitri Phule asked the anti-social elements, in a most gentle and polite manner not to obstruct her way, on that dark night and in that totally deserted spot. The rowdy-elements, however, had no desire to yield or to see reason. On the contrary, they came still closer to her. Even after repeated endeavours, when the misled mischief-mongers did not allow her to move an inch forward, the silence of the night was broken by a most resounding/extraordinary sound. Savitri Phule had slapped the anti-social criminals in the most powerful manner, not once or twice but three times.

The drama had ended. The obstruction had vanished. There was perfect peace and silence all around.

The slapping was indeed bold and full of supreme self-confidence. It was perhaps the most courageous, slappingof, its kind, in the entire century.

That was Savitri Phule in her greatness and her glory. Savitri Phule, it may be remarked, was not required to slap anyone thereafter. She continued to serve the country, in her own inspiring manner, throughout her life till 1897, even after the death of her husband in 1890.

45

Sir Joseph Bamfylde Fuller: Don Quixot of India's Struggle for Independence

Mirza Ghalib, the greatest Urdu poet of the nineteenth century India, writing about the British reign of terror and endless inhuman tortures, inflicted by the British Government during the Great Indian Revolt of 1857, remarked:

Now every English soldier that bears arms
Is sovereign and free to work his will,
Men dare not venture out into the street,
And Terror chills their hearts within them still,
Their homes enclose them as in prisonwalla,
And in the 'chauk' the victors hang and kill.

The reign of terror did not end in 1858, when the East India Company fell like a huge castle of sands. The British inhumanity and tortures continued unchecked even after that great uprising.

Many top ranking officials of the British Crown continued to behave in the most arbitrary and highhanded manner. Their attitude towards the Indian people did not undergo a radical change and they did not mind even displaying their own conflicts and clashes. There was open hostality, defiance, intrigue, indiscipline *ad nauseum* in the British top corridors of power. Some officials indulged in mindless suppression of Indian national sentiments and in vulgar display of imperial power. To many Indians they looked silly, stupid blockheads and a ludicurous laughing stock.

One such individual was Sir J. Bamfylde Fuller, born in 1854 and who entered the ICS in 1875.

Sir J. Bamfylde Fuller, Lt. Governor of East Bengal and Assam in 1905, was considered not merely by the Indians as the supreme Don Quixot of India's struggle for Independence but also by some British administrators, who considered him as a nuisance and a danger.

Sir Bamfylde had some unique wonderful ideas and his every administrative measure or policy appeared to the people as the greatest acts of stupidity, insanity or abnormality.

Sir Bamfylde had no tolerance for Indians singing 'Vandematram' and other patriotic songs. He disliked their processions and public meetings for the achievement of swarajya. Under depression or frustration, he banned the singing of Vandematram and even the public meetings.

He was not satisfied with all these repressive measures. He threatened the Viceroy and Governor General Lord Minto. He told the Government in the most unequivocal terms that if Banwarilal High School and Victoria High School were not immediately disaffiliated from the University of Calcutta, it would be diasterous for the administration. It would result in his immediate resignation from the Lt. Governership. Sir Bamfylde was of the opinion that in those educational institutions the students were totally indisciplined and had assaulted some British Bank official Carberry.

Lord Minto was totally perplexed. He did not know how to put a check on Sir Bamfylde's brainlessness or unimaginative policies. The Viceroy could not understand how to deal with this kind of unreasonableness or vegetability, every now and then.

The Government decided not to pay any heed to the throats of Sir Bamfylde, who appeared to it nothing more than a clown or a stupid simpleton. He was emerging as a great nuisance, to Lord Minto's administration. He was a threat and a constant strain on the nerves of Lord Minto.

After endless toleration, Lord Minto sent an immediate telegram to London for the removal of Sir Bamfylde from his Government and India.

Sir Bamfylde resigned and his resignation was immediately accepted by the British Crown on August 5, 1906.

Sir Bamfylde was an extraordinary individual. He never wanted to leave India without putting his permanent stamp on the minds of the Indian people.

Before the acceptance of his resignation, he had put such a powerful stamp of his personality on India, which could never be forgotten.

He wanted to fulfil his dreams.

He, therefore, did something extraordinary and he was condemned and criticized by the press and the people. The newspapers described him as tactless, irresponsible and without any judgement. He was described as 'the seventh incarnation of Shaisth Khan'.

A youngman Udai Patani was sentenced to death in 1906, in connection with his nationalistic activities. He had sent a powerful appeal to the Viceroy Lord Minto against the terrible judgement. Everyone around him felt that Udai Patani would be pardoned and he would be able to escape the cruel hanging. His appeal reached the Viceroy Lord Minto on May 21, 1906, for reconsideration. There was a lot of hope and excitement everywhere.

The people were optimistic. They hoped that Lord Minto would consider the appeal in the most humane and sympathetic manner.

Sir Bamfylde however was made of a different clay, and before the Viceroy Lord Minto could consider the appeal, the whole country was taken aback. The people were stunned.

On May 21, 1906, the people were astonished when they heard the heart-rendering news:

'Sir Bamfylde Fuller had Hanged Udai Patani Today at 7 AM.'

The people were furious. They wanted to take revenge against British tyranny. Two bombs were thrown on Lord Minto in Ahmedabad on November 13, 1909.

46

Sister Nivedita and 'Vandematram'

Sister Nivedita or Margnet Elizabeth Noble, born on October 28, 1867 at Dunganou, Ireland, was a remarkable educationist, social reformer and politician, who dedicated her life to the cause of enlightenment in India. She was a great disciple of Swami Vivekananda, who gave her the name "Bhagini Nivedita" on March 25, 1898. She came to India on January 28, 1898 and devoted herself wholeheartedly to the welfare of the Indian people. She worshipped Goddess Kali and Lord Shiva and felt inspired by the teachings and ideas of Ramakrishna Paramhansa.

Sister Nivedila travelled throughout India to arouse national consciousness among the people. She condemned the British Government for its autocratic and tyrannical ways. She attacked Lord Curzon for the Indian Universities Act of 1904 and for his Calcutta University Convocation Address in 1905. She supported the Swadeshi Movement and attended the sessions of the Indian National Congresss and the Dawn Society. She was closely connected with Gopalkrishna Gokhale, Bipanchandra Pal, Taraknath Das, and Aurobindo Ghosh,

She wanted the whole country to be educated on national lines. Rabindranath Tagorc and Sir Ramsay Macdonald were appreciative of her work in India. She edited the *Karmayogi* of Aurobindo Ghosh.

Tall, well built, with deep blue eyes, wearing while long gown and a rosary of rudraksha around her neck, Sister Nivedila was an image of purity and intense spiritual powers.

Swami Vivekananda described her a lioness and to Aurobindo Ghosh she was a flame or Agnishika. My task is to awaken the notion she said, and for most of the time, during her stay in India, she worked for the enlightenment of the people.

Swami Vivekananda presented a short poem to Sister Nivedita, while they were together in France and spent some days in Brittany towards the close of 1899. It's title was 'A Benediction'.

The mother's heart, the hero's will,
The sweetness of the southern breeze,
The sacred charm and strength that dwell
On Aryan alters, flaming, free;
All these be yours, and many more
No ancient soul could dream before
Be thou to India's future sons
The mistress, servant, friend in one.

The British Government banned the singing of 'Vandematram' in public places immediately after the Partition of Bengal on October 16, 1905. It was in sheer panic and utter lack of confidence that the British Government adopted such an extreme measure. It was almost a kind of madness. Many people, who violated the Government orders, were cainned, whipped and flogged. The Government considered 'Vandematram' as the root cause of 'sedition' and violence during the Swadeshi Movement.

Most of the Indians did not like this kind of blatant prohibition of the greatest patriotic song ever produced by Bankimchandra Chatterjee. They felt sad and completely disappointed.

Sister Nivedita did not like such tyrannical attitude of the British colonialism. She did not like the way the Government was shamelessly torturing the people involved in Vandematram-processions.

Sister Nivedita was bold and courageous. She wanted to find a way to teach the British Government a lesson. She introduced spinning and other such swadeshi activities in her Calcutta Girls School. She requested the Calcutta artists to paint the pictures of Ram, Krishna and Buddha for her school.

She wanted to defy the Government orders. In a bold and courageous manner, she introduced Bankimchandra Chatterjee's 'Vandematram' as daily-prayer in her school.

No educational institution in Calcutta had introduced 'Vandematram' as every day prayer. Perhaps, no other institution in India had adopted Vandematram as a daily prayer. That was unprecedented and inspiring.

That was a demonstration of extreme boldness and the objectives Sister Nivedita wanted to accomplish. That showed her passion for the unity and welfare of the people.

Everyone was surprized and astonished. Udai Patani was hanged for singing 'Vandematram' and other patriotic songs in 1906.

But Sister Nivedita did not stop the singing of 'Vandematram' in her school throughout her life.

She died on October 13, 1911. That was Sister Nivedita in her greatness.

47

Mysterious Whispers and Fatal Shots, Professor W. Knox Johnson, British Repression and India's Struggle for Independence

Immediately after the ruthless suppression of the Great Indian Revolt of 1857, the greatest anxiety in England was how to hold India as a part of the British Empire. England was small, with a small population and extremely limited natural resources. The people were poor, illiterate and extremely backward. Without a continuous drain of Indian wealth, England deeply involved in the Industrial Revolution, would have remained completely underdeveloped. Women had no representation in the British Parliament and the Government had not granted them even the voting rights.

The Revolt of 1857 had shattered the economy of England. It had proved a great military and financial disaster.

Frantic efforts, therefore, were made in England to retain its hold over India.

Bahadurshah Zafar was thrown out of India, Maharani Jind Kaur was forced to leave India and go to London, where her son Maharaja Dilip Singh, a Christian convert, was already leading a life of total seclusion. Amar Singh had died a tortuous death in captivity in Gorakhpur, a Mughal prince had to run away to Udaipur from

Delhi to escape immediate death, Rao Tula Ram had died in Afghanistan, Bhaskar Rao Nargundkar, Tatiya Tope were mercilessly hanged and Nana Saheb and Begum Hazrat Mahal had no alternative but to go to Kathmandu to escape the British tortures.

Countless Indian revolutionaries had gone underground. They were anxiously awaiting a suitable opportunity to throw the British out of India.

The British Government had completely destroyed its image in India by indulging the gross savagery and endless barbarianism.

The British Government was not prepared to take any chance or risks. They had shot dead countless Indian soldiers and hanged all those Indians, whom it suspected of revolts or rebellions. Properties were confiscated without varification. Even women and children had been tortured and killed.

The British Empire wanted its control over India by any means, fair or foul. It continued to interfere in the Indian states and maltreat the sovereigns. It taxed the people. Many Indian battalions were disbanded and an attempt was made to thoroughly disarm the people, from one end of India to the other. All the top responsible positions, both civil and military, became the monopoly of the Britons.

Such inhumanity was unparalleled and unprecedented. A great concern of the British Crown was to check the recurrence of another powerful violent rebellion in India.

The Indian revolutionaries, who participated in the Great Indian Revolt of 1857 continued to be hanged even till the establishment of the Indian National Congress in 1885.

Lord Lytton had already imposed a heavy censorship on vernacular newspapers and other publications. Lord Curzon was so much upset at the rising tide of nationalism in India that out of total panic he committed an unpersonable crime by partitioning Bengal in 1905. He committed that political blunder to check the dangerous revolutionary, terrorist activities.

The partition created a commotion. There was violence and an anti-partition movement, everything British became obnoxious and untouchable to the Indians. They boycotted the British goods and attempts were made to kill the British individuals in power.

The Indian revolutionaries manufactured powerful bombs and collected huge ammunitions. Their aim was to "Rain Death and to make the British Administration an impossibility in India." The British officials, including academicians, also received countless threats.

Their life was always in danger. Many secret, underground revolutionary, terrorist organizations, which believed in the doctrine of daggar and bomb sprang up in quick succession.

The people of India wanted an immediate termination of the foreign imperialist tyranny and the achievement of swarajya. The result was a widespread swadeshi movement.

Professor W. Knox Johnson, an eminent educationist, who had served as Professor of English Literature at the Queen's College, Banaras in 1902 and who had become the Principal of an educational institution in Jabalpur, was fully aware of the wave of violence and terrorism in the country. Perhaps, the teachers, students and other Indian revolutionaries were not prepared to tolerate the presence of this English scholar any more. There were perhaps some conspiraries and plots to eliminate him—some mysterious whispers all around him.

Professor Knox Johnson immediately left Jabalpur and reached Piparia. At Piparia, he heard once again the same mysterious whispers.

Knox Johnson was terribly upset. He left Piparia and reached Panchmarhi.

The mysterious whispers followed him like a shadow. He heard the same mysterious whispers at Panchmarhi, time and again.

Professor Knox Johnson was bold and upright. Though puzzled, perturbed and perplexed, he remained calm, cool and composed. His behaviour looked absolutely normal.

On June 19, 1906 something extraordinary happened. Professor Knox Johnson wrote an "Epitah" for himself he wrote how a stone could be put in his graveyard, and what should be the text of the inscription on the tomb. How the cost would be met. He left a lot of money so that his survirors had no problem at all in his burial.

Knox Johnson then said farewell and greetings to everyone around. He met his people as if that was his last meeting with them.

Everything looked absolutely normal. There was hardly any scope for anxiety, suspicion or fear.

The Professor went to a far off, secluded place—a spot which perhaps he had selected for his own burial.

Knox Johnson stood there in complete silence for a moment. The nature was calm. There was complete tranquillity everywhere. He whispered something to himself. All of a sudden, he took out a loaded revolver and within moments, he fired some fatal shots ... and Knox Johnson was no more.

No one knows what was the real mystry of those whispers. Why did Knox Johnson ended his precious life in an alien country, thousand of miles away from his homeland.

48

Poor Village Boy from Tirutani and 'The Ethics of the Vedanta'

A poor village boy from Tirutani was asked by his teachers at the University of Madras to write a Dissertation on Indian Philosophy, as a part of his M.A. studies. The student displayed a remarkable sense of responsibility, and took his assignment in an extremely serious manner. He made an extensive study of every possible source and produced within an extremely short period an outstanding dissertation: 'The Ethics of the Vedanta'. It was an excellent work, scholarly and analytical, full of select, interesting and deep extrats from the Vedic Literature. The originality of interpretation and effectiveness of style were indeed—commendable. The Professors of the University described it as a great work. Everyone hailed the youngman as a great scholar and his work, which he produced in 1908, as admirable.

Soon a miracle happened. Such a miracle had never happened in the history of the university, or that of any other university in India or the world. 'The Ethics of the Vedanta' was published even before the youngman obtained his MA degree.

Critics, commentators, and reviewers described 'The Ethics of the Vedanta' as an extraordinary work and its author a genius.

'The Ethics of the Vedanta' was sold out within no time and

other editions had to be brought out. Soon many more miracles happened. 'The Ethics of the Vedanta' was followed by many more scholarly works: Eastern Religions and Western thought; Indian Philosophy; Contemporary Thought; Idealistic View of Life; Future of Civilization, etc. by the same author, who could establish himself as one of the most celebrated scholars of the world.

Oxford, London, Manchester, Calcutta, Mysore, Banaras, Madras, Chicago and many other world-famous universities and other learned institutions showered endless praise and honours on this legend of Literature and Philosophy. Wherever he went, he was heard with utmost respect and reverence, and the greatest countries of the world vied with each other in immortalizing him with the highest distinctions of life.

The country of his birth was not lagging far behind. In 1962, the first Prime Minister of India, Pandit Jawaharlal Nehru requested him to accept the highest honour, which the country could bestow upon an individual: The Presidentship of the Indian Secular Democratic Republic.

The poor Brahmin boy from Tirutani, born on September 5, 1888, was Dr. Sarvepalli Radhakrishnan, the world renowned Indian philosopher-statesman and one of the most powerful and extraordinary speakers of all times.

Dilipkumar Roy was full of great admiration for Dr. Sarvepalli Radhakrishnan. Describing him as a noble judge, he wrote:

O noble judge, who declinest to condone
The demon passions that blur God's sky of peace
And yet canst understand why men are prone
To outlaw the heights and acclaim the dread abyss:
Thy windows are open to the soul's pure white
Vast firmament of faith no doubt can mar;
A contemplative of compassion's light,
Thou sing'st: None but true lovers win the Star
Of Love whose unique miracle alchemy
Can resolve Hale's discord into a Harmony.

49

Total Fearlessness and Rationalism of Madanlal Dhingra

Madanlal Dhingra, born in Amritsar in 1857, said before his execution in London on August 17, 1909 that he was proud of having the 'honour of laying down his humble life' for the freedom of his motherland: India. He wanted his execution so that the "spirit of vengeance" of Indians became strong and powerful. He made it absolutely clear that the British had 'no right' to occupy or rule over India. He said:

> "The only lesson required in India, at present, is to learn how to die and the only way to teach it is by dying ourselves."

Madanlal Dhingra wanted immediate freedom for India in 1909, because according to his calculations the British were responsible for plundering or taking away £ 100,000,000 every year from India. He was opposed to British tyranny in India because, according to his calculations in 50 years, the British had murdered 80,000,000 Indians.

Madanlal Dhingra was an extraordinary fighter for India's freedom because after murdering Sir Curzon Wyllie on July 1, 1909, he did not engage any advocate to plead his case, and wanted to be executed so that his sacrifice created a political storm in India and India became free within the minimum possible time.

Many other freedom-fighters, before and after Madanlal Dhingra, showed examplary courage at the time of their execution, but most of them wanted to survive, after their heroic accomplishments. But Madanlal Dhingra wanted to be executed so that there was a storm or a tornado in India. And indeed Madanlal Dhingra's sacrifice served as a powerful inspiration to Bhagat Singh, Rajguru, Shahdev, Chandrashekhar Azad and countless other fighters for India's Independence.

On July 1, 1909, Madanlal Dhinga, a youngman of 22, shot dead Sir Curzon Wyllie, ADC to the Secretary of State for India. He had gone to London to study Engineering.

He fired 5 shots at Sir Curzon Wyllie, who had come to the Imperial Institute for a 'Talk', alongwith his wife. Madanlal Dhingra used his Belgian revolver to shoot him down. Sir Curzon Wyllie fell on the ground and died. Madanlal Dhingra was arrested; tried by a court, and hanged on August 17, 1909, within less than 50 days of the shooting.

What is remarkable about Madanlal Dhingra is his total fearlessness and determination. Madanlal Dhingra did not employ any advocate to plead his case. He confessed that he had murdered Sir Curzon Wyllie. He said that he did not want any mercy, and that he wanted to die for the country's freedom. He wanted to highlight, through his shooting the British maladministration, tyranny and torture in India. According to Madanlal Dhingra the British Government was responsible for the killing of countless innocent Indians. The British Government was also responsible for plundering India and for the drain of its wealth, in a constant manner. He said that he had murdered Sir Curzon Wyllie because Indians were not prepared to tolerate the British autocracy and colonial exploitation.

Madanlal Dhingra wanted to be hanged, because he felt that his hanging would provide inspiration to the freedom-fighters of India and it would also provide a stimulus to India's struggle for freedom. He was, therefore, determined to sacrifice himself for the freedom of his country.

Madanlal Dhingra was rational and convincing to the core. He had a total justification for involving himself in violence. He made it absolutely clear that he was a freedom-fighter and fighting for the liberation of one's own country could never be a crime. He raised an interesting hypothetical question. He told the British Government and the people that in case Germany captured England, the people of England would make every possible effort to liberate England, and those who killed the German imperialists would be honoured in England as great patriots.

Madanlal Dhingra was absolutely rational and convincing. He had discussed these matters in detail with Shyamjikrishnavarma, Veer Savarkar and many other Indian revolutionaries in Europe. He was also inspired by Lala Har Dayal.

Madanlal Dhingra was convinced that without sacrifice or death, India could not achieve its freedom in a short time. He told everyone around him that he wanted to die so that India could be immediately liberated. In his message to Indians, before hanging, he made it absolutely clear that Indians must immediately learn how to die. By setting such examples they would contribute immensely for India's immediate freedom.

What is outstanding about Madanlal Dhingra is that he never wanted any mercy from the British Government. He never wanted any advocate to plead his case. Many freedom-fighters who sacrificed their lives for the freedom of India submitted mercy petitions, pleaded for their release but this great freedom-fighter from Amritsar was completely different. He was fearless and wanted to be executed.

In the history of freedom struggle for India in England, there was perhaps no other Indian who did not want to survive. Such examples are rare even in the struggle for India's Independence in India or in any other country of the world, while fighting for freedom.

Madanlal Dhingra's supreme desire for sacrifice and his execution was indeed a heroic fearless and daring demonstration that India had completely awakened and wanted 'swarajya' and the immediate destruction and downfall of the outdated British colonial superstructure.

It was a bold, brave and powerful warning to the British Empire that the gallant people of India would not mind even storms of violence and bloodshed for the immediate realization of their pious long cherished dreams.

It was a danger-signal to England to stress that the loin-hearted Indians were fully prepared to heroically offer their lives—as an act of supreme divine service—for demolishing the obsolete and redundant sand-castles of misgovernment, corruption, injustice, tyranny and torture in India.

Madanlal Dhingra's sacrifice is perhaps unprecedented, unparalleled and unique. Madanlal Dhingra would remain an inspiration to all the fighters for freedom for all times to come.

50

Mira Richard: The Mystic Beauty-Queen from France and India's Struggle for Independence

Mira Richard, who was born in Paris on February 21, 1878, played a memorable role in India's struggle for freedom. She considered Patriotism or Nationalism as the highest aspiration of an individual. It was divine. She had great love for India. She wanted India to be free from the British imperial shackles so that it could emerge as a powerful nation. She worked day and night, not merely as a yogi or a spiritual mystic, but also as a fighter for India's freedom.

It is unfortunate that scholars have not adequately studied or analyzed her glorious role in the field of politics. Most of the people—who surrounded her—prayed and worshipped her for her extraordinary mysterious, occult powers. They felt that she was capable of providing immense happiness to the people and putting an end to all human miseries, misfortunes and sufferings.

Mira Richard embarked for India from France on March 7, 1914 and made Pondicherry her home and the centre of her incredible spiritual and political activities. She was well-informed and maintained countless documents, including press-chippings on political developments in India, France, England, Germany, Japan and other parts of the world.

She went to Paris from Pondicherry and remained there for some time during the first world war. She had horrible experiences of the war, when she had to live in trenches and there was horrible bombardment and violence all around. She also went to Japan from London on March 13, 1916 with her husband Paul Richard and stayed there for four long years meeting countless leaders there, including Gurudev Rabindranath Tagore and Shumei Okawa, the moving spirit behind the notable Black Dragoon Society.

In Paris earlier a member of her Occult-group and poet, who led an extremely gloomy sexual life, was found murdered on a Wednesday night. Mira held regular meetings of her Occult-group in her fifth-floor apartment every night on Wednesdays.

On April 24, 1920, she was again in Pondicherry—her sweet, loving home. An outstanding achievement of her life was her meeting with a great, dynamic Indian Revolutionary and Yogi Sri Aurobindo —on March 20, 1914—whom the British Empire considered as "the most dangerous man in India". Sri Aurobindo was indeed extraordinarily dangerous. He was raining bombs and bullets on the British Empire through his fearless speeches and writings since the cruel partition of Bengal in 1905 or even earlier.

He was connected with powerful underground, secret revolutionary organizations—which wanted to overthrow the British Government in India, without a moment's delay, through the most effective violent ways.

Sri Aurobindo was connected with *Vandemataram, Kannayogin, Dharma,* Dr. Annie Basant's *New India* and many other fire-brand revolutionary newspapers and periodicals.

He was involved in Alipore Bomb case, Mannicktolla Bomb case and perhaps with the manufacturing of bombs and other arms and ammunitions. Sri Aurobindo was arrested and imprisoned two times. When he was released in 1909, the British Government, wild with panic, once again issued warrants for his arrest. Sri Aurbindo got information about the British Government's orders for his immediate arrest. He, therefore, left Calcutta swiftly, silently and secretly by a fast steamer and reached a French territory Chandranagore and from there he reached Pondicherry, which was also a French territory, on April 1, 1910 under a secret name Jyotindranath Mitra.

In 1914, he met extremely beautiful, attractive, graceful and stylish Mira Richard in Pondicherry. Mira Richard entrusted the task of editing a new news-magazine *The Arya,* to Sri Aurbindo—who desperately needed some money to maintain himself in Pondicherry. The first issue of *The Arya* came out on August 15, 1914.

After return from Japan, Mira wanted that Sri Aurobindo should continue his wonderful revolutionary activities from Pondicherry for the freedom of India, without being caught by the British Police or its intelligence net-work, She, therefore, did her utmost to provide a total cover to Sri Aurobindo. Her success was brilliant, and Sri Aurobindo continued his great work completely unhampered. He was neither caught nor hanged by the British till August 15, 1947, when India became independent.

Even around 1914, Mira saved this "Most dangerous Man" from arrest, imprisonment or even execution.

The British Government was terribly afraid of the Indian revolutionaries. The Government of England, therefore, requested the Government of France not to allow Indian revolutionaries to operate from French territories, particularly Pondicherry.

It, therefore, sent a top secret, confidential file regarding: Indian revolutionaries to France. The Government of France would have taken fast severe action but because of Mira and her brother, Matteo—who was an important officer in the Ministry of Foreign Affairs in France, the Government of France did not take any action. This was a great service rendered by Mira to India.

The other ways, sophisticated and blatant, adopted by Mira to save the life of Sri Aurobindo were as follows:

1. Maintenance of dog-sized, dangerous, furious-looking, attacking Wild Cats at the 'Ashram', where she lived with Sri Aurobindo.
2. There was a tremendous fear of Sri Aurobindo's arrest any moment by the British police and intelligence network, who were always shadowing him. Therefore, one Indian

revolutionary in Pondicherry: Vara, grew beard, dressed up exactly like Sri Aurobindo, spoke like Aurobindo, moved from place to place in Pondicherry to completely befool or confuse the British Government. Vara acted as Sri Aurobindo—as his duplicate. Whether Vara was a product of Mira's mind, or that of Sri Aurobindo and his followers requires a deep study. Bejoy Nag [Alipore Bomb Case], however, could not escape arrest.

3. Mira Richard did not allow anyone to meet Sri Aurobindo. His whereabouts were not known to anyone. He remained in hiding most of the time. It is well known that Bijoy Kumar Nag, Nolini Kanta Gupta, Suresh Chakrovarty, Philippe Barbier, Barindra Kumar Ghosh—a revolutionary and Sri Aurobindo's younger brother, Dorothy Hodgson, K. Ranjangam, A.B. Purani, K. Amrita, Kanailal Ganguli, Purushottam Patel, Nani Bala, Dr. Upendranath Banerjee continued to meet Sri Aurobindo, secretly but frequently. His sadhaks or Indian revolutionaries were allowed to meet him for yoga and sadhana, perhaps for political guidance after thorough inquiry, investigation and scrutiny.

   Mira had divorced her first husband Henri Morrisscy before coming to India. She divorced her second husband Paul Richard around 1924 after separation for more than 2 years, because she considered Sri Aurobindo as her 'inseparable' 'Lord'. She not merely did her yoga exercises with Sri Aurobindo alone in the Ashram but she also washed his long hairs. At the time of 'darshan' to the sadhaks she did not mind kissing the Mahayogi's hands.
4. Sri Aurobindo's house was searched thoroughly by the French Government, but no "Seditious Literature", bombs or arms could be discovered. That was perhaps, due to Mira's presence in the house or Ashram. Mira also knew the French Government officials and politicians, who were active in Pondicherry.
5. Mira provided employment and financial assistance to Sri Aurobindo, who had, at times, no money at all, by

requesting him to take up the editorship of *the Arya.* She also helped him in writing or revision and the productions of the *Life Divine, Savitri, The Lights on Yoga, The Riddle of this World, the Brain of India, Renaissance in India, Objects of Yoga, Yogik Sadhana, Superman, Ishopnishad, the Mother, Self-Determination, Essays on Gita, Love and Death, the Ordeals of Karma-yogin.* These spiritual and literacy activities were perhaps absolutely imperative to demonstrate to the entire world that Sri Aurobindo has turned into a yogi or a literary genius. He was not a dangerous man any more. One year after her return from Tokyo in 1921, *The Arya* was stopped because even the publication of this journal could be detrimental to Sri Aurobindo's interests—that could lead to his arrest—when after the commencement of Mahatma Gandhi's non-cooperation movement, hundreds and thousands of freedom-fighters were tortured, arrested and imprisoned on mere suspicion.

6. Mira had put a lot of restrictions on Sri Aurobindo, of course with mutual consent. It was decided that he would not go to Calcutta or British India—even when requests were made by Deshbandhu Chittaranjan Das, Lokmanya Balgangadhar Tilak, Purushottam Das Tandon, and even Mahatma Gandhi. Even earlier, Aurobindo did not go to Calcutta when Miralini was ill—or even when she died in December 1918.
7. Mira kept Sri Aurobindo properly informed about the political developments all over the world, through newspapers, radio, press-chippings, etc. Sri Aurobindo was in complete touch with the Indian National Movement, and the World Wars—which drew his great attention. Mira planned political strategies with Sri Aurobindo every now and then.
8. And finally, Mira took complete charge of his correspondence which included 4000 letters to D.K. Roy alone—and his articles and comments for publication in the Indian newspapers openly or anonymously.

9. Mira discussed every new move by Mahatma Gandhi, J. Nehru, Netaji Subhas Chandra Bose with Sri Aurobindo—and the strategies to be adopted for the immediate liberation of India.

Mira did not allow anyone to meet Sri Aurobindo, without total scrutiny, after November 24, 1926, because she knew such meetings could be fatal to the Mahayogi—from political point of view. In Chauri Chaura (1922) already there was a terrible demonstration of Indian anger against the British. Mira was with Sri Aurobindo when India achieved Independence on August 15, 1947.

51

Lord Hardinge's Invaluable Inspiration and India's Struggle for Independence

The British Viceroy Lord Hardinge was a great inspirer. In his brilliant speeches and addresses, he tried to provide a new direction to the people of India. On March 16, 1912, Lord Hardinge, who was the Viceroy of India and the Chancellor of the University of Calcutta, delivered an excellent, historic and inspiring convocation address at the University of Calcutta. He talked about the great role the Indian youth or the scholars of the universities in India could play in the progress of the country. He said:

> "My concluding words are: be true to your god; ... true to your country and true to yourself. Follow these precepts and have no fear of the future of your country or of yourself."

These golden words served as a wonderful inspiration to the people. The People of India realized in full measure the utmost significance of highest integrity, indomitable courage and total fearlessness.

The people realized that they were indeed half-asleep and they were not indeed completely true to their God, true to India and true to themselves.

There was a realization among the people that without India's Independence, the peace, prosperity and progress of the country could never be realized. The greatest impedment or the stumbling block was the British Empire, which was coming in the way of realization of their noblest dreams including "swarajya".

Lord Hardinge had opened their eyes. The same year, within less than 10 months, on December 23, 1912, when the Viceroy Lord Hardinge was marching in a magnificent state procession, with elephants and horses, through the streets of Delhi, some Indian young revolutionaries tried to assassinate him. They considered him the greatest stumbling block in the way of India's Independence. They threw powerful bombs on Lord Hardinge in Chandni Chowk.

The great inspirer Lord Hardinge was seriously wounded. It was a terrible bomb-blast. It was frightening and most disasterous. A guard died in the bomb-blast within no time. Countless people received serious injuries. There was panic everywhere. Lady Hardinge was in a state of tremendous shock. She was shaken and completely nervous. She decided to leave India without any delay, but died in July 1914, after reaching England.

The University of Calcutta convocation address proved a great inspiration to the fighters of India's freedom. It proved disasterous to the British Viceroy Lord Hardinge and in years to come, fatal to the British Indian Empire.

52

Sri Aurbindo's Metamorphosis

Sri Aurobindo was an outstanding philosopher and a remarkable revolutionary. He was considered as the most dangerous man in India by the British Government in India. Sri Aurobindo wanted an immediate overthrow of the British Government in India. His contribution in the field of literature and philosophy is outstanding. His philosophy can serve as an instrument for the realization of world peace and human happiness. His ideas about Yoga and Sadhana can also help in self-realization and in the attainment of 'anand' or the Supreme bliss.

It would, however, be most appropriate to understand the fundamental basis of the evolution of his entire philosophy, particularly after 1910, when he left Calcutta and reached Pondicherry, a French territory. Was his philosophy a product of utter helplessness, phobia or fever? Was it an outcome of British-horror or dead of execution or death?

How a powerful revolutionary, who wanted an immediate termination of British tyranny in India, and who had a conviction in 'Nisha Kama Karma Yoga' decided to spend countless hours, days and years, completely aloof, almost in total isolation, in Samadhi or Sadhana in Pondicherry?

How did he completely neglect Miralini, his noble, selfless wife, who died of influenza in Calcutta endlessly awaiting the arrival of Sri Aurobindo, in December 1918?

How did he decide to keep himself cut-off from his great ambition and did not actively participate in India's great struggle for freedom? How did he decide to spend some most valuable 37 years of his life, till 1947, in editing journals of philosophy, in revising his manuscript and in creating some literary, philosophical gems, such as the 'life Divine' and Savitri.

It would be worthwhile examining if his total metamorphosis from a revolutionary fighter for freedom to a 'maharishi' or a philosopher in total isolation or a yogi in meditation, cut-off from the world, was not a product of some extremely compelling political events or developments. He ran away silently, secretly, when someone whispered into his ear a report about his immediate arrest. He went to Chanderanasore in a fast steamer, with his closest associates and after a short hiding there, he reached Pondicherry under a secret name: Jyotindra Nath Mitra, on April 1, 1910.

India wanted Sri Aurobindo to return and take active part in the struggle for 'swarajya'. He was offered be editorship of a newspaper. He was promised all protection and support. Sri Aurobindo, however rejected the offer to Deshbandhu Chittaranjan Das to return to politics. He rejected the most invaluable suggestions of the great Indian National Congress leader Dr. Annie Basent, who felt that Sri Aurobindo's return to India's struggle for freedom was absolutely indispensable.

The apostle of Indian unrest and the greatest extremist leader of the country Lokmanya Balgagadhar Tilak's request to Sri Aurobindo to join India's struggle for Independence could not create any impression on Sri Aurobindo's mind. He was determined not to return immediately to India's struggle, his answer was an emphatic 'No'. That Sri Aurobindo was interested in Indian politics and in India's struggle for independence every moment of his life till August 15, 1947 is axiomatic. He wrote his comments for Dr. Annie Basent's New India on Minto Morley reforms in 1918 anonymously, and he also approved the Crips's Proposals in 1942.

Deshbandhu Chittaranjan Das wanted his cooperation, when

the Swarajya Party was formed Lala Lajpatrai and Rajrishi Purushottam Das Tondon reached Pondicherry after a couple of years to persuade Sri Aurobindo to return to India's struggle for independence, but Sri Aurobindo was adamant. He was not prepared to return any time under any circumstances. What was at the root of his adamancy?

The factors which might have forced Sri Aurobindo not to return to India or to join the mainstream of India's struggle for freedom could be as follows:

1. Sri Aurobindo's arrest and imprisonment and inhuman torture for one long year for seditious writings in 1908-09. He was humiliated and ridiculed.
2. His description as the most dangerous man in British Government circles and a cruel constant close watch over all his political activities and writings by the blood hounds or under-cover, plain-clothed secret-agents.
3. His acute lack of financial resources, after reaching Pondicherry for many years. At one time during 1910 to 1914, he had barely one rupee and four annas for survival.
4. His constant shadowing by British intelligence network and the planting of a spy in Sri Aurobindo's rented house in Pondicherry. The name of this British spy was Virendra Roy, a domestic servant to a TB patient who had gone to Sri Aurobindo for some guidance.
5. The British Government's warning to Sri Aurobindo to stop indulging in politics or seditious activities.
6. Surprisingly, even the Government of France was not kind to Sri Aurobindo. His Pondicherry house was thoroughly searched by French Government.

   The French Government was absolutely sure of finding some inflammatory, seditious documents or some most dangerous items of revolutions, including bombs and bullets in Sri Aurobindo's house, but most surprisingly it found only some invaluable gems and diamonds of literature: the Latin and Greek manuscripts produced by Sri Aurobindo in Pondicherry or elsewhere.

7. Paul Richard—a French politician and his wife Mira Richard's long, unnecessary stay with Sri Aurobindo for endless years, depriving him of his total privacy and active support to India's Struggle for freedom from a French territory.
8. Inhuman treatment or torture of Barindra Ghosh, Sri Aurobindo's Brother and other revolutionaries, including deportation to Andaman etc. Particularly those involved in Muzaffarpur bomb case in India—the manufacture of bombs at Maniktollah and the Assassination of Narendra Goswami, the approver in Muzaffarpur bomb case.
9. Offer or acceptance of honorary editorship from Paul Richard and Mira Richard for editing the *Arya* from 1914 onwards.
10. And finally Sri Aurobindo solid conviction that the British Government would not tolerate his presence in British India for a single moment and his return would mean his immediate arrest and imprisonment and that his liberty and 'peace' would be axed.

Sri Aurobindo, therefore, led a horrible life in Pondicherry, some times in BB Lele's uncomfortable house and later on in Shankar Chhetty's house on rent, with no meals, no furniture, no comforts, only tap water for bath.

Around 1920 and later, Sri Aurobindo decided to meet sometimes secretly and sometimes at appointed hour a countless 'Sadhaks' and 'Yogis' including his own brother Barindra Ghosh.

Was Sri Aurobindo secretly guiding the revolutionaries and terrorists? Movement in India from a French territory is not yet properly known. It is also not clear whether he was secretly conveying some messages to his followers and other Indian revolutionaries through his poems and writings on Yoga, Indian Literature and Spiritualism?

These questions require a trough investigation and a scholarly probe.

His confinement in a French territory, however, proved a blessing in disguise. It gave to the world a philosophical interpretation of 'Yoga' which is unique and matchless; the 'Life Divine' and a work of English poetry 'Savitri' which is unparalleled.

It gave to the world a highest mystic "adwaitta".

"Around me was formless solitude,
All had become one strange, unnamable.
Topless and fathomless forever still".

53

Dr. Har Dayal and a most Powerful Violent Movement for the Overthrow of the British Government in India

Dr. Har Dayal, 1884-1939, was not merely an intellectual progedy, a powerful-creator, a fearless journalist and a profound scholar of Indian Literature, Philosophy and History, but he was also an extraordinary fighter for India's Independence. He was born and brought up in Delhi and went to Panjab, Oxford and London for his studies. He wrote excellent books and articles on a variety of subjects including politics, society and education. His approach to problems confronting India was absolutely original and brilliant. He was thoroughly acquainted with world politics and the political ideas of Plato, Aristotile, Jeremy Betham, John Stuart Mill, Karl Marx, etc. The political ideas of Lokmanya Balgangadhar Tilak, Sri Aurobindo, Dadabhai Naoroji, Vinayak Damodar Savarkar, Bhikaji Cama, Shyamji Krishnavarma, and Madanlal Dhingra provided him the highest inspiration of life. He went to England, America, Germany, Sweden, Switzerland, France, etc. and tried to influence the people about the immediate need for India's freedom from the British colonial yoke.

Dr. Har Dayal was extremely optimistic. He felt that India's Independence could be achieved within no time if the people of India prepared themselves for utmost sacrifice. He was convinced that India could achieve the overthrow of the British Imperialism only through 'daggar and bomb' or the most heroic violent ways. He looked at the question of India's Independence slightly differently. He felt that the number of British officials in India was so small that they could be thrown out of the country, within a short time.

Dr. Har Dayal's outstanding accomplishment was the establishment of Yugantar Ashram in Stockton on November 1, 1913. It was an excellent organization, which preached nothing but revolution or an armed struggle for India's immediate Independence. It was an extremely powerful centre with endless support from thousands of Indian revolutionaries. Dr. Har Dayal felt that there was a greater opportunity for organizing an armed struggle for India's freedom outside India than in India, where the British Government was almost ruthless in the suppression of nationalistic ideas or movements. Dr. Har Dayal appealed to the Indians in USA, England, Germany, France, Sweden, Switzerland, etc. to sacrifice their lives so that India became an Independent nation.

Shaheed Madanlal Dhingra'a assassination of Sir Curzon Wyllie in London and an attempt to assassinate Lord Hardinge in Delhi, on December 23, 1912 had created extreme panic in the whole British Empire. These violent incidents convinced Dr. Har Dayal that in case there was a powerful armed revolt in India, the British would quit India without any loss of time.

Dr. Har Dayal was a practical philoaopher. On November 1, 1913, through his powerful paper 'Ghadar', Dr. Har Dayal declared his open War Against the British Rule. He wrote: "The time will soon come when rifles and bombs will take the place of pen and ink." An appeal was made by many revolutionaries to massacre all the British in India.

Dr. Har Dayal wanted all the Indians in America etc. to reach India immediately for organizing an armed revolt against the British. On May 31, 1914 Dr. Har Dayal wrote in the Ghadar, "Sweep all the Whites from India." He further wrote: "Cut all the whites, cut them to pieces."

Dr. Har Dayal's comments were full of fire and thunder. Such a bold, open condemnation of the British Government was almost unprecedented and unparalleled in the annals of India's struggle for Independence.

Dr. Har Dayal's appeals had a wonderful impact. He created a wonderful stir in the realm of ideas. And there was a miracle. Countless Indian patriots immediately left the foreign shores for utmost sacrificc in India. It was all unimginable or incredible.

Countless Indian revolutionaries had to sacrifice their lives on reaching India in fighting against the British forces. Dr. Har Dayal had written in the Ghadar:

'Wanted: Enthusiastic and heroic soldiers for organizing Ghadar in Hindustan Remuneration: Death. Reward: Martyrdom. ... Pension: Freedom'.

The Indian revolutionaries from abroad reached different parts of India and inspired countless people to sacrifice their lives for India's immediate freedom. There was a lot of brutal repression and torture. The British Government was not prepared to tolerate open defiance of its authority and violence.

Countless revolutionaries were tortured, arrested, imprisoned, shot dead, transported to Andaman or executed. Bir Singh, Ishwar Singh, Panjha Singh, and Uttam Singh were hanged to death in Lahore. These were followed by the execution of Babu Ram, Balwant Singh, Hafiz Abdullah, Kartar Singh Saraba was hanged on November l6, 1915. Bhag Singh, Didar Tera Singh, Jetna Singh, and Budh Singh could also not save themselves from execution. Harnam Singh, Dar Singh, Chotta Ram—all had to part with their precious lives.

The Ghadar Revolution was indeed a great accomplishment of Dr. Har Dayal. It was an open defiance of British authority and violence. It was an act of supreme self-sacrifice. Attempts were made to assassinate the British officials and damage the Government properties. The British continued their unethical game of brutal repression including the April 13, 1919 Jallianwallahbagh Massacre. Attempts were made to arrest Dr. Har Dayal. He moved from one country to another propogating his violent ideology. He also served as a Professor of Literature and Philosophy in California.

Even during the Non-cooperation, Civil Disobedience, and Quit India Movements violence could not be stopped. An attempt was made to kill Lord Irwin.

Dr. Har Dayal came to India for a short while in 1933 but returned immediately to USA, where he died a mysterious death as a "sanyasi" in 1939 in Philadelphia. The spirit of supreme self-sacrifice, which he created among the Indians resulted in India's Independence on August 15, 1947.

This was indeed a great contribution of Dr. Har Dayal.

54

Sarojini Naidu's Indomitable Courage and Jallianwallahbagh Massacre

On April 13, 1919, the Jallianwallahbagh Massacre took place. There was Martial Law in Punjab. One British officer, who had abused Indian women as 'Witches', 'Flies' and 'She-Asses', shouted in anger at the totally defenceless women in Punjab in 1919.

"Swine, if I shoot you
What will you do?"

The British officials had already crossed all bonds of decency and culture by beating the Indian women with sticks and by using the filthiest language—unprintable—on earth. One of them said, "Now your skirts will be looked into." The women were indeed unveiled and assaulted.

Sarojini Naidu, who had visited the Jallianawallahbagh and the crawling of Amritsar, could not tolerate such humiliation and uncivilized behaviour of the British Power—Mad Officials.

She knew that if she condemned the British atrocities and attacked the British Tyranny or Reign of Terror, she could be hanged, deported or imprisoned. But she was a lady of tremendous courage and bravery. She decided to attack the British Empire and pay the British in their own coins.

She went to England.

At a huge public meeting in London on June 8, 1920, she said that the British had no moral justification to retain their Indian Empire.

She decribed the British as 'Swine.'

In her bold and courageous speech she said:

"Swine, if you shoot us,
We shall live.
You can kill our bodies,
But our souls go Free."

That was Sarojini Naidu in her greatness.

55

British Control over Indian Educationist and Scholars, Sir Asutosh Mookerje's Unique Device, 1922

The British Government tried to purchase the Indian educationists and scholars. It gave them knighthood; it gave them powers and privileges. It appointed many scholars involved in the struggle for freedom as Vice-Chancellors and Justices. But all these tricks could not enchain the Indian mind. These could not create "unbounded" loyalty towards the British colonialism among the intellectual elites.

Indian scholars showed a remarkable sense of patriotism both in their writings and speeched. They continued to inspire the people in India's struggle for freedom, whenever they got an opportunity to do so.

Sir Asutosh Mookerje (1864-1924) served as Vice-Chancellor of the University of Calcutta for countless years. He converted this centre of education into the largest university of the British Empire and perhaps the whole world.

He was not interested in politics.

He did not participate actively in India's struggle for freedom, but whenever he got a chance he did not allow it to go waste. He inspired the people. He wanted them to work wholeheartedly for the progress of the motherland.

The British Government consulted him time and again on educational problems of the country. He was considered as an outstanding education expert.

He was always in search of opportunities for inspiring the people without offending the British Empire. It was not possible for many educationists and bureaucrats to sing 'Vandematram' or 'Sare Jahan Se Achcha Hindostan Hamara' in convocation addresses. The British Government had banned the singing of 'Vandematram' even in the beginning of the 20th century.

Sir Asutosh Mookerji wanted to pay his homage to the motherland and inspire the people, in a convocation address in 1922. He therefore invented a unique device instead of singing 'Mother, I bow to thee' or 'Vandematram'. He quoted a most inspiring patriotic poem written by a "warrior" poet in English. It was written by an Englishman. It said:

"I vow to thee, my country; All earthly things above
Entire and whole and perfect the service of my love
The love that asks no question, the love that stands the test
That Ways upon the alter, the darest and the best
The love that never falters, the love that pays the price
The love that makes undaunted the final sacrifice."

The poem had the desired effect. It was even reproduced in another convocation on December 5, 1936 at the University of Nagpur.

56

British Colonial Trap and Sir Asutosh Mukherjee

The British colonialism during its hold on India played tricks even with those on whom it conferred its highest honours, such as the knighthoods. It treated them shabbily and considered the honours, positions, and awards as a political game, a trick and a bluff. The Indian knights, etc. were required to act almost as British spies, agents or slaves. Whenever they condemned or criticised the British colonial policies, they were humiliated, discarded or tortured.

The most interesting case is that of Sir Asutosh Mukherjee, a great patriot and an outstanding scholar, who was appointed a judge of the Calcutta High Court by Viceroy Lord Curzon in 1904 and who was offered the Vice-chancellorship of the university of Calcutta, soon after the Partition of Bengal and the commencement of the powerful Swadeshi Movement in 1906. Perhaps the British wanted to divide the educated elite or to weaken the national movement and therefore Sir Asutosh Mukherjee was tried as an experiment.

Scholarly by temperament, Sir Asutosh was so much overwhelmed with his academic appointment that he could not participate in the Swadeshi Movement and kept himself aloof from the Indian National Congress and the revolutionary organization, the Anushilan Samiti.

He kept himself away from Dadabhai Naoroji, Aurobindo Ghosh, Mahamana Madanmohan Malaviya, Gopalkrishna Gokhale, Lokmanya Balgangadhar Tilak. He kept himself away from Dr. Annie Besant, Satishchandra Mukherjee and Subodhchandra Mallick.

Earlier October 16, 1905 was observed as the day of fasting and protest in many parts of the country, but Sir Asutosh, who was quite friendly with the British, kept quite. He was also silent when the Indian revolutionary Khudiram Bose, who had thrown bomb on the British on April 30, 1908, was hanged to death. Lokmanya Balgangadhar Tilak's deportation for 6 long years in 1908 could also not move Sir Asutosh. He continued to serve the Viceroy's Council which he had joined in 1903.

The British transferred their capital from Calcutta to New Delhi and Sir Asutosh was soon awarded the knighthood in 1911. Knighthood had a magical effect. Sir Asutosh, quite an enlightened mind, refused to join the mainstream of the national struggle. He had tremendous sympathy with Lokmanya Balgangadhar Tilak and Sir Surendranath Banerjee, but he would not condemn the British policies of savage ruthless repression.

The British tried to use him for their colonial game. He did not kill his conscience, but because of his excellent academic orientation, he continued to justify his support to the British colonial exploitation.

The whole world was stunned when the British, without any justification, involved India in the World War and threw its soldiers into the vortex of that fatal conflagration. Millions of Indians were either killed or wounded. India had to spend crores of rupees on the war. Most of the national leaders violently, attacked the British inhumanity or madness. The press threw bombs and rained bullets on British colonialism, through its articles and editorials. There were protest meetings and demonstrations in some parts of the country.

Ultimately Sir Asutosh broke his silence. The British policies were becoming completely intolerable and he said boldly that the British had absolutely no justification in putting such a heavy financial burden on India. It was in 1914.

The same year Sir Asutosh ceased to be the Vice-Chancellor. The year 1915 passed away but Sir Asutosh did not hear anything from the Government. 1916 also passed away. In 1917, the same story was repeated by the British. It was indeed a great humiliation for Sir Asutosh.

No one expected such total indifference or apathy on the part of the British. Under tremendous popular pressure, the Government was compelled to accommodate Sir Asutosh and he was made a member of the Calcutta University Commission in 1917. But even as a member of the Commission, he was not honoured. His views and opinions about the university education were never faithfully recorded.

This was perhaps the beginning of Sir Asutosh's downfall as regards his bureaucratic career.

Sir Asutosh was humiliated. He was also humiliated by the people, who wanted him to participate boldly in India's struggle for freedom. Sir Asutosh, for reasons best known to him, was not prepared to utter even a single word in favour of Swarajya or the struggle for freedom. In fact, he had hardly much interest in politics.

Earlier for his appointments in the University of Calcutta as Vice-Chancellor, Sir Henry Sharp and Sir Harcourt Butler had threatened him. He was condemned by the British officials for what they termed as his arrogant and hauty attitude. They threatened to stop all aid to the University of Calcutta if he did not change himself.

But the Sir Asutosh did not condemn the British colonial policies or pressures openly.

He signed the Sadler Commission Report—a report which denigrated him and his university; a report which crippled or paralysed the greatest University of the British Empire or the World.

Even earlier, when the Jallianwallahbagh Massacre took place and countless Indian leaders protested against the British inhumanity and Rabindranath Tagore renounced his knighthood, Sir Asutosh remained unmoved.

When his own students and colleagues compelled him to join the freedom struggle and to boycott the British controlled educational institutions, Sir Asutosh adopted a different attitude. He described the Government-controlled University of Calcutta as a 'national' institution. He opposed Mahatma Gandhi's Non-cooperation Movement and refused to boycott the British educational institutions.

The Indian nationist leaders Swami Shradhananda, Aurobindo, Lokmanya Balgangadhar Tilak, Dr. Annie Besant, and the National Council of Education had established a network of educational institutions all over the country financed wholly by the Indians and also managed by them. Sir Asutosh did not feel concerned about these institutions. He continued to support his masters and he forced Sir Taraknath Palit and Sir Rashbehari Ghose to donate Rs. 50,00000 to the University of Calcutta—an amount which the nationalists wanted to get for the smooth-running of their newly established 'national' institutions.

The Sadler Commission completely paralysed the University of Calcutta. It took away much of it's academic autonomy and tried to reduce it to a residential, unitary institution. It also crippled the university financially, when the Act of 1919, put the university under the provincial control of the Government of Bengal. The powerful university was further weakened when intermediate classes were separated and put under a separate Board. Without any advantage three years' degree course was introduced and worst of all, against the wishes of Sir Asutosh, who wanted to promote the vernaculars, English was made the sole medium of higher education and research.

The Sadler Commission Report was a torture to Sir Asutosh. It was a political trap, a delusion or a snare.

When Mahatma Gandhi's powerful Non-cooperation Movement had created an unprecedented stir, all over the country, the British once again made an offer of vice-chancellorship to Sir Asutosh in 1921. Forgetting and forgiving all past insults and humiliations, Sir Asutosh accepted the offer.

It was a disgrace for Sir Asutosh, and a humiliation to the University of Calcutta. It was a setback to the struggle for freedom, and the movement for national education launched by Aurobindo, Rabindranath Tagore, Annie Besant, Dhondokeshav Karve and Mahamana Madanmohan Malaviya.

On March 24, 1923, Lord Lytton, Governor of Bengal, tried

to compensate Sir Asutosh for his silence. He offered him the Vice-Chancellorship once again, provided Sir Asutosh behaved like a slave and did not oppose the British colonialism. In a preposterous, insulting letter, he was discourteously asked to change his attitude and to support the Government.

Sir Asutosh was almost in tears. He could now understand the British colonial game in its stark nakedness.

There could not have been a greater humiliation for Sir Asutosh, who had opposed the Non-cooperation Movement and Mahatma Gandhi and had demonstrated his total loyalty to the British colonialism.

He had not even joined the Indian National Congress or the Anushilan Samiti, inspired by Lokmanya Balgangadhar Tilak and Aurobindo.

Sir Asutosh was completely dejected and demoralized.

He was in deep anguish. He felt betrayed. He declined the offer and left for Patna, where he died suddenly, on May 25, 1924.

57

Pandit Motilal Nehru's Thunder—An Open Warning to the British Empire

Mahatma Gandhi's nation-wide Non-cooperation Movement had created a fierce fire for freedom in India's heart. People had no more any tolerance for the colonial yoke. They wanted to throw the British out of the country. 'Jallianwallahabagh' and 'Chaurichaura' had already shown to what extent the Government could be mad and repressive and also to what extent the Indian demonstration, protest and anger could go.

Countless people were hanged, arrested, sent to Andeman and tortured by the government. Some British officials had also to lose their lives.

The government had realized that it would not be possible for England to hold India any more. It could, however, delay through diplomacy, deceit and design.

The government felt that if it announced certain "administrative" reforms, perhaps, it could create some peace in India. But it was impossible to extinguish the fire of nationalism.

There were cause of bloodshed and violence. There was inhuman repression.

Pandit Motilal Nehru, the leader of the Swarajya Party, could not tolerate the British apathy and indifference. The government was completely neglecting the India's determination for Swarajya. The government was blaming Indians for anarchy and violence.

Motilal Nehru, therefore, staged a walk-out from the Legislative Assembly, along with his followers, on March 8, 1926. He remarked:

> Violence for any sort does not enter our ethics. We resort to no menace or threat. We go out today not with the object of overthrowing the mighty empire. We will try to devise those sanctions which alone can compell any government to grant the demands of the nation. We do not give up the fight.

If you do not care, you will find the whole country from end to end, honeycombed by these anarchical societies.

The Government did not take up the challenge wisely. The result was Civil Disobedience Movement and the Quit India Movement.

58

Mahatma Gandhi's Powerful Dandi March and Sir Winston Churchill's Open Condemnation of British Policies in India

On May 25, 1915, Mahatma Gandhi established his world-renouned Sabarmati Ashram at Ahmedabad. He had become a legend even before he started his powerful mass-movements in India. He was becoming more and more powerful with every rise of the sun. His ideas of satya, ahimsa and satyagraha' were becoming more and more acceptable to the people of India, as sharp instruments for the achievement of swarajya.

The Non-cooperation Movement, started on August 1, 1920, had rudely shaken the foundations of the great British Empire, Mahatma Gandhi had taken a pledge to destroy the 'satanic' British Government in India and had advised his friends and followers to completely 'noncooperate' with the British.

When Mahatma Gandhi commenced his Dandi March on March 12, 1930, there was tremendous anger and panic in the entire British Empire. It had come after Ram Prasad Bismil's execution on December 19, 1929 and the British assault on Lala Lajpatrai and his death in Lahore on November 17, 1928. Shaheed Bhagat Singh and Bhatukeshwar Dutt had already threatened the British

Government in India by throwing bombs in the Legislative Assembly in Delhi on April 8, 1929. Jatindranath Das had also demonstrated India's great desire for Independence through his fast unto death on September 13, 1929.

Due to Dandi March, the Government of Great Britain was wild and nervous. It did not know what to do. It was an impossibility to put a check on the nationalistic aspirations of the people of India. The cry for 'swarajya' was loud and crystal clear. It was being heard in the highest corridors of power in England, including the Buckingham Palace and the British Parliament.

Many parliamentarians and intellectuals in England were convinced that the British viceroys and other prominent Britons in India would not be able to save themselves against Indian fury and fire. They were talking of granting 'dominion status' to India, without a moment's delay. It appeared that the British control over India was swiftly slipping away from England.

Sir Winston Churchill was uncontrollable. He was furious and wild with extreme anger. He never wanted that the brightest diadem of the British Empire. India should become independent of the British Empire. He criticized openly the British 'unimaginative, absurd and unwise' policies in India. He wanted that Mahatma Gandhi and his ideas should be completely crushed.

He lost his balance of mind when the British Emperor inaugurated the Round Table Conference in London on November 12, 1930.

Sir Winston Churchill did not like that the Indian freedom-fighters were not thrown out of India when at Lahore the Union Jack was burnt Mahatma Gandhi was not arrested or severely punished through a trial immediately when he broke the laws. Not crushing Gandhism in the bud was the greatest blunder committed by the British policy-framers, in Churchill's mind.

In a powerful speech on December 11, 1930, therefore, Sir Winston Churchill condemned and criticized his own country for an absolutely fatal policy towards India. He said:

"If instead of raising alluring hope of speedy 'Dominion Status',

> we had concentrated on practical steps to advance material condition of Indian masses, if the Congress at Lahore, which burnt the Union Jack, had been broken up, its leaders deported, if Gandhi had been arrested and tried immediately, he broke the law, there would have been no necessity for immense series of penal measures. The truth was that Gandhism and all that it stood for must sooner or later crippled with and crushed. It was useless to satisfy the Tiger by feeding him on cat's meal."

The Civil Disobedience Movement, however, could not be repressed. It took a violent turn when Jawaharlal Nehru took up a fast on December 18, 1930 in Naini Jail, Allahabad, in protest against the inhuman torture and flogging of political prisoners etc. In December itself, the students of the University of Punjab became uncontrollable and shot the British Governor of Punjab, while he was delivering the Convocation Address at Lahore, on December 23, 1930.

Sir Winston Churchill's 'imperial' dreams were shattered to pieces when Mahatma Gandhi launched his Quit India Movement on August 8, 1942 and India became Independent on August 15, 1947.

59

Motilal Nehru, the Freedom Fighter, who was not Prepared to Move in the Shadow of others

Motilal Nehru was born on May 6, 1861. He spent his early life in Khetri in luxury and affluence. He had his education in Kanpur and Allahabad.

He lived in an extraordinary age—an age in which the British Empire was emerging as the greatest political power in the world and in which after the powerful Indian Revolt of 1857, the forces of nationalism, national unity, and patriotism and passion for India's Independence from the British Colonial Yoke were becoming extremely powerful.

Maharani Laxmibai, Nana Saheb, Tautiya tope, Mangal Pandey, Bhaskarro, Nargundkar and Bahadurshah Zafar had emerged as great inspirers.

Queen Victoria had apolozied to the People of India for the British misrule and injustice through the Queen's Proclamation of 1858.

Motilal Nehru was a unique individual, who could not be easily influenced. He was thoroughly aquainted with the contribution of Rammohan Roy, Keshav Chandra Sen, Dadabhai Naoroji, Swami

Dayananda Saraswati, Sir Firozeshah Mehta, Ramakrishna Paramhansa and Bankimchandra Chatterji, yet he adopted his own course in Indian Politics.

Extremely active and hard working, Motilal Nehru was well-built tall, fair and dynamic with an extremely attractive and dominating personality. He was an aristocrat by temperament and lived in total affluence and luxury in his grand palace—like Anand Bhawan at Allahabad, like a representative of the Great Mughals.

His standard of living was fantastic, and because of his involvement in the municipal administration, the Home Rule League of Dr. Annie Besant, and the membership of the Indian National Congress, he lived like an Uncrowned Sovereign in Allahabad.

He wanted Independence for India and the downfall of the British Empire and yet he was friendly with the highest representatives of the British Empire in India. He was against violence and bloodshed but in the heart of his hearts he was friendly with the Indian Revolutionaries and Extremists, who wanted to achieve Independence for India through bombs and bullets. For quite sometime he knew that it would be difficult for India to achieve Independence through the Gandhian way of Satyagraha and Non-Cooperation, yet he was friendly with Mahatma Gandhi and participated in the Non-cooperation Movement. He was arrested and imprisoned. Even his son Jawaharlal Nehru was also arrested and imprisoned. He was friendly with his own son Jawaharlal Nehru who was not prepared to accept anything except Complete Freedom for India. He was friendly with Netaji Subhash Chandra Bose.

Without adopting violent, illegal ways, he wanted to achieve Independence for India. He also wanted to protect the revolutionaries against execution. In fact, he wanted to provide them a legal cover.

He had a thorough understanding of the western political ideas and policies—the politics of England, France, Germany, Denmark, Norway, Spain and even that of America.

He tried to adopt a rational, peaceful course of action, though he had to remain in prisons for his participation in the national struggle for freedom.

Motilal Nehru was greatly respected in Indian Politics and

Society. Besides his affluence, a thorough understanding of world politics and society, including his numerous visits to Europe, his legal expertise and his flourishing legal practice, his understanding of the Indian states, his involvement in municipal administration, his most-modern princely style of living, the factors responsible for his tremendous respect was his age.

He was senior to Swami Vivekanand, to Sri Aurobindo, to Deshbandhu Chittranjan Das, to Mahatma Gandhi's political inspiration Gopalkrishana Gokhale, Sir C.F. Andrews, Sarojini Naidu, and Maulana Abul Kalam Azad.

Obviously, he was senior to the political sensations and leaders of India's Struggle for Freedom, his own son Jawaharlal Nehru, Netaji Subhash Chandra Bose.

Motilal Nehru, therefore, commanded supreme respect in Indian politics. He was also quite intimate with Dr. Annie Besant, who had a powerful popular support throughout the country.

Motilal Nehru has remained a puzzle in Indian Politics. Till today he has not been properly evaluated as a fighter for India's Freedom.

Motilal had his own political strategies and his own silent, sophisticated, far sighted, camouflaged ways of working in Indian Politics.

The British Government had made great promises to India during the World War 1914-18. India's contribution was indeed extraordinary both in men and material during that Great War. The people expected some rewards, but the British Government forgot all about India's hopes and aspirations. There was therefore, anger, blood shed and violence in India.

Motilal Nehru wanted to remove the British Empire and to educate the people about India's Independence. He therefore, adopted a subtle way. He started his daily the 'Independent' from Allahabad on February 2, 1919.

The British rewarded the People of India for their sacrifices during the World War with Jallianwallabagh Massacre of April 13, 1919.

Along with Mahamna Madan Mohan Malviya and M.R.

Jayakar, Motilal Nehru went to Amritsar, and after a thorough study submitted a detailed report about the bloodshed and violence in Punjab. The report was a great contribution of the three great leaders.

Motilal Nehru participated in the Non-cooperation Movement fearlessly, but he felt that through Non-cooperation alone India might not achieve Independence immediately. He therefore, established the Swarajya Party. Chittranjan Das, M.R. Jayakar and many others cooperated with Motilal Nehru in this great venture.

Pandit Motilal Nehru, the leader of the Swarajya party, strongly opposed the British repression.

Pandit Motilal Nehru staged a walkout from the Legislative Assembly along with his followers on March 8, 1926 in protest against the British repression. He made a fiery speech in the Legislative Assembly against the Raj.

"Violence of any sort does not enter our ethics. We resort to no menace or threat We will try to devise those sanctions which alone can compel any government to accept the demands of the nation. We do not give up the fight"

The government did not pay heed to the challenge and the result was civil disobedience movement and the Quit India Movement.

And soon, Jawaharlal Nehru, who had declared at Lahore on December 31, 1929 Complete Independence as the main objective of the Indian National Congress, founded with Netaji Subhash Chandra Bose in 1929, Independence For India League at Allahabad.

Motilal Nehru was not a camp follower. He cast his own shadow and was not prepared to move in the shadow of others. He therefore, did not follow a single ideology all the times. According to the situation; he adopted both moderatism and extremism as his *modus operandi* for the achievement of 'Swarajya'.

His summon bonus was the Independence for India and the welfare of the people of India.

Motilal Nehru was convinced that India could no longer remain in imperialist chain. It was bound to achieve its Independece. A bomb was thrown in the Central Legislative in Delhi by Bhagat Singh and his associate Chandra Shekhar Azad was active in Allahabad. Mahatma Gandhi had started his Dandi March.

Motilal Nehru, therefore, was quite hopeful of India's Independece. The movement for India's Independence had assumed uncontrollable proportions.

Motilal Nehru, with utmost sense of fulfilment died on February 6, 1931, in the presence of two great leaders of the twentheth century: Mahatma Gandhi and Jawaharlal Nehru.

Motilal Nehru was the head of a remarkable family, which has shaped and influenced the politics in India for almost one long century.

He has the rare distinction, unknown in the history of the human race, of being the father of a Prime Minister grandfather of a Prime Minister and the great grandfather of a Prime Minister.

Himself the President of the Indian National Congress, he has in incomparable distinction of being the father of a Congress President, the grandfather of a Congress President, the great grandfather of a Congress President, and the great grand-father-in-law of a Congress President.

60

Ganesh Shankar Vidyarthi's Sacrifice for Harmony and Love, 1931

"I would like to die while doing my duty"
—*Ganesh Shankar Vidyarthi*, March 25, 1931.

Ganesh Shankar Vidyarthi (October 26, 1890—March 25, 1931) was a unique leader of India's struggle for freedom. He was the editor of 'Pratap' and he wrote excellent editorials and comments—full of fire and thunder—on politics, religion, society and culture.

He was greatly inspired by Mahabir Prasad Dwivedi and the summum bonum of his journalism was 'jisko na apne desh aur nij jati ka abhiman hai, woh nar nahi hai, pasu nira hai aur mratak samaan hai'.

He was full of patriotism and wanted to keep India united for the achievement of swarajya and for social reconstruction. He however, could not survive for long.

When a terrible riot broke out in Kanpur, on March 25, 1931, since morning, he moved from place to place frantically, to save the lives of innocent men, women and children. He succeeded in pacifying hundreds of people. He succeeded in saving countless lives.

At about 4 p.m. in the evening he was surrounded by a violent mob between Makar Mandi and Naya Chowk. He did not make any attempt to run away or escape. He tried to pacify the people. But there was anger and violence in the air. People started attacking Ganesh Shankar Vidyarthi from all sides with lathis. They dragged him and took him to a narrow lane. One of his companions had already been stabbed to death. That was followed by the death of a volunteer who was mortally wounded with a sharp knife. There was a lot of opportunity for Ganesh Shankar Vidyarthi to run away and escape but he continued to do his duty and to save the lives of the innocent people. Soon one assassin stabbed Ganesh Shankar Vidyarthi in the back and within no time another rushed towards him. Ganesh Shankar Vidyarthi was axed to death at about 4 p.m.

His body remained untraceable till late in the night, His crimination took place in Kanpur on March 29, 1931 at 7.30 a.m. He was barely 41 years of age.

The last words of Ganesh Shankar Vidyarthi were: "I would like to die while doing my duty".

61

When the Indian National Congress Fired 'Amogh Brahmastra' on British Imperialism during India's Struggle for Freedom

The decline of the British Empire during India's struggle for Independence, at the time of Mahatma Gandhi's powerful 'Civil Disobedience Movement' became completely intolerable to the people of India.

An attack on British tyranny and torture on British injustice and total absence of ethical or moral considerations became imperative.

The Indian National Congress, therefore, at its Karachi session in 1931, under the presidentship of Sardar Vallabhbhai Patel fired a unique, most powerful and fatal 'amogh Brahmastra' against the British Empire.

The whole British Empire bled and lay prostrate in utter helplessness.

The Brahmastra fell like a storm, shattering the foundations of British colonial tyranny and the British Crown, the British Prime Minister and the British Parliament shed tears of utter helplessness and ridicule.

The entire British Empire had neither the capacity nor

competence to face this mighty challenge. In the entire British Empire, there was not even a single statesman, scholar, philosopher, diplomat or economic expert, who could cool the fire of this Brahmastra or extinguish the powerful flame of this 'swarajya' burning in the hearts of Indian revolutionaries or freedom fighters.

The British king George, the British Prime Minister Ramsay Macdonald, the Indian Viceroys Lord Irwin and Lord Wellingdon—none had any answer for this mighty assault.

What was this 'Amogh Brahmastra' from where did it come how did it originate.

When Mahatma Gandhi's most powerful, peaceful non-violent mass-movement the Non-cooperation Movement could not achieve the destruction of British Colonial structure in India or achieve Swarajya for India, Pandit Jawaharlal Nehru made a bold declaration of FULL FREEDOM FOR INDIA on the banks of Ravi in Lahore in 1929 and soon in 1931, Sardar Vallabhbhai Patel decided on behalf of Indian National Congress to appoint a Tribunal known to the entire world as Indo-British Financial Obligations Committee.

The committee, after a lot of study and investigations came to certain startling and extraordinary conclusions. The findings of committee were extremely explosive. They produced powerful flames of revolution in India. The idea shook, in a most disastrous manner, the deep foundations of British tyranny and exploitation.

The idea came as a bombshell and created unimaginable panic in the British administration in India.

The committee felt that the autocratic policies of the British Empire in India were completely indefensible, unethical, irrational and without any solid moral foundations.

It was an impossibility to find any justification for such exploitative policies.

The committee felt that the British policies in India were not meant for serving the interests or welfare of India, on the contrary these were a fatal blow to India's progress and welfare, an attempt to blackmail and exploit India, both blatantly and in a secret, subtle and sophisticated manner. These polices were making India weak and helpless. The policies were a total misuse of India's grand resources.

The committee questioned why the Indian resources and capital which should be used for India's progress, prosperity and development was being wasted by British Empire over England in Eden, Persia, Nepal, Burma, and China. The misuse of India's capital in Egypt, Afghanistan and Abbyssinia was completely intolerable to the members of the committee.

Why did India spend 37,000,000 pounds on Abbyssinian Expendition, etc.

The committee felt that all these expenditures were the financial responsibility of England. Why the burden fell on India? This money should have been used for the progress of the Indian people.

The committee went to the extent of condemning England for wasting 45,000,000 pounds during the revolt of 1857.

Many Indian statesmen, thinkers and social reformers had already pointed out how England was responsible for the drain of Indian wealth, which ultimately resulted in poverty, unemployment, backwardness, famines, starvation and death, Dadabhai Nauroji, Gopalnari Deshmukh, Bhartendu Harishchandra had attacked the British exploitative economic policies even during the nineteenth century.

Many Indian intellectuals and revolutionaries felt that the sole solution of termination of economic exploitation was 'swarajya'.

The British had also wasted India resources during the First World War. Even after the findings of the committee were made public, the British Empire continued its colonial game and wasted huge Indian resources on second World War. Countless Indian soldiers and others, had to part with their lives. India, it must be pointed out, had absolutely friendly relations with Germany, Italy and Japan.

Ultimately India's struggle for freedom took a different turn and the Indian freedom-fighters took pledge to sacrifice their utmost for India's immediate freedom and soon on August 15, 1947, India's Tricolor flag started fluttering on the Red Fort.

Thus it is axiomatic that 1931 INC 'Amogh Brahmastra' played a significant role in India's Independence. The British could not defend themselves against that fatal assault.

62

When Indians Slept and Burma was Separated

Burma was an inseparable part of India, after its conquest by the British. It was administered from Calcutta and later on from New Delhi exactly in the same manner as Madras, Bombay or NWP. Most of the educational institutions in Burma were affiliated to the University of Calcutta, the Graduates and Postgraduates of Burma received their degrees, diplomas and certificates from the University of Calcutta, etc. till the establishment of the University of Rangoon in 1920.

When Bengal was partitioned in 1905 by Lord Curzon there was a lot of bloodshed and violence. In fact the whole Swadeshi Movement received a new momentum due to the separation of certain part of Bengal from rest of it. The People were not prepared for any partition or separation. They were prepared to sacrifice their lives but not accept this British injustice. As a result of the bloodshed and the Swadeshi Movement, the British had to surrender and in 1911, the Partition was undone.

After the Partition of Bengal, there were attempts on the lives of Lord Minto, Lord Hardinge and many other top British officials. Many British officials were shot dead. There was a powerful Terrorist Movement in this country. Countless secret revolutionary societies and underground organizations, meant for turning the British out of the country, were formed. There was so much of consciousness in this country that the British could not think of any partition or separation.

Lokmanya Balgangadhar Tilak, Dr. Annie Beaant, Bipinchandra Pal, Aurobindo Ghosh, Shyamjikrishna Varma, Lala Har Dayal, Lala Lajpatrai, Motilal Nehru, Pandit Jawaharlal Nehru, Swami Shraddhananda, Chandrashekhar Azad, Bhagat Singh, and Mahatma Gandhi all had joined the national struggle for freedom.

These leaders were so much sagacious that it was impossible for the British to play their diplomatic or political tricks. Newspapers like the *Statesman*, the *Times of India*, the *Bombay Chronicle*, the *Hindustan Times*, the *Leader*, the *Pioneers*, the *National Herald* were condemning and criticizing every act of injustice or highhandedness.

The whole country was wide awake. In 1920, Mahatma Gandhi further awakened the People through the Non-cooperation Movement. In 1930s the Civil Disobedience Movement further awakened the People. But the British played their trump card in 1935. They played a great diplomatic trick. They befooled the entire country. They turned the tallest leaders into dummies. They played a miracle. It was a magical trick.

The leadership was caught napping. It slept and slumbered as if nothing had happened.

The British through their top political management and diplomacy partitioned Burma from India. Burma was seperated. It became a part of the British Empire. It was no more a part of India.

Through the Government of India Act of 1935, Burma was separated from India.

Surprizingly there was no massacre. No British Viceroys or Governors-General were shot dead. No political movement or agitation was organized.

The entire intellectual and political elite of the country closed its eyes and slept.

There was no murmur; no ripple.

Crores of people who were an inseparable part of India, who had the same culture as that of India, who had participated actively in India's struggle for freedom from the British yoke were separated from India.

It was a remarkable diplomatic trick. It was a wonderful political management.

63

Indian Leaders Hypnotized: British Diplomacy Succeeds during the World War

Adolf Hitler attacked Poland on September 1, 1939 and the Government of Great Britain declared war against Germany on September 3, 1939. That was the beginning of the Great War. In 1939, the whole of Europe was afraid of Adolf Hitler and the threatening striking-power of Germany, which had emerged as a great power.

The British Government in India and the British Prime Minister Winston Churchill, understanding the gravity of situation, never wanted any disturbance in India during the war. They never wanted even the slightest interference in England's war-policies and military-operations. Both Germany and Japan had emerged as a colossal threat to the British Empire. Germany was so powerful that England was nervous and in a tremendous panic.

Through subtle and sophasticated diplomacy, England succeeded in involving India in the World War. It is well known how England recruited countless Indians—approximately 200,000 soldiers for sacrificing their lives for England's victory all over the world.

India had also agreed tacitly to finance the war according to its resources. Through diplomacy, England wanted to completely silent the Indian National Congress during the war. England had succeeded and the Indian National Congress agreed to cooperate with the British throughout the war. They agreed to participate in the war to support the British power. Some Indian leaders also decided not to press England for India's 'swarajya' or for their political demands till the termination of the war.

England was still afraid. It was still afraid of India's non-cooperation, or revolutionary outburst.

The most prominent reason behind England's panic was that the British Government in India in a large number of provinces was under the powerful control of the Indian Ministers.

England's greatest desire was to paralyze the Indian Ministries or to anasesthetize them. Some kind of analgesia hyponosis or narcosis was urgently required.

The situation was extremely interesting and critical. The British played all their trump-cards. There were secret, subtle, sophisticated diplomatic moves, tricks and traps. The greatest challenge for the British was how to stop Indian interference in the British policies during the war with Germany. India could have easily exploited the situation to demand full 'swarajya' during that war time. It was an impossibility to byepass or ignore the Indian ministers during that time of stress and strife.

Astonishingly, England succeeded in its diplomatic endeavours. It was a miracle, England succeeded in befooling the entire leadership or the country. Mahatma Gandhi, Sardar Vallabhbhai Patel, Maulana Abul Kalam Azad, Madanmohan Malaviya, Sarojini Naidu, Chakravarti Rajagopalachari, Dr. K.M. Munshi, J. Kripalani and Dr. Rajendra Prasad—all were stupefied, drugged or turned insensitive. The Indian National Congress suffered a terrible stroke of coma.

Within a short time from the commencement of the war, till the end of October 1939, all the Indian ministers in six provinces were knocked out. As a bolt from the blue, the Indian ministries resigned.

The Indian ministries, deaf, blind and unconscious, fell like sense-bereft monkeys, falling down from tall trees, after seeing wild furious tigers or other animals in a forest.

It was a great blunder.

The Indians were completely out of the decision-taking mechanism of the Government. They were reduced to total helplessness or inertia. For all practical purposes, they became cold or dead.

Indian had now practically no role in the formation of Government policies.

They lost their voice. The leadership had failed, beyond any measure.

On August 8, 1942, Mahatma Gandhi had to start his Quit India Movement for the freedom of India from the terrible British colonial yoke.

64

Gurudev Rabindranath Tagore and University of Oxford Honour

Gurudev Rabindbmath Tagore was a literary genius. Even in the beginning of the 20th century, he had countless admirers in India and abroad. Mahatma Gandhi was so much impressed by this outstanding scholar that he described him as Gurudev. His Literature is Immortal. He wrote not merely the world famous Geetanjali but also the Jan Gan Man Adhinayak Jaya Hae.

Even before meeting Rabindranath Tagore, C.F. Andrews wrote a poem about him in 1912. He described him as a pure soul, whose poetry had swept the darkness and gloom away and had awakened joy and mirth:

Rabindra, Lord of a new world of song,
Heir to the sacred rishis of old time,
This homage comes from a far distant clime
To hail thee crowned amid the immortal throng.
Where words have power to make man's spirit strong;
For thou has reared a citadel of rhyme
Great and majestic, which to this world belong.
Heaven sends to every people one pure soul,
Filled with the spirit of music, who can sway,

The hearts of countless multitudes, till they
Love at his bidding. Age on age may roll,
Voiceless, but when the singer comes, the whole
People awake to greatness. Nought can stay
The might of song on that Victorious day,
When nations find at length their appointed goal.
So wast thou sent to give thy nation birth,
Such was the power that brought back life again.
To this dear country. Like a gracious rain
Thy songs poured forth upon the weary earth.
And thirsting souls parched dry with arid dearth
Revived. The magic of thy mighty strain
Echoed in all men's hearts and swept
Darkness and gloom away and wakened joy and mirth.

S. Chordia wrote:

O dreaming Laureate of the dreaming East!
You stand head-high among the poets and sing
In sweetest voice that ever breathed in spring
Of love and life and death. O Nature's priest!
Death holds no fears for you when life is told
As the altar-place beyond the sunset-land
Is richer with the offerings from your hand,
God ever thirstyeth for your music's gold.
Your tree of fame has touched the skiey height,
The stars that shine—they are its blossoms bright.
The moon, the folded glory time unfolds,
In spell of soothing light the wide earth holds.
These buds, when they shall burst in golden light,
Will drive from hence the blackest monster Night.

Deeply impressed by the outstanding literary accomplishments of Rabindramath Tagore, the University of Oxford took an excellent decision in 1940 to confer upon him the degree of Doctor of Literature. A special convocation was held at Shantiniketan to honour the eminent Nobel Laureate.

The formal benediction sent by the University of Oxford was in Latin. Employment of Latin on such significant ceremonial occasions of utmost academic importance was a tradition with many notable learned institutions of England.

When the degree of Doctor of Literature was presented to Gurudev Rabindranath Tagore, who was , perhaps, not an expert in Latin, he thought for a while. He wanted to honour the University of Oxford and the great, glorious Indian Tradition. He wanted to accept the honour in the most appropriate manner. He stood up with a smile on his face, and delivered his wonderful speech, accepting the great honour, not in English, not in Latin or Greek, not even in Hindi or Bengali, but in Sanskrit—the language of Great, Glorious Indian Tradition.

The People were delighted.
The People were full of admiration for the great scholar.
The People stood up and gave a thunderous applause.
There was nothing but SMILES everywhere.

Rabindranath Tagore had succeeded in honouring the University of Oxford as well as the Indian Tradition. This was the most appropriate reply to the British academic world.

65

Chakravarty Rajagopalachari and India's Restlessness during Struggle for Independence

Chakravarty Rajagopalachari, born at Thorapolli, Salem in December 1875, was a great link between India's struggle for Independence and the British Empire. The British Government in India was so much impressed by his outstanding scholarship and competence that it honoured him time and again. He served as a member of the Governor-General's Council before India's Independence, and immediately after Independence he was appointed by the Government of India as Governor-General. He was honoured with a 'Bharatratna' in 1954.

C. Rajagopalachari was greatly influenced by the ideas of Dadabhai Naoroji, Dr. Annie Besant and Mahatma Gandhi. He served as the President of the Indian National Congress and participated in the Non-cooperation Movement.

He was a powerful speaker and a great writer. His study of Indian religion, literature and philosophy was profound. Though he wanted India's support to the British Government during the World War, he continued to inspire countless people through his speeches and writings.

He had serious differences of opinion with many leaders but the Independence of India was always uppermost in his mind.

When Adolf Hitler attaked Poland on September 1, 1939 and Great Britain declared War against Germany on September 3, 1939, and the British Government declared India's participation in the World War on September 4, 1939, there was nothing but disappointment, dejection and discontent everywhere in India. There was irreconciable heart-burning, hostility and restlessness among the people.

The people did not want that India should fight against Germany or the Indian soldiers should sacrifice their lives for the victory of England, which was blackmailing India through its abnoxious policy of 'divide and rule'.

The Indians were frustrated because they felt that now India's Independence would become an unrealized dream. It would be postponed. They feared that the sacrifices of Chandrashekhar Azad, Bhagat Singh, Rajguru, Sukhdev, Ramprasad Bismil, and countless other patriots would go in vain.

Before the commencement of the World War, the British colonialism had clearly demonstrated that it had no respect or love for the sentiments of the people of India. Even from 1930 to 1940, it had hanged or shot dead countless Indians in quick succession. Vishnu Lele was shot dead in July 1930; Benoy Krishna Bose was shot dead on December 13, 1930. These were followed by the sacrifices of Jagannath Shinde, January 12, 193I, Tarkeshwar Sengupta, September 13, 1931; Surya Sen, January 11, 1934, Mahbir Singh Rathore, May 17, 1933, S.K. Pillai, 1938, R. Rahavan, 1938, R.B. Krishnan Nadar, September 21, 1938, and Ajaib Singh, July 1940.

The people were unhappy and embittered when Udham Singh was hanged in England on July 31, 1940 for murdering Sir Michael O'Dwyer on March 13, 1940, who was responsible for the massacre at Jallianwallahbagh on April 13, 1919.

The People had absolutely no love or sympathy with the British at the commencement of the World War. Around 1940, more than 25000 freedom-fighters had been arrested.

People had lost faith even in their national leaders, who were fighting among themselves. The Indian revolutionaries were critical of those leaders who were prepared to support the British imperialistic forces during the war. Many top leaders of the country were trying to pacify the Indian freedom-fighters but it was an impossibility to please or satisfy them.

How to inspire the people of India at that critical time was a great challenge. It was absolutely imperative that the youngmen and women should not be allowed to sink under the strain of frustration and they continued their constructive nation-building endeavours. They were to be told that India would emerge as a great nation within a short time, and it would play an extremely significant role in the comity of nations. Its freedom could not be delayed. The need was their total commitment and dedication.

Where many leaders had failed completely, Chakravarty Rajagopalachari saw a glimmer of hope. He knew the pulse of the nation. He understood the fundamental restlessness, anxiety and fear prevailing throughout the country. He knew how to inspire and put the people on the fast highway of struggle for India's freedom.

Chakravarty Rajagopalachari was determined to put the people on the right track. It was not possible to tell the people at the commencement of the world war to throw the British out of the country through bombs and bullets.

On December 13, 1941. C. Rajagopalachari got an opportunity to realize his dream. He wanted to rekindle a ray of hope among the Indian people. He had to deliver a convocation address on that day.

In his historic convocation address, C. Rajagopalachari spoke at length, in a bold manner, about India's freedom, about the greatness of India and about the great task of national reconstructions. He said:

> The greatness of India is not dead.
> That India shall be free one day and great again, leading an Asiatic Federation of Great Nations is certain.
> Build.
> Build daily.

The whole country heard these inspiring words and on August 8, 1942, the world-famous Quit India Movement was started, and India achieved its Independence on August 15, 1947.

66

Mahatma Gandhi, the Apostle of Nonviolence and the Revolutionary Movement in India

Mahatma Gandhi was an outstanding apostle of truth, nonviolence and satyagraha. He out-rightly rejected the cult of 'dagger and bomb' for the realization of India's Independence. He considered the British Rule as 'satanic' but never compromised with his great glorious ideas of passive resistance, nonviolence and love. And finally, when India achieved its Independence, on August 15, 1947, it became axiomatic to the entire country that Mahatma Gandhi had tremendous conviction, wisdom and foresight in selecting the most appropriate methods for the realization of 'swarajya'. The entire world, today, is grateful to Mahatma Gandhi for his great contribution of nonviolence as a means for the realization of the most cherished ideas or dreams.

The Prophet of peace and apostle of nonviolence, Mahatma Gandhi wrote:

> 'Nonviolence is the greatest virtue, cowardice the greatest vice. Nonviolence springs from love, cowardice would always inflict suffering.
>
> Nonviolence is not an entirely personal quality. It is an easy way

of spiritual as well as political action, for all individuals, society and the country.

It is my firm conviction that nothing endearing can be built upon violence.'

The people were so much impressed by Mahatma Gandhi that they wanted him to lead the nation towards swarajya. H.W.B. Moreno wrote after the well-known Noncooperation Movement:

Martyr and Saint of India, now to thee
The masses turn, in all their silent pain.
To rid them of their woes, Swaraj to gain,
On thee thy love thou pourest. full and free.

Apostle of the home-spun garment, clad
In loin cloth, armed with spindle in thy hand,
Thou showest Freedom's path to all the land-
While idlers scoff, the people's heart is glad.

Thine is the clarion call to every heart,
To the deep-seated-scarred and bleeding sons of toil,
The sun-burned serfs that wrestle with the soil.
To sweating slaves that labour in the mart.

O Great Mahatma, lift thine eyes and see,
Her shackles India snaps—she shall be free.

Although Mahatma Gandhi had full faith in the efficacy of satyagraha and nonviolent ways, countless people had lost all faith in such methods because of the brutal British repression and total disregard for Indian national sentiments and their demand for swarajya or self-rule. They wanted Indian leaders to adopt more effective ways of 'daggar and bomb' or violence so that India could attain freedom within a short time.

Some hardboiled, hardcore, young revolutionaries, therefore, wanted to seek an interview with the great political leaders, who was almost a legend, and convince him to discard the policy of nonviolence and adopt violent ways for the immediate achievement of India's long-cherished dream of independence.

Mahatma Gandhi was not at all interested in meeting the Indian revolutionaries or terrorists. He rejected their request for interview, out-right.

Mahatma Gandhi was not prepared to move an inch but on repeated requests he finally told the revolutionaries to meet him for a short while in his Ashram at the dead of night. He never wanted that such a meeting should ever come to the notice of the British Government, which always considered the Mahatma as the Greatest Danger to the British Empire and whom even Winston Churchill wanted to be crushed or eliminated from the political scene at the earliest.

One hundred select, most patriotic revolutionaries, full of fire and who wanted the immediate termination of the British rule, reached Mahatma Gandhi's ashram on the appointed day, at the dead of night, as directed by the apostle of Nonviolence.

They all collected themselves on the backside of the Ashram, in an open space. Practically nothing was visible except the total darkness.

After some time, the Mahatma came out of the ashram and asked the revolutionaries, in a straightforward and stern manner, what exactly they wanted from him. The revolutionaries told him in the most enthusiastic manner that they wanted Mahatma Gandhi to lead the revolutionary, terrorist movement so that India became Independent without any loss of time.

Mahatma Gandhi was told that the Revolutionaries were prepared to 'rain death' and spread utmost violence to achieve their goal.

Mahatma Gandhi was deeply impressed by the patriotic fervour of the young revolutionaries. But he was never convinced about the effectiveness of the violent ways. He stood motionless before the revolutionaries. He did not know how to tackle the uncontrolled nationalistic fire. He bowed his head in silent admiration.

All of a sudden a brilliant idea flashed in his mind. He told the revolutionaries to stand straight in a row, and after a few moments said with almost a commanding voice. "Look, suppose I meet the Viceroy tomorrow for India's immediate freedom and he agrees to grant us Independence but in return asks me to offer the heads of one hundred Indian patriots, how many of you are prepared to cut-off their heads and offer them to the British Government. Please raise your hands".

There was a dead silence. It was a total calm. All the revolutionaries were standing like a statue. There was no murmur, no stir.

Like a military marshal Mahatma Gandhi, shouted at the pitch of his voice: "Raise your hands immediately. Are you prepared to cut down your heads and offer them to the British Government."

Again there was total silence. Hardly any movement was visible in that total darkness.

After a few moments Mahatma Gandhi shouted again: 'Raise Your Hands'.

Mahatma Gandhi was totally stunned. He was astonished. There was not even a single revolutionary who did not raise both his hands in affirmation.

Mahatma Gandhi never expected such a powerful patriotic, sacrificing response.

He bowed his head in total admission at the dedication and devotion of the revolutionaries.

Mahatma Gandhi told them to disperse immediately and leave the Ashram without a moment's delay. He said, "You are free to do whatever you like, but I cannot provide any direction or leadership. Even today, I have not developed the courage and conviction to sacrifice myself for the freedom of the country, in that manner. Suppose the Viceroy demands 101 heads in return for the freedom of India, I will not be able to cut-off my head as an offering. I, therefore, cannot provide you the leadership. Thanks."

This brief interview was obliviously extremely interesting, exciting and astonishing. It was simply beyond the understanding of the great Indian revolutionaries, who felt shocked and stunned. It showed Mahatma Gandhi's unwavering commitment and conviction. He never wanted to deviate from the path of nonviolence. It was also a demonstration of Mahatma Gandhi's extraordinary understanding of the nature of the autocratic, repressive British Empire and a deep insight into human psychology or human nature. It was an outstanding manifestation of Mahatma Gandhi's brilliant tact, soundness of vision or foresight. It showed his political maturity and wisdom.

Perhaps Mahatma Gandhi also wanted to avoid violence and bloodbath in the country. He was well aware of the fate of Damodar Chapekar, Vasudev Chapekar, Balkrishna Chapekar, Mahadev Ranade, Brahmamadhav Upadhyaya, Khudiram Bose, Prafulla Chaki, Satindranath Basu, Madanlal Dhingra. Anant Kanhere, Indu Bhushan Ray, Amir Chand, Avadh Bihari, Mewa Singh, Harnam Singh, Ganesh Pingle, Uttam Singh and Dr. Mathura Singh, who had adopted the violent ways even before the Jallianwallahbagh massacre, of April 13, 1919.

On August 8, 1942, Mahatma Gandhi launched his most powerful Quit India Movement and achieved his great cherished goal.

67

Mahatma Gandhi, Nation-Building and the Philosophy of Total Involvement

Mahatma Gandhi was not merely a freedom-fighter but he was also an outstanding political thinker. He wanted an immediate termination of the British rule in India because he considered the colonial administrative superstructure as "satanic" and totally indefensible. Through his three powerful mass movements—the Non-cooperation Movement, the Civil Disobedience Movement and finally the Quit India Movement, he compelled the British Empire to surrender and India achieved its long-cherished dream of Swarajya on August 15, 1947.

The three most revolutionary and fundamental principles of his struggle for freedom, as is well known, were 'satya, ahimsa and satyagraha'. For the first time in the history of the entire human race, these principles were tried in the most successful manner in India. This demonstrated clearly that even without bloodshed and violence many objectives of life and society could be achieved.

The entire world felt grateful to Mahatma Gandhi for propounding these ideas. These ideas remain an inspiration to humanity even today and in all probability these would continue to inspire the people for all times to come.

For the success of the principles of 'satya, ahimsa and

satyagraha', Mahatma Gandhi's philosophy of total involvement or total commitment was greatly responsible. He wanted the involvement of men, women and children in all his movements, mentally, morally and physically, with a sense of total commitment, dedication and self-sacrifice. He considered the total involvement of the people as absolutely indispensable in the task of nation-building.

It was also the greatest secret of his tremendous success.

Mahatma Gandhi was totally involved in his powerful movements for 'swarajya' but at the same time he never wanted to neglect his other programmes of nation-building, so that India could emerge as a peaceful, prosperous and progressive country in the shortest possible time.

Professor Nirmal Kumar Bose, an eminent anthropologist, who served as Mahatma Gandhi's secretary in Mahatma Gandhi's ashram for some time, was deeply impressed by the philosophy of total involvement. It was a total philosophy with tremendous psychological foundations and insights. Mahatma Gandhi wanted that a small road between his 'ashram' and the 'mahila ashram' should be immediately constructed, despite financial constraints. He ascertained from the contractors the financial investments required for the purpose. The contactors and engineers were extremely cooperative and they assured Mahatma Gandhi that in case the building material could be arranged, the cost of construction would come down drastically. Mahatma Gandhi, therefore, decided to provide the contractors the necessary construction-material through physical endeavour. Early in the morning, Mahatma Gandhi started going for the morning walk, along with all other ashramites and returned to the ashram, every day, loaded with huge, heavy blocks of stones on the 'shoulders and covering about half a mile of distance'. The exercise, no doubt, was extremely tiring, hard and painful. But Mahatma Gandhi was successful in providing the required construction-material to the contractors.

Professor Nirmal Kumar Bose was furious. It was almost unbearable for this academician to carry huge blocks of stone on his shoulders, every day, for half a mile. He asked an ashramite Khan Abdul Ghaffar Khan who used to carry the heaviest blocks of stone on his shoulders, on the first day, what was the idea behind all this tortuous exercises. Why funds could not be raised for the purpose both from the rich and the poor. To the Professor this painful work was completely intolerable. This must be immediately stopped, he felt.

Looking at the uncontrollable anger of Nirmal Kumar Bose, the Frontier Gandhi Khan Abdual Ghaffar Khan told him that efforts were being made to make the whole project successful through every possible way, but Mahatma Gandhi had told him that he wanted the total involvement of all the people in the work. This had also deep psychological implications. When asked what exactly Mahatma Gandhi was involved in or wanted to accomplish, the Great Apostle of swarajya satya, ahimsa and satyagraha himself said in the most unequivocal terms:

"We are not constructing a road.
We are building a nation.
The total involvement of everyone
therefore is absolutely indispensable."

Based on Dr. B.M. Sankhdher's interview with Professor Nirmal Kumar Bose.

68

Netaji Subhaschandra Bose and Reports about his Air-Crash Death

Netaji Subhaschandra Bose, born on January 23, 1897, was an outstanding fighter for India's Independence. Within an extremely short time, he emerged as a legend in leadership and a frightening peril to the entire British colonialism in India. He served as the President of the Indian National Congress and as the founder of the Forward Bloc. The British Government could not tolerate the presence of this firey patriot and put him in a prison in July 1940.

Netaji was not merely an extraordinarily popular national leader but he had also become a powerful stir, a deep sensation and a deathless inspiration to the people, fighting for India's liberation.

Netaji was brave and courageous and he moved like a fast missile. Before his superb, brilliant escape to Germany via Afghanistan on January 26, 1941, before the commencement of the Quit India Movement, under the dynamic leadership of Mahatma Gandhi, from his Elgin Road residence in Calcutta, he had made it an impossibility for the British Government to breathe.

He was boldly talking about the immediate establishment of a National Government, total noncooperation with the British Empire, during the World War, which had started menacingly in September

1939, a six months' ultimatum to the British Government in India, and "Purna Swarajya' or complete Independence to India.

The British Government in India looked helpless, defenceless and resembled a castle of sands.

Netaji's contribution to India's Independence was indeed unique and extraordinary. Paying his highest tributes to Netaji Subhaschandra Bose, Dilip Kumar Roy wrote:

O son of strength, who spruned on earth the lures of lesser love's delight,
And, to help us worldlings, gave up all for which we clamour, fret and fight
You lived to achieve India's freedom in our homeland and abroad
And we hailed you as our country's leader, by your sunrise overawed.

You chanted the Gita's deathless hymn: Wage war we must to do His will
And quell the embattled alien hordes and dying to night, His Morn reveal;
We'll cross the seven seas, ride the storm and rule the waves, may bless us God:
We'll stake our all for the All-in-all redeem our Motherland with our blood."

REFRAIN:

You sang the Gita's song: "Arise, deal death to the shadows of tyranny"
And so our Lord of dawn booned you with the Crown of Immortality.

Netaji Subhaschandra Bose miraculously disappeared from India because he never wanted to sail too close to the repressive winds of British tyranny and torture. His secret escape to Germany, through Afghanistan, on false passport etc. was a threatening Danger Signal to the British administration in India. It was a shameful total failure of the British intelligence-network. Astonishingly, till November 1941, the British Government was completely in the dark about the nationalistic activities of Netaji Subhaschandra Bose, who had also married his secretary Emily, before his departure to Tokyo, for taking up the leadership of the Indian National Movement from Rashbehari Bose there.

Subhaschandra Bose was an outstanding visionary, planner and a man of action. He was determined to obtain the maximum help and cooperation of Afghanistan, Germany, Italy, Russia, Singapore, Burma, Korea, and Japan, etc. for the immediate overthrow or destruction of the British colonial superstructure in India. He wanted to discuss his plans and sophisticated strategies with Adolf Hitler, Benito Mussolini, Joseph Stalin and the great Japanese leader Tojo.

Netaji was a Threat and a Danger to the British Empire. England looked completely unguarded and unequipped and was in utmost predicament because of the brilliant secret, subtle and sofisticated statesman-like moves of the great Indian revolutionary leader.

Netaji wanted that countless Indian soldiers, who were defending England in the World War, should immediately revolt and fight for India's freedom as they did during the Indian Revolt of 1857. It was absolutely certain that if the Indian soldiers had revolted, when Germany was bombarding England, the British Imperialism in India would have reached the dragon's mouth, effortlessly. It would have been a fatal death-trap for England. Subhaschandra Bose was raining bombs and bullets on British Empire through his Berlin Radio broadcasts since January 1942, in the most planned manner.

After the commencement of the World War in September 1939, England had reached the edge of a volcanic disaster. It was a critical time of "sweat, toil and tears" for England. Germany had brilliantly captured Poland, in September 1939. Germany had powerfully attacked Denmark, Norway and Holland and had captured all those countries. Germany had captured Belgium. It had, by June 14, 1940, captured even France after heavy bombardment.

England had nothing but tears in its eyes. It was completely disappointed, dejected and demoralized. It looked helpless, when

Germany had started its frightening bombardments. In August 1940, England had lost even Somaliland.

It must be stressed that Germany, Japan, Italy, France, England and many other powerful countries of the world were trying to win the war through political management, through publicity and propaganda and through every possible strategy, including media-management-subtle, sophisticated, secret, blatant and even menacing. They were not ashamed of using dodge, deceipt and deception.

In India, Japan had captured Andaman and it was planning to attack many other parts of British India.

India, therefore, was the greatest hope for England, provided the Indian forces could remain loyal to the British Empire. According to an estimate more than 2 lac Indian soldiers were defending England's honour in different parts of the globe. India was also financing England's participation in the war, in an extremely substantial manner.

England's supreme concentration therefore was on Netaji Subhaschandra Bose. It wanted to capture Netaji-dead or alive. It wanted Netaji's immediate elimination or extinction from the political scene.

Something extraordinary happened on March 24, 1942. It was shocking, painful and unbelieable. There was a sensational report, far and wide that Netaji Subhaschandra Bose had died. It was reported that he was moving from Saigon to Tokyo and he died in an air crash.

The report was disheartening. It was a setback to India's struggle for Independence.

Next day, there was yet another sensation broadcast from Berlin. It said:

> 'This is Subhaschandra bose, who is still alive, speaking to you over Azad Hind Radio. the latest report about my death is perhaps an instance of wishful thinking'.

Netaji further remarked how the British Government, during that critical war time, wanted the immediate death of Netaji

Subhaschandra Bose. The British Government according to Netaji wanted to win over India for the Imperial War. It wanted no hinderances.

Thus Netaji had succeeded in defeating England in its own game of diplomacy and propaganda. Who planted this air crash report is still a mystry.

On August 23, 1945, a similar report, prepared by INA Government Publicity Minister, with the help of great Japanese military experts, about Netaji Subhaschandra Bose's air-crash death, while flying over Taiwan to Tokyo—on August 18, 1945—was given world-wide publicity.

Till today, no one has completely contradicted it to the total satisfaction of the People of India. It is still a mystry. The People for a long time, awaited a broadcast to the Nation from Berlin or through some other channel, from anywhere in the world.

69

Mahatma Gandhi's Extraordinary Magnetism

Mahatma Gandhi was a unique individual. He had an extraordinary magnetism. His ideas and movements for India's Independence were a source of inspiration to countless people all over the world.

Much before, he reached India on January 9, 1915, after his successful civil resistence movement in Transvaal, he had become a legend and a source of inspiration in India. A unique characteristic of his satyagraha movement in Transvaal was the participation of 129 women and 57 children besides thousands of men, for the achievement of their highest goals and aspirations.

When Mahatma Gandhi reached India, there was a flood of articles and comments in the Press on his non-violent methods for the achievement of political ends and on his experiments in the field of civil resistence and satyagraha. While the masses looked at him as a "miracle" man, he appeared to the poets and men of literature as a true "Messiah". Poems in almost every important Indian language started occupying the coveted columns of the newspapers and journals. Poems in English were no exception. When the struggle for India's freedom was at its height, H.W.B. Moreno wrote:

"Martyr and Saint of India, now to thee
The masses turn, in all their silent pain,
To rid them of their woes, Swaraj to gain,
On them thy love thou pourest, full and free.

Apostle of the home-spun garment, clad
In loin-cloth, armed with spindle in thy hand,
Thou showest Freedom's path to all the land—
While idlers scoff, the people's heart is glad.

Thine is the clarion call to every heart,
To the deep-scarred and bleeding sons of toil,
To sun-burned serfs that wrestle with the soil,
To sweating slaves that labour in the mart.

O great Mahatma, lift thine eyes and see,
Her shackles India snaps—she shall be free."

The poet's prophecy came true and India became free on August 15, 1947, when, as described by another English poet Omesh Saigal in his *Bapu: A Study in Verse*:

"The Union Jack came down the mast
And up there rose a shining star-
The star of India's hopes and wills
The guardian-angle of her dreams...
The Indian soul now rose again
Freed from these chains of bondage, fear."

But what followed soon after India achieved its Independence was an irrepairable loss, as the poet further describes:

"Three shots rang out, few drops of blood
Flowed out ... And ere a hundred human eyes
The body of Ahimsa fell. ...
The symbol of the humble, weak

Lay prostrate, bowed to Mother Earth:
"He Ram", he sang, then shut his eyes."

Gandhi had died and yet the flow of poems still continued. According to Omesh Saigal, Bapu'a death was a sacrifice at the alter of peace and freedom. He wrote, after Gandhi's martyrdom:

"But Bapu's death was not in vain,
It was the final sacrifice
Offered by Hindustan to He
Who over peace and Freedom rules;
It was the culmination of
The fire of anguish, despair
That raised in every hut in Hind.
For blood of Bapu flowed like drops
Of "amrit" from the sky above
And quenched these fiery, razing flames."

K.P. Roy drew his own poetic portrait of Gandhi's martyrdom. He recollected the day when on January 30, 1948, Gandhi was shot dead in the Birla House, in New Delhi. He says:

"I recall the day
I recall the moment
The horror of horrors e'er imaginable
The petrifying horror
The dead stop and standstill of human activity."

"The world's breath was almost stopp'd to hear it
Words were chocked in the mouth
India lay in a swoon;
Grief first froze her soul
Froze and then thawed
And flowed in non-stop torrents to seek relief
The tragicality of the tragedy was tremendous
The scene at Golgotha was re-enacted on Indian soil."

Gandhi was an inspiration during his life-time. Gandhi is an inspiration today and in all probability he will remain an inspiration for the posterity. K.P. Roy writes:

> "He was for three generations, the Grand Supremo
> The friend, philosopher, guide, guru
> Of the three hundred fifty million Indians."

While Dilip Kumar Roy—another poet—describes Gandhi as the "fearless Priest", whose "loved gleamed like a star", M. Ramakrishna Rao holds him responsible for the "priceless prize" of India's freedom, in his poem, which appeared in October 1982, in *'Treveni, Journal of Indian Renaissance'*: He says:

> "Hail the hero, hail his praise
> In whose command the nation did rise
> And achieved its freedom, the priceless prize."

70

Bharat Ratna Purushottamdas Tandon's Unique Sense of Commitment and Ramlila in Allahabad

Rajrishi Purushottamdas Tandon, August 1, 1882–July 1, 1961, was not merely an outstanding fighter for India's Independence, but he was also a man of highest integrity, commitment, and self-sacrifice. He was a patriot to the core and could sacrifice anything for the welfare of the people of India. He served as the President of the Indian National Congress and the Government of India, under the presidentship of Dr. Rajendra Prasad was so much impressed by his utmost courage, and purity of life that it conferred upon him the Bharatratna. Around 1960 President Dr. Rajendra Prasad went to Allahabad and presented him 'Rajrishi Purushottamdas Tandon Abhinandan Grantha.

Rajrishi Purushottamdas Tandon was a remarkable fighter for India's Independence. He was arrested and imprisoned more than half a dozen times during India's heroic struggle for Independence. He was not prepared to compromise and held the motherland in highest esteem. Even before completing his Post-graduation in History and LLB, he was expelled from the University of Allahabad for his radical ideas and uncompromising attitude.

Inspired by his contemporaries—Mahamana Madanmohan Malaviya, the Lion of Punjab Lala Lajpatrai, and Mahatma Gandhi, Rajrishi Purushottamdas was the moving spirit behind the Servants of People Society, Ratrabhasha Prasar Samiti, and Hindi Sahitya Sammelan. He worked day and night, as a member of the Indian Constituent Assembly and succeeded gloriously in installing Hindi as Rashtrabhasha. That was his great achievement and the fulfilment of his long-cherished dream.

While Dr. Rajendra Prasad, Dr. S. Radhakrishnan, Jawaharlal Nehru, Sarojini Naidu, Rajkumari Ambit Kaur, Dr. K.M. Munshi, Dr. B.R. Ambedkar, Dr. Sampurnanand, and Vallabhbhai Patel signed the Constitution of India in English, Rajrishi Purushottamdas Tandon, along with Ravishankar Shukla, signed it in Hindi.

Purushottamdas Tandon wanted to replace English with Hindi after the Independence of India. He was convinced that without a National Language, the country could not make great progress in a short time. Like Mahatma Gandhi, Purushottamdas Tandon considered foreign language English as a mental burden, for the people of India.

In 1926, at the Indian National Congress session at Kanpur, Rajrishi Purushottamdas appealed to the party to conduct its proceedings in Hindi. He wanted that Hindi should be adopted by the INC as its medium.

Purushottamdas Tandon had a remarkable understanding of Law. In fact for some time he served as a lawyer in Allahabad. His politics, as his life, was pure, unadultrated and absolutely transparent.

He was a bold and fearless journalist. He wrote excellent comments on politics and society in the Abhudaya, Allahabad. As Speaker of the UP Legislature, he played an excellent role and every member was overwhelmed because of his impartiality, objectivity and courage.

He was above all rigidities and narrowness and wanted India to emerge as a classless, casteless, secular society without any distinction between Man and Man.

He was convinced, like Mahatma Gandhi, that without the participation of women, no nation, no society could be considered as advanced or progressive. He was an advocate of universal elementary education and advancement in the field of science and technology.

When India's Independence was almost in sight, there was a furious, maddening storm of violence in Allahabad. The situation was explosive and everywhere there was an outburst of wild oppression, brute barbarianism, explosion, and it looked as if the fury of bloodshed would burst its banks. Dragons of death, devile of destruction and demons of demolition had created a *havoc* in Allahabad. People were running amock on the roads of ruin and it had become an impossibility even to stage the annual 'Ramlila'.

The Ramlila procession was surely to be bombarded and knocked down. There was mischief, vandalism and mass-murder in the air. No one, therefore, was prepared to play the role of Ram and Lakshman in the Ramlila, which could become a scene of genocide any moment.

Rajrishi Purushottamdas Tandon was the chief organizer of such religious and cultural activities or festivals in Allahabad. All the organizers had come to him and expressed their total helplessness in organising the festival. Rajrishi Purushottamdas Tandon, however, was a man of steel. He was made of an extraordinary clay. He was an apostle of tremendous courage, commitment and self-sacrifice. He was not afraid of the wild Thunder, the stupid Hurricane and the rude cloudburst, which were breaking the peace of Allahabad, in an unbridled manner.

He called an emergency meeting of the Allahabad Ramlila Committee. He told them in the most heroic manner that under no circumstances, the Ramlila could be postponed or cancelled. It would be staged in the usual manner whatsoever the consequences. He told them to leave immediately and make the necessary arrangements.

Looking at the acute nervousness, diffidence and anxiety of his co-workers, Purushottamdas Tandon thundered:

> "I have four sons. Take two and make them Ram and Lakshman. If the two are killed, take the remaining two. Ramlila cannot be dropped."

The Tempest and turmoil of violence continued in Allahabad.
But the Ramlila was held in the usual manner.
There was no slaughter, no butchery and no interruptions.
That was Rajrishi Purushottamdas in his greatness.

71

An Extraordinary Convocation: When Jawaharlal Nehru was Awarded a Doctorate

Jawaharlal Nehru, it is well known, was an outstanding scholar. He had a remarkable understanding of science, literature and world history.

He had a sharp analytical mind and a scientific temper.

Immediately after India's Independence, the University of Allahabad took an excellent decision to invite Jawaharlal Nehru and to confer upon him the degree of Doctor of Law.

An extraordinary Convocation, therefore, was organized about 120 days after India's Independence on December 13, 1947.

The University honoured itself by conferring Doctor of Law, Doctor of Science and Doctor of Letters degrees on some of the most outstanding scholars and leaders known to human history.

The chancellor of the university Sarojini Naidu and the vice-chancellor Dr. Tara Chand had the unique privilege of welcoming the great scholars and leaders.

The Galaxy Introduced:

India's first Prime Minister

Jawaharlal Nehru,
Rajrishi Purushottamdas Tondon,
Maulana Abul Kalam Azad,
Pandit Govindballabh Pant,
Sir J.R.D. Tata, and
Mrs Vijaylakshmi Pandit.

The University also Conferred Doctorates on:

Professor Dhodokeshav Karve,
Founder of the SNDT National Women's University,
Sri Tej Bahadur Sapru,
Sir Mirja Ismail,
Professor Meghnad Shah,
Professor Birbal Sahani,
Dr. Bidhanchad Roy,
Dr. Shanti Swarup Bhatnagar, and
Professor Amarnath Jha.

Others who Received the Doctorates were:

Dr. K.S. Krishnan,
Professor K.V. Kane,
Sir S. Vardhachari,
Dr. B.C. Law,
Professor R.D. Ranade, and
Mafjaraja of Nepal.

Sir Visveswarya and Dr. Kailashnath Katju received the Doctor of Sciecne and Doctor of Letters respectively *in absentia.* Never in the History of India or of the world has such a galaxy of outstanding leaders been awarded Doctortes on a single day. The Convocation was indeed unique and unprecedented.

Index